POSTCOLONIAL GRIEF

· JINAH KIM ·

POSTCOLONIAL GRIEF

THE AFTERLIVES *of the* PACIFIC WARS *in the* AMERICAS

Duke University Press Durham and London 2019

Printed in the United States of America on acid-free paper ∞
Designed by Courtney Leigh Baker and typeset
in Garamond Premier Pro and Futura by
Tseng Information Systems, Inc.

Library of Congress Cataloging-in-Publication Data
Names: Kim, Jinah, [date] author.
Title: Postcolonial grief : the afterlives of the
Pacific wars in the Americas / Jinah Kim.
Description: Durham : Duke University Press, 2019. |
Includes bibliographical references and index.
Identifiers: LCCN 2018027899 (print) |
LCCN 2018041030 (ebook) | ISBN 9781478002932 (ebook)
ISBN 9781478001355 (hardcover : alk. paper)
ISBN 9781478002796 (pbk. : alk. paper)
Subjects: LCSH: Asian diaspora. | Asians—United States. |
Grief—Political aspects—United States. | Postcolonialism
and the arts—United States. | Decolonization—Pacific Area. |
Imperialism. | United States—Race relations—History—
20th century. | Pacific Area—Relations—United
States. | United States—Relations—Pacific Area.
Classification: LCC E184.A75 (ebook) |
LCC E184.A75 K53 2019 (print) | DDC 973/.0495—dc23
LC record available at https://lccn.loc.gov/2018027899

COVER ART: Tomiyama Taeko, *At the Bottom of the Pacific*, 1985.

· CONTENTS ·

· ACKNOWLEDGMENTS ·

This book would not have come into being without the support and love of my friends, family, colleagues, and teachers. First my teachers. Lisa Lowe and Lisa Yoneyama are extraordinary feminist scholars and mentors. They have supported my intellectual development since graduate school and as a junior scholar. I am indebted to them and other members of my MA and dissertation committee at the University of California–San Diego who inspire me to build upon hemispheric, transpacific, and decolonial knowledge production and archive: Rosaura Sanchez, Shelley Streeby, Denise Ferreira da Silva, Jack Halberstam, Nayan Shah, Takashi Fujitani, and Nicole King. I would not have gone to graduate school if I hadn't met David Eng as an undergraduate at Columbia University. This book began there, and his formative lessons on the power of loss and racial melancholia is clearly saturated into every corner of this book. The best thing I did after graduating from college was to go to work as a union organizer at the United Auto Workers, Local 2110. There I learned one of my most powerful and enduring lessons, how to overcome fear. Thank you, Maida Rosenstein, June Benjamin, Michael Cinquena, Danny Ferman, Eden Shultz, and my comrades on the Museum of Modern Art strike line.

Characteristic of her extraordinary mentorship, Carolyn Chen organized a book manuscript workshop for me convened by Ivy Wilson, Lisa Marie Cacho, and Dylan Rodriguez at a crucial point in the writing of the book. I am indebted to their careful reading and generous engagement with my work. Nitasha Sharma, Peter Holderness, and Rekha Radhakrishnan have read every word of this book and have helped me give this book life.

Throughout my work and academic life I have been surrounded by fierce, brilliant women and feminist leaders who have modeled for me how to live an uncompromised life and speak the truth even when it makes people uncomfortable. Thank you: Tai Soo Kim, Maida Rosenstein, Lisa Lowe, Lisa

Yoneyama, Ji-Yeon Yuh, Carolyn Chen, Nitasha Sharma, Judy Wu, and Kathryn Sorrells.

The brilliance of the Korean Studies Working Group, Anne Joh, Ji-Yeon Yuh, and Elizabeth Son shine through this work. Thank you for the advice, company, and good food. In addition, I have been a part of several writing groups, and their comments have made this project stronger: Thank you, Aimee Carrillo Rowe, Lynn Itagaki, Erin Suzuki, Aimee Bahng, Pavi Prasad, Carolyn Chen, Joshua Chambers-Letson, Yu-Fang Cho, Camilla Fojas, Neel Ahuja, Simeon Man, Andrew Leong, Daniel Immerwahr, Sylvester Johnson, Kathleen Belew, Gerry Cadava, John Alba Cutler, Mónica Rodríguez y Russel, John Márquez, Frances Aparicio, Caroine Hong, and Kent Ono.

I have had the great privilege to work with wonderful students at Northwestern University and California State University, Northridge. At Northwestern I am particularly grateful to the members of the Colloquium on Ethnicity and Diaspora and the graduate cluster on Comparative Race and Diaspora. My research assistants, Colleen Kim Daniher and Stephanie Bergren, at Northwestern, and Xuejing Xao and Calvin Abbassi, at CSUN, offered valuable research and editorial help. At CSUN I thank my graduate students in the Performance and Violence Seminar for their companionship and intellectual engagement as I finished this book.

My colleagues at Northwestern's Asian American Studies Program, Latina and Latino Studies Program, and the Department of African American Studies are the best. I thank them for their intellectual genius and their courage in continuing to fight for critical ethnic studies at the University: Ji-Yeon Yuh, Greg Jue, Cheryl Jue, Carolyn Chen, Nitasha Sharma, Shalini Shankar, Frances Aparicio, Ana Aparicio, Mónica Rodríguez y Russel, John Marquez, Martha Biondi, Michelle Wright, and Ivy Wilson. My colleagues at CSUN have been immensely supportive of my work and have offered intellectual companionship throughout the final stages of finishing this book, in particular Melissa Brough, Pavi Prasad, Aimee Carrillo Rowe, Kathryn Sorrells, John Kephardt, Gina Giotta, Kevin MacDonald, Frances Gateward, and Tae Hyun Kim.

Time and support for the book was made possible by an Andrew W. Mellon Postdoctoral Fellowship in Asian American Studies and English at Northwestern University. Due to several fellowships during graduate school I was able to research and conduct interviews with Korean small business owners in Lima, Peru, Rio De Janeiro, Argentina, São Paolo, Brazil, and Ciudad del Este in Paraguay, during which I learned how deep transpacific fantasies between Asia and Latin America structure the neoliberal cultural imaginary. All this travel was made possible by the Joseph Naiman Japanese Studies Fellowship, Calcultures Fellowship, California Cultures in Comparative Perspectives Fellowship, and Tinker Travel Research Grant from the Center for Immigration and Latin American Studies, UCSD. At CSUN I have received the support of Research, Scholarly, and Creative Activities fellowships that gave me release time from some teaching to enable me to make the final push to finish. I have benefitted from the audience of the American Studies Association, Association for Asian American Studies, National Women's Studies Association, and American Studies Association of Korea, as well as the Newberry Library Seminar on Borderlands.

I had access to an extraordinary education. I am lucky to have had the companionship of my fellow graduate students at UCSD. The insights I gained during our seminars are scattered through this book. They have offered me lifelong community and friendship, without which I would find our field unlivable. Thank you, Neda Atanasoski, Julietta Hua, Neel Ahuja, Kyla Schuller, Elizabeth Streeby, Aimee Bahng, Gabriela Nuñez, Su Yun Kim, Jake Mattox, Justin Wyble, May Fu, Morelia Portillo, Choung-Dài Võ, Yu-Fang Cho, Blu Barnd, Helen Jun, Grace Hong, and Heidi Hoescht.

I am particularly grateful to the support of the Duke University Press for their assistance. Courtney Berger was unflagging in her support of this project and made the entire review process painless and encouraging. I thank Sandra Korn, and Susan Albury for shepherding this book through the review and publication process. Sohinee Roy was an incredible editor—she helped my words shine through.

Finally, but not least, I am indebted to my family who supported me, loved me, and took care of me during the time I wrote the book. My parents, Tai Soo Kim and Jai Kwon Kim, have always believed in me. My parents never had the chance to go to college and follow their intellectual passions the way I have been fortunate to do. Words cannot express how much I owe them for everything I have been able to accomplish. I am lucky to have a supportive and warm family in Susan and Jerry Holderness, my brother, Sejin Kim, Mae Masow, Maggie, Mike, Marshall, and Mason Pratt, and my extended family in Seoul. Peter Holderness has my heart and is my rock. Our sons, Miles and Junho, were born while the book was being written, and they have shown remarkable good cheer even when I was too busy to play. Our cat Mao warmed my lap while revised the thorniest sections. This book is dedicated to them.

· INTRODUCTION ·

MOURNING EMPIRE

> We Americans are unhappy; we are not happy about America. We are not happy about ourselves in relation to America. We are nervous—or gloomy—or apathetic—as we look towards the future—our own and that of others.
>
> —HENRY LUCE, "The American Century"

> The dead in this story come to me not so that I can speak of distant sorrows. / They come to me so vividly because they are my own sorrow: / I am the sister whose hands were tied by fear.
>
> —TERESA RALLI and JOSÉ WATANABE, *Antígona*

This book explores moments when the present is so bloated with dead bodies demanding mourning that their claims threaten to overtake life. I ask what kind of transformative politics is enacted when we name the deaths of those considered unworthy of mourning and remembering. Answering this question means finding out which lives count. Fundamentally, then, such mourning is potentially insurgent, challenging the liberal nation-state's claim to sole right to violence. *Postcolonial Grief: The Afterlives of the Pacific Wars in the Americas* directs this inquiry by focusing on narratives about Korean and Japanese diasporas across the Americas, as well as how they intersect with other displaced and marginalized peoples. Although they are surrounded by unexpressed deaths and losses, as Lisa Yoneyama argues in *Cold War Ruins*, "the necropolitics of Asia are occluded" within knowledge production and erased from Japanese, U.S., and Korean national histories.[1]

Cold War U.S. liberal governance, its disavowal of military violence and colonialism, narratives of rescue and liberation, and monopolies over justice are enabled by the interimperial confrontation, connection, and complicity between U.S. and Japanese imperialisms. This explains how the violence in the Pacific Arena is compelled to silence, despite the intimate and deeply embedded nature of U.S. imperialism there. Instead of disappearing, this violence emerges as a bloated, palimpsestic haunting. Rather than just a bad memory that cannot be shaken, this describes living with the fear that a future of violence is inevitable.

This book is part of a long tradition of critiques of colonialism and war, challenging the ways that mourning and melancholia are theorized. From Sigmund Freud's reshifting of his notion of melancholia to Fanonian anticolonial psychoanalysis, which arises in the midst of insurrection against French colonialism in the 1950s, to feminist and queer anti-neoliberal reconceptualizations of mourning, loss, and trauma in the twenty-first century, I direct my inquiry into the long history of American militarism in the Pacific Arena. In the nineteenth, twentieth, and twenty-first centuries, the United States has been in a constant and accelerated state of opening markets, war making, and empire building in the Pacific Arena, spanning the continents of Asia, Australia, the Americas, and the islands in the Pacific, including Guam, American Samoa, the Commonwealth of Northern Marianas, Hawai'i, the Marshall Islands, Okinawa, and Pitcairn. America's transpacific empire is constituted by a "homogenizing force and collaborative alliance among various colonizers at different historical moments under shifting geopolitical configurations."[2] Judith Butler has argued that we are a "public created at the prohibition to mourn" those whose deaths implicate the nation-state.[3] This prohibition to mourn American empire building in the Pacific Arena is structured by historical amnesia and upheld by the ritualistic production of the Asian body as one in pain and in need of rescue.[4] The dead victims of American military violence in the Pacific Arena are rendered unmournable as "spectral being[s], between real and unreal."[5] However, this prohibition to mourn is occurring at the height of the signifying power of the Pacific in the U.S. geopolitical imaginary. The pressure of these spectral beings whose death is the condition of possibility for American prosperity in the twentieth and twenty-first centuries may cause an "insurrection at the level of ontology."[6] Their names, claims, and stories are at the center of the creative and political engagements and narratives on which *Postcolonial Grief* is based.

Given the interimperial and interracial entanglements I engage with in this book, I turn to the aesthetic and creative works of the Japanese and Korean diasporas in the Americas to map how they engage and contest postcoloniality and the deferment of decolonization.[7] The memories of those murdered come unbidden in Hisaye Yamamoto's short story "A Fire in Fontana" (chapter 1); grief threatens to turn into morbidity in Dai Sil Kim-Gibson's film *Sa-I-Gu* and Héctor Tobar's novel *The Tattooed Soldier* (chapter 2); colonial violence willed into disappearance haunts the American imaginary in the genre of noir (chapter 3); and the disappeared refuse burial in Teresa Ralli and José Watanabe's play *Antígona* (chapter 4). In these works, living closer to death also means living closer to statelessness, marked by the shifting of status from citizen to more liminal categories such as "enemy non-alien," "*kibei*," "*zanichi*," "refugee," and "undocumented." Mourning them makes the present feel risky and creates a sense of uncertain futures.

The epigraph from Henry Luce's "The American Century," with which I begin this book, captures how melancholy violence is constitutive to the American Century. This document seeks to direct U.S. consciousness away from Europe and toward the Pacific Arena. Through taking leadership over new markets and fallen empires, Luce argues, American lives will come to have value and matter over all other bodies. Luce was the head of a publishing empire and one of the most influential Americans of his time. "The American Century" sought to spur an American internationalism that urged a reluctant President Franklin D. Roosevelt to enter World War II.[8] This article foreshadows Luce's association of the American Century with the Pacific Century and his sense that the United States must step up to its destiny as the commander of Asia, which is only possible by dominating the Pacific world. "The American Century" is a cipher for an American colonialist vision, here particularly the lure of Chinese markets that would expand American power and might. A policy document and cultural text, this essay, along with Luce's lobbying, profoundly influenced U.S. priorities within the Pacific Arena during the Cold War and continues to inspire reflection in the neoliberal period. Published on February 17, 1941, just months before the bombing of Pearl Harbor by the Japanese Imperial Army would propel Americans into World War II, Luce begins his essay lamenting American unhappiness: "We Americans are unhappy; we are not happy about America. We are not happy about ourselves in relation to America. We are nervous—or gloomy—or apathetic. . . . As we look toward the future—our own future and the future of other nations."[9] His gloominess stems from the diagnosis that Roosevelt's refusal to enter the war means the loss of an immense opportunity and possibility. He continues, "Now all our failures and mistakes hover like birds of ill omen over the White House, over the Capitol dome and over this printed page."[10] Racial anxieties expressed through the language of negative affect pervade the text. Here the image of hovering black birds threatening the white symbols of U.S. imperium heightens the sense of pathos that will define the American mind should the United States fail to take the helm as the new global arbiter. For Luce, the decline of European empires in the Pacific Arena means the Third World is threatened with a potentially dangerous interregnum in which Communism may take root. Roosevelt's failure to prime the nation for international involvement and global investment, especially in light of the opportunity provided by the decline of European empires, particularly the British in Asia, has created an America of mental ill health.[11] Repeatedly using the words *sickness* and *failure* as cognitive anchors throughout the article, Luce seeks to move a currently impotent people into leadership. Luce highlights that without entering the war and conquering Asian markets, the United States would decay in significance in the modern world.

Luce's American Century further develops the intractable idea that the future of the Pacific is meant to be an "American Lake," as termed by the nineteenth-century expansionist Whitelaw Reid. The Pacific's draw and luminosity as the oceanic extension of the American western frontier has been represented in fiction and in political and economic treatises by Robert Louis Stevenson, Mark Twain, Herman Melville, Henry Luce, and numerous American politicians. As a source of creative engagement and shoring up of national ideologies, the idea and image of the Pacific Ocean as an American Lake reemerges again and again in the American canon as an abstract space outside of history where American enterprise can flourish. The dominant U.S. representation of the Pacific is as the engine for a future of capitalism everlasting.[12] This has meant that the Pacific is forcefully evacuated of meaning for itself, existing only for others.[13] On Luce's account, for example, the entirety of the Pacific Ocean disappears under the lure of continental Asia. Ronald Reagan's declaration in a 1984 presidential debate that the Pacific Basin "is where the future of the world lies" is haunted by previous and future utterances.[14] Former Secretary of State Hillary Clinton similarly situates the Pacific in the future in her 2011 statement that the "American future of prosperity lies in becoming a Pacific power."[15] In 1903 Theodore Roosevelt also envisioned the Pacific as a future site of American capitalist rejuvenation, remarking that "the Mediterranean Era died with the discovery of America; the Atlantic Era is now at the height of its development and must soon exhaust the resources at its command. The Pacific era, destined to be the greatest of all, is just at its dawn."[16] In 1944, General Douglas MacArthur told a group of war correspondents, "The history of the world for the next thousand years will be written in the Pacific."[17] What is shared across these statements is that the Pacific must remain free in order for free-market capital to flourish and innovate, and, in order for the Pacific to remain free, it must be an extension of the U.S.

It is remarkable that Luce's brief opening paragraph, comprised only of two sentences, reveals the biopolitics and bioeconomics that will structure U.S. investments in the Pacific Arena in the period following World War II. Luce's article anticipates U.S. modernization programs and containment policy where the uplift of Asia was imagined as a necessary counter to an insidious Asian Communism led by Mao Zedong.[18] Christopher L. Connery argues that this uplift was a collusion between states' interests and that of U.S. financial markets, concluding that "the particularly Cold War ideologies of internationalism and containment theorized and practiced by Acheson, Kennan, Forrestal, Dulles, Rusk, Nitze, Harriman, among others, [has a] root in their own careers on Wall Street and in other institutions of U.S. financial capital that stood to benefit from an international economy free of trade barriers, anchored by strong regional economic powers." Central to the accompanying "Cold War geo-imaginary" was a psychologism that tended to pathologize Asian Communism and that was "shared by the psychic structures of the most developed stage of international capitalism. This kind of essentializing psychologism combined with the strategic character of nuclear warfare to de-spatialize the globe."[19]

This Manichean and binaristic Cold War psychic structure is anticipated by Luce, who manages to connect bodies across immense scales, starting from the American self to global others, and to demand a commitment to a world order-structure in which only the mental health of the American self ensures the future health of the world.[20] For the rarely mentioned Asian bodies in his essay, unhealthiness, illness, and brokenness define their experience of living through the violence of U.S. wars and the institution of capitalism in the region. The "others" referenced in this essay float variously between a Europe besieged by Hitler and an Asia that "will be worth to us exactly zero — or else it will be worth to us four, five, ten billions of dollars a year. And the latter are the terms we must think in, or else confess a pitiful impotence."[21] Luce cannot imagine a space or quantity that is between nothing (down there) and infinite and ever-expanding fullness. The American self is forebodingly described as a person in deep depression and driven only by negative affect — unhappy, nervous, gloomy, apathetic — and only by finding its release for its frustrated desire for enterprise across the Pacific Arena can Americans regain happiness.

Asian diasporic literature is bloated with the pressure that the dead put on the living due to the afterlives of Japanese imperialism and American World War II–era war violence, ongoing war, settlement, and expanding U.S.-led militarism and capitalism in the Pacific Arena imagined as necessary for American survival. There are shared themes in how various U.S. wars in Asia and the Pacific Arena are represented in American popular culture as a rare opportunity for Americans to rejuvenate and gain new vitality. This rejuvenation is so tied to American hegemonic influence over the Pacific that, even when there is no one to rescue, an Asian figure in distress must be produced again and again, to be rescued or destroyed again and again. This Asian figure in need of rescue is not unique to the World War II era or Korean War but is a structure of feeling across the transpacific. In the context of the Vietnam War, for example, U.S. cultural politics fixates on the "figure of the Vietnamese refugee," whose imagined rescue by the U.S. military "has been key to the (re)cuperation of American identities and the shoring up of U.S. militarism in the post–Vietnam war era."[22]

The repeated destruction and rescue in popular cultural representations of war and Asian bodies function to affirm Ann Laura Stoler's argument that the colonizing presence is not automatically recognized as a colonizer but must be made into one through fantasy: "Their identity as a colonizer needs to be repeatedly affirmed in the *fantasized* situations of colonial encounter."[23] Elaborated and made into fantasy, most prominently through the medium of film, the "microphysics" of war — that is, the specific encounters that happen during the time and space of combat and occupation — shape the colonizers' sense of their dominance. These are national fantasies. These conditions make more salient the ways that literature, film, and the arts are a critical alternative archive for the recuperation of the forgotten, the unseen, and the unhealed. The analyses in *Postcolonial Grief* span the language of treaties and policies to literary and filmic archives because ruptures and abject subjects can only be seen and heard when disciplinary constraints are transgressed. This requires epistemological practices that reassemble places and meanings previously taken for granted.

Literature and film are central to building a national consciousness and are imagined to aid in the cultivation of a self who cares for an other, can feel for an other whose experience they do not share but with whose difference they can empathize and sympathize.[24] However, *Postcolonial Grief* reveals a desire not only to expand contacts with the Third World other, but also to set limits within what seems (as a result of the erosion of former boundaries) like an infinite and uncontrollable contact. This requires that neoliberal cultural politics "set the limit of *how much* otherness is required, as opposed to how much is excessive, disruptive, disturbing, in ways that damage us, rather than enhance our lives."[25] Under such conditions, unless contested, empathy finds its limits in narratives that enhance the life of the First World over all others.

In Luce's reflections on the American Century, obviously missing is the recognition that the American Century can only be built on the ruins of Japanese imperialism. By the time Japan bombed U.S. naval bases at Pearl Harbor on the island of Oahu on December 7, 1941, almost all French, British, and Spanish territories had come under Japanese control. In the period after Japan surrendered to the United States in August 15, 1945, the United States gained possession of Japan's former empire in the Pacific and Asia. Luce refuses to see the United States as absorbing Japan's dominion and represents the collective will that seeks to render the recognition of U.S. imperialism in the Pacific Arena verboten. But Naoki Sakai cautions that unless we recognize how "Japanese imperialism was grafted into American imperialism . . . we will remain enslaved to the legacies of past colonialism in East Asia."[26] Like the missing Asian bodies in his text, Luce's refusal enables empire to be reframed and energized as a matter for health and happiness, demonstrating the colonialist investment in narrating the history of empire and imperialism in affective terms.[27] Luce rhetorically positions colonies as necessary for the sublimation of American unhappiness. Only once these colonies have been established can Americans tend to the unhappiness of these Others, now under American dominance, by transforming the potential zero value of Asia to "four, five, ten billions of dollars a year,"[28] a positive effect for U.S. racial colonialism.

These closing sentences of Luce's essay are the most famous, but this triumphant tone comes only after much tortured treatise on the threats of decline and the emasculated future awaiting America: "[I envision] America as the dynamic center of ever-widening spheres of enterprise, America as the training center of the skillful servants of mankind, America as the Good

Samaritan, really believing again that it is more blessed to give than to receive, and America as the powerhouse of the ideals of Freedom and Justice.... It is in this spirit that all of us are all called, each to his own measure of capacity, and each in the widest horizon of his vision, to create the first great American Century."[29]

Luce describes colonialism in terms of universal human liberation. The American Century seeks to shape not only the biopolitical—bringing others the gift of freedom—but also the production of the bioeconomic and the raising of American human value as *homo oeconomicus* across the globe.[30] U.S. visions for the Pacific were always stated in terms of "capitalist rejuvenation," whether through capital from new markets and consumers or through the idea of "free enterprise and progress" (fundamental to U.S.-led capitalism).[31] However, as I explore in this book, this racial capitalism is anchored to a racial-colonial logic and to structures of white supremacy. There are moments in the U.S. colonial archive when the colonial project is codetermined, if not primarily determined, by the racial substructure of American "civilizing missions," of which capitalism is a component.[32] Here, the conquest period in the post-1898 years of the U.S. colonial invasion of the Philippines is instructive. It was generally the case that the archipelago was less important for its capitalist potentials than it was as a material template for the making of modern American racial civilization into a global work-in-progress.[33] Hence, the frequent destruction of ecology, land, and people was not centrally guided by the imperative of preparing the colony for capitalist relations, but was structured by both pacification and assimilation as violent—and empowering—racial-colonial logics.[34]

The power of Luce's call for war as an injunction against a feeble future forcefully demonstrates how narratives of wounds stand in danger of being co-opted to uphold military nationalism as well as a regressive rhetoric of therapy that encourages individuals to focus on themselves as opposed to addressing structural problems. The biopolitics and bioeconomics of neoliberalism fetishize vitality and flexibility, against which grief appears as a melancholic attachment and as an unhealthy hyperremembering of a past best forgotten.[35] However, this is premised on a temporality of neoliberal reason that ignores the "palimpsest" between the United States and the Pacific Arena. Colonial forms never die out but are adapted or go into fugitive mode.[36] The present time in the Pacific Arena is one in which postcolonialism, settler colonialism, military occupation, and liberal nation-state forms coexist concurrently. This palimpsest challenges a neoliberal temporality that fetishizes closure and linear progress, thus seeking to force a refusal to see how the past, present, and future exist simultaneously.[37] But that simultaneity is impossible to ignore when thinking of how past wars and the violence of colonialism shape the postcolonial present. Thus, although the political form and political imaginary encouraged by neoliberalism promise to secure freedom and reinvigorate the body politic, they end up undernourishing it and placing it in ever more precarious states.[38]

Postcolonial Grief

Mourning is described as occupying a spatiality and temporality of ambivalence because it is not a state that one is supposed to maintain. Mourning is meant to be a temporary journey, wherein the grieving self must learn to replace a loss. Grief, when thought about in the most liberal and positivist way, can be linked to the liberal humanist process of reconciliation – that is, the notion of letting go of the attachment to grief as like letting go of grievance, which is resolved through a new attachment to a proper replacement. However, as my turn to melancholia demonstrates, this replacement may be impossible, as some losses cannot ever be replaced, but rather are erased or lived as loss. It is, for instance, important for a state waging war that people do not replace their loss of loved ones or homeland with resentment for the nation-state.

My discussion of postcolonial grief, afterlives, and the related terms of mourning, loss, and melancholia emerges from several intellectual shifts and interventions. These revolve around a radical critique of liberal humanism and its attendant institutions through grief, grievance, loss, and injury as central rubrics. I follow two particular and related iterations of this critique that are connected in their emergence of a theory of grief and mourning. These are rooted against war, militarism, and colonial and liberal state's violence: Fanonian anticolonial psychoanalysis and twenty-first-century transnational feminist and queer challenges to neoliberal statecraft and escalating wars.[39] *Postcolonial Grief* covers new ground by offering a comparative look at mourning practices at different sites within the Pacific Arena. Politicizing the structure of grief simultaneously requires the recognition that the force of grief does not itself imagine or desire freedom. And yet it is impossible to think about grief and mourning without imagining freedom from loss and thus the impasses and the incommensurability facing the insurgent drive for freedom.

Engaging with mourning and loss means negotiating memory. It is through the terrain of both personal and cultural memory that survivors and others negotiate their traumatic past. I focus on how this unresolved violence and loss create a fear and dread of an uncertain future, in a sense drawing one's memory forward. Based on her sociological study of how the trauma of the Korean War is silenced within the Korean diaspora, Grace M. Cho terms this fear of an uncertain but violent future "dread forwarding": "Just as a new trauma can trigger an older one, inducing a flashback, it can also flash forward, projecting itself into a future haunting."[40] Dread as an orientation toward the future is painful. Dread creates intense anxiety and makes the future feel unbearable. Depending on the depth of dread and the nature of that which is dreaded, some people would do anything, even experience great pain, rather than have to live with dread of the thing they fear. Abating this dread forwarding requires addressing the conditions that caused this fear in the past. The narrative blocks, limits, and incommensurabilities I describe in the texts I study mirror the impasses found within transpacific redress movements in the 1990s and the twenty-first century. In their attempts to address the violent past, Korean comfort women and Korean forced workers, for example, have consistently encountered obstacles and the fact that war reparation issues against Japan and the United States have already been "settled."[41] As affective presences, the unmourned dead and the fear of a future return of violence make the particular memories held by the Japanese and Korean diaspora potentially insurgent. But the refusal of the dead to leave also makes the present melancholy.

David L. Eng and David Kazanjian's edited volume *Loss* exemplifies the shift in discourse and the kinds of intellectual and political communities that are forming around the reconceptualization of loss that I have been discussing.[42] Eng and Kazanjian identify a compulsion of the "regressive fate of historicism," which demands that subjects "resolve" their loss through the adoption of a new object of desire. This call for resolution sees "proper" mourning as leaving behind historical memory. Eng and Kazanjian's text is prescient in its intervention against a regressive rhetoric of therapy that we have seen in particular since 9/11, one that authorizes more violence. Arguing that the individual and the West are traumatized by the violent insertion of Others into the Self, this regressive rhetoric of therapy creates a value and hierarchy out of our trauma.[43] The wounded Western self is named as preemptive war is enabled. Preemptivity is a continuation of détente upheld by the stockpiling of a nuclear arsenal. Under certain conditions melancholic subjectivity becomes a valued positionality for the U.S. military hegemon. This means that we are living in a time when we are encouraged to be in a state of melancholic attachment to our own sense of loss as opposed to the loss we cause others.

In the twentieth and twenty-first centuries, defined by "historical traumas and legacies of, among other things, revolution, war, genocide, slavery, decolonization, exile, migration, reunification, globalization, and AIDS," the rendering of certain subjects as melancholic and affective means not only silencing the historical conditions that led to the loss, but also pathologizing that which "remains"—that is, the present and future shaped by the loss.[44] Defined in relationship to their loss and its unhealthiness, these melancholic subjects are also pushed toward the liminal borders of society as unfit. Eng and Kazanjian revise this dominant idea in politics and culture, which continues to render certain subjects and their losses inarticulable.[45] A critical lens situated around mourning is a rejection of the precepts that underlie psychoanalytic theory and neoliberal biopolitics.

Residing in loss is dangerous not only because it is imagined to lead to a state of melancholic, unending mourning, but also because of the proximity such a state allows between violence and insurgency, death and the living, the past and future. Thinking too much about loss generates a state of morbidity and grotesque attachment in which the dead are allowed to dictate present and future relations. This is what happens when grief is in and for itself, when it does not "seek," but sits in the morass of melancholia, or never-ending mourning. The dialectical temporality of historical materialism can also lead to what Wendy Brown cautions is "a certain narcissism with regard to one's past political attachments and identity that exceeds any contemporary investment in political mobilization, alliance, or transformation."[46]

Rather than engaging mourning and melancholia as a general condition of possibility for subjectivity, I focus on how the "politics and ethics of mourning lie in the interpretation of what remains—how remains are produced and animated, how they are read and sustained" in part by thinking about grief and loss temporally (as memories that return unbidden) and spatially (across different kinds of states and being).[47] Postcolonial grief is pathologized as a kind of mental and physical contagion that should be avoided because it is insurgent in the context of a postcolonial and settler colonial Pacific Arena that, in the twenty-first century, has remained "locked and loaded."[48]

Given America's variegated empire across the Pacific Arena, *Postcolonial Grief* analyzes the loss and its disavowal in the postcolonial period by putting the experiences and representations of Korean and Japanese diasporas in the Americas in conversation with a large constellation of actors and historical situations that are not obviously postcolonial. Throughout this project, postcolonialism refers to the complex processes through which decolonization is deferred after formal colonialism ends. Although they may not be populated by American racial others, Pacific Islanders, and the Korean and Japanese diasporas evenly or in the same way, when we start our inquiry with America's "empire of bases" and move toward the U.S. continent, we can see how military occupation, settler colonialism, and postcolonialism—as states and in terms of governance—operate palimsestically in the heterogeneous temporality that is the U.S. liberal nation-state.[49]

Drawing on a specific Third World postcolonial genealogy that insists on the "living on" of colonialism in all arenas, including the field of postcolonial studies, I treat "deferred decolonization" and postcolonialism as interchangeable terms. "Living on" describes the dialectic between the living on required of the survivor and the living on of colonialism in the postcolonial period. Addressing this dialectic requires a way of meaning making that generates "commensurabilities from incommensurability" in attempts to resolve the damages related to the violence of the past and ongoing violence.[50] This way of treating "what remains of loss" means that what is to come does not have to be defined solely by what was lost.

From the onset of the field in the 1970s, postcolonial studies was not concerned with the settler colonial states in the Americas, Australia, and the Pacific; it focused instead on British, Dutch, and other European franchise empires that sought to extract surplus value from their raw material–rich colonies in Africa and Asia.[51] Postcolonial theory is inherently fragmented, emerging from anticolonial and anti-imperialist struggles in the African continent and diaspora, on the one hand, and from the heritage of Western philosophy and of the disciplines that constitute the European humanities on the other.[52] Scholars from the global south, including Gayatri Chakravorty Spivak, Néstor García Canclini, and Sylvia Wynter, have continually critiqued how Euro-American humanities produce differential levels of humanity.[53] Within U.S. scholarship Anne McClintock's "Angel of Progress and Pitfalls of Postcolonialism" is fundamental to rejecting the conservative consensus in postcolonial studies, arguing that "post" should not be temporalized as meaning "after," but to define an altered state of colonialism where colonial domination lives on. Otherwise colonial domination becomes replicated by the field's refusal to hear this criticism from Third World feminist and global south scholars.[54] Ann Laura Stoler terms this ongoing status "ruins."[55]

What is to be gained by starting from the premise of living on as a condition of resisting deferred decolonization in the Pacific Arena? For one, it is the recognition of a radical intimacy—due to the temporal heterogeneity and spatial dislocation that is a condition of shared being—between the postcolony and the U.S. liberal nation-state.[56] In describing the condition of contemporary South Korea as postcolonial Chungmoo Choi argues that the "actual landscape of the postcolonial space is a contestatory one" where postcolonial subjects understand the colony to be inferior to the metropole.[57] This is not to say that the postcolonial is not different from the colonial period, as U.S. Cold War liberal governmentality "relied on a new technology of governance that targets life and the bodies without territorial possession or coercive force."[58] But, this noncoercive force is upheld by territorial occupation that enables U.S. military dominance and unfettered access to Asian, Pacific, Oceanic, and Pacific Rim markets, revealing the intractability of old forms at the same time that new forms of domination are instituted.[59]

It is not enough to say that this living on of colonialism in the Korean and Japanese diasporas in the Americas and the Pacific Arena impacts American racial others and Pacific Islanders passively. Instead, these U.S. racial others, which include displaced peoples and descendants of slaves, were always imagined to have a role to play in the domination of native lands within the continental United States, as well as in the colonies. Candace Fujikane asks are, "[Migrants'] descendants are not settlers?"[60] For critics of Asian settler colonialism in Hawai'i, Asian migrants and their descendants "are beneficiaries of U.S. settler colonialism . . . and early Asian settlers were both active agents in the making of their own histories and unwitting recruits swept into the service of empire."[61] In Hawai'i, Asians and Asian Americans have often gained political and economic dominance due to their overwhelming population and the need for their labor by the capitalist leaders on the island and mainland. Their political and economic needs often, and sometimes deliberately, seek to erode native Hawaiian articulations for political sovereignty. The goal of settler colonialism is the total and complete eradication of indigenous beings and total occupation of their land.[62] The native population is not necessary for producing surplus value; territorial occupation is most significant.[63] Eventually, memory of the people and the land should also ideally disappear. Not denying the important histories and legacies of interracial solidarities and alliances, I agree with Fujikane that "settler status is a mixture of both self-determination and structural contingency."[64]

The beginning of Craig Santos Perez's *From Unincorporated Territory [Guma']* describes Guam's necropolitical connection to the United States and highlights the ongoing expansion of its military dominion over the Pacific Arena: "Guam is 'Where America's Day Begins.' . . . Guam is a U.S. citizen ever since the 1950 Organic Act. . . . Guam is an acronym for 'Give Us American Military.' . . . Guam is America's front porch to Asia. . . . Guam is no longer 'Guam.'"[65] He powerfully illustrates how rethinking postcolonialism in the twenty-first century in the U.S. context requires taking stock of the breadth and scale of ongoing U.S. military occupation in the Pacific Arena into which almost all facets of American being is conscripted. Evoking where and how Chamorro culture and history is threatened throughout *From Unincorporated Territory* this ongoing U.S. aggression is always already positioned in relation to Guam's history before its entanglement with the U.S. This means that what came before Guam became a "U.S. citizen in 1950" is central to what Guam's future beyond the U.S. can be.[66] As with Guam, the installation of U.S. military bases throughout Asia and the Pacific Arena at the end of World War II means that other former Japanese colonies have "never had an opportunity to decolonize in the true sense of the word."[67]

U.S. and Japanese empire building in the Pacific are shaped by intertwined forces.[68] America's empire across the Pacific begins to consolidate after 1898: Hawai'i's monarchy is overthrown and the island nation made into a U.S. territory; additionally, seized from Spain after the Spanish-American War, Guam becomes an unincorporated territory.[69] Meanwhile, Japan's formal empire building began "in the wake of the Sino-Japanese War in 1894 and 1895 with its colonial expansion into Taiwan and Korea, building on Japan's annexation of Hokkaido (1869) and Okinawa (1879)."[70] Beyond territorial overlaps Takashi Fujitani compares the treatments of Koreans by the Japanese Empire and Japanese Americans by American Empire during the World War II era to argue that their treatment of racialized others becomes increasingly similar to that of the other.[71] This wartime racial management cannot be seen as solely connected to the World War II era but as building on pre–World War II–era imperial entanglements between Japan and the West. Japan, for example justified its empire through the attempt to overcome the Euro-American empire in the Pacific under the "Greater East Asia Co-Prosperity Sphere" and called for "pan-Asian solidarity." Starting in 1914, Japan formalizes its empire in the Pacific with the purchase or acquisition of former German colonies in Micronesia, which included the Caroline, Marshall, Palau, and Northern Mariana Islands. These territories are then seized during World War II and legally acquired by the United States through a successive series of defense- and security-geared treaties related to the San Francisco Peace Treaty and the division of the Korean peninsula, among others. This is what enables a South Korean citizen who is a resident of the United States (a Green Card holder) to live in South Korea but update their right to U.S. residency by stepping foot on the U.S. territory of Guam (rather than traveling to the continental United States). The American "empire of bases" has created specific and new conditions for deferment of decolonization.[72]

The culture of loss and mourning studied here demonstrates that this past violence requires addressing the impossibility of making up for what was lost. This is clearly the case with any kind of battle for reparations or restitution. However, what is to come does not have to be defined solely by what was lost. Jodi A. Byrd and Michael Rothberg argue for the need to "generate commensurabilities from incommensurability," as "decathecting from empire is a multi-levelled process that involves confronting head on the fact that the logics of colonization are often contradictory and even incommensurable."[73] By "incommensurable," they are pointing out how "both 'subaltern' and 'indigenous' name problems of translation and relationality; or, to put it slightly differently, subaltern/indigenous dialogue is, among other things, a dialogue within and about incommensurability."[74] When both sides recognize that the two sides do not share the same language—both in terms of that which is being referenced (variant genealogies) and the symbols used—there is potential to destabilize meaning and the system in which it is made. "Incommensurability" means recognizing that things will never quite be okay because of what happened and that something will always remain broken. Thus, the economy of incommensurability is drastically different from liberal humanist representations that see "proper" healing in terms of a moving on from the regrettable past by bringing the two communities together into a new collectivity.[75]

It is particularly urgent to think about incommensurabilities given the necessarily relational, comparative, and critical juxtaposing nature of decolonial and antiracist scholarship and activism that is required across the transpacific. The bitter history of Japanese imperialism and inter-Asian racisms, in addition to the immense physical distance between places, has proven a significant barrier in forming and sustaining transpacific movements in support of anti-base and decolonization movements. In light of this, Setsu Shigematsu and Keith L. Camacho argue that it is "imperative to understand local demilitarizing efforts *in relation to* other movements to decolonize Asia and the Pacific Islands," pointing specifically to President Barack Obama, who in 2010 authorized the move of 8,000 to 55,000 American military personal and hardware from Okinawa to Guam.[76] Since 2007, the growing majority of residents in the small village of Ganjeong in Korea's Jeju Island have maintained a relational movement with other antimilitary activists in Okinawa and Guam, as well as the United States, against the establishment of a naval base there—a global movement sustained in part by the refusal to allow the U.S. Navy to establish a foothold in the Korean peninsula.[77] Anticolonial alliances span Oceania that requires actively defying the U.S. formulation of the Pacific as an "American Lake." For example, on October 2012, when the Rapa Nui Council, a representative of the indigenous people of the island of Rapa Nui, also known as Easter Island, filed a lawsuit for independence and sovereignty from Chile, "they drew inspiration from similar movements elsewhere in Polynesia," identifying with the peoples and movements across Polynesia bearing the scars of competing European, New World, and Asian imperialisms.[78]

Stoler's edited volume *Haunted by Empire* is guided by her development of intimacies and comparisons as conceptual frameworks, arguing for an innovation in how we organize our archives of study and asserting that only by moving away from discrete cases to "lumpy comparative analytics" can we expose the links that may have been previously erased, as between the liberal nation-state and postcoloniality.[79] Yen Le Espiritu calls for a critical juxtaposing in her formulation of critical refugee studies: "Whereas the traditional comparative approach conceptualizes the groups, events, and places to be compared as already-constituted and discrete entities, the critical juxtaposing method posits that they are fluid rather than static and need to be understood in *relation* to each other and within the context of a flexible field of political discourses."[80] All three perspectives—relational, comparative, and critical juxtaposing—exhibit a utopic belief that the attempt to make commensurability out of incommensurabilities does not have to be defined solely by what was lost.[81]

Postcolonial grief describes a structure of feeling across the Pacific Arena. The growing body of cultural products that attempt to reckon with state violence and military imperialism across the Pacific Arena cross-reference each other's histories and aesthetics, giving shape to postcolonial grief as a structure of feeling.[82] This is why the story of Antigone, the sister who defies the state to embrace and bury her brother's body—left publicly to rot by a despotic king (Creon) in order to terrorize—is resonant across the transpacific, including the United States, Peru, and South Korea.

Postcolonial Space: Perverse Archives and Dossiers

The question of terminology and terms of engagement over the study of the transpacific is neither settled nor neutral. In addition to the idea of the "American Lake," the "Pacific Rim" is another dominant powerful U.S. economic imaginary and utopic discourse that draws on the Pacific as a rejuvenating site for U.S. capitalism.[83] The term first emerged in the 1970s to try to describe a new capitalist global relation that includes formerly communist countries, most notably China, back into relationship with each other and the capitalist economies under free-market terms. The Pacific Rim discourse and idea is "a celebration of the end of the Cold War, but it is also an anxious discourse that attempts to rim in that which is unknown. It is anxious about third spaces and non-alignment."[84] Primarily an American idea, the cultural imaginary around the term also negotiates the rising anxiety in the seeming decline of U.S. hegemony globally faced at the end of the 1970s, connected to domestic racial unrest, loss of the Vietnam War, the Saudi Oil Embargo, and the end of the gold standard for the U.S. dollar.[85] The idea of the Rim soothed these anxieties. As Connery has described it "The Rim is a horizon, a thin line that connects spaces along the rim, but also implies a lack of center."[86] It appears as a homology for a "decentered unity" that enables an enlightened mode of capitalist relations that defies older models of colony/metropole and center/margin binaries. However, the centrality (geographically and geopolitically) of the United States also allows for new forms of hegemony over Asia, the Americas, and the Pacific.

To draw attention to this ongoing contested process, I develop the term *Pacific Arena*. *Arena* references the tendency to refer to zones of combat as *theaters of war*. Unlike a theater, however, an arena more accurately describes the conditions of war and the ways that it is made into violent fantasy for consumption. Arena historically references the Roman Coliseum and is physically a large amphitheater with raised seats and a field in the center where sports games or large concerts are showcased. Figuratively, *arena* etymologically refers to a "place of combat" or "scene of contest,"[87] and the term's meaning is laden with histories of violence. One root of *arena* may be in Latin (*harena*) for the sand that cleaned up the blood of gladiators in the Roman Coliseum. The physical structure reinforces this relationship: the arena is circular, and the spectators not only watch, but encircle and bound the play happening on the field below. As a metaphor for the space and history I describe, *arena* seeks to make visible how the extant economic geo-imaginaries like "American Lake" and "Pacific Rim" are a part of a larger discursive field that upholds Cold War knowledge production that forswears colonial atrocities and ongoing militarized occupations.

While taking a transpacific approach may make it appear that I treat the Pacific Islands, Asia, and the Americas evenly, this work is weighted toward processes that occur in the Americas and Asia. In the process of revealing the links between and across the transpacific, I hope to demonstrate how "Asia, Americas, and Pacific Islands are themselves problematic terms, whose boundaries and locales have been shaped by competing histories of colonialism and militarism."[88] Los Angeles is the critical node through which the book enters and engages the militarized Pacific Arena. Starting from Los Angeles enables exposing how militarized encounters exist not only across the Pacific Ocean, but also within the Americas and along the Pacific Rim.[89]

As I explore in chapters 1 and 2, Los Angeles is produced through encounters that invite comparisons between American militarism in the Asia-Pacific and in Latin America, comparisons that bring "into 'sharper resolution' the kinds of knowledge generated—and on which people might draw—across imperial terrains and within them."[90] In addition to studying the links between U.S. and Japanese empires, this book considers how U.S. military intervention in Latin America and Central America shapes the injunction to prohibit mourning that is linked to U.S. Cold War liberal governance and resistance to it in Asia, the Americas, and across the Pacific Islands. Theodore Roosevelt's vision of the Pacific as an American Lake free for American dominance by growth of the U.S. Navy is central to establishing U.S. dual geopolitical power in Latin America (as seen in the seizure of the Panama Canal Zone in 1903) and across the Pacific to Asia. The history of covert wars in Latin America, like the American empire of bases across the Pacific and Asia, is denied and willed into invisibility. The Asian/diasporic literary and cinematic texts analyzed here make visible the centrality of the Pacific Arena to U.S. global hegemonic influence and a consistent and systematic erasure of this imperialism.

A key tension that arises in *Postcolonial Grief* is between the reassembly of the Pacific Arena into shared memories and desires for futures, defined by retribution, closure, and justice and my understanding of the productive nature of unresolved or unresolvable grief. The reassembly is not guided by my detection of a vindicated future within the archive, but by the political vision(s) we read and imagine through it.[91] The colonial archive is important not only in terms of its evidentiary value—for example, when it is used as evidence during special commissions and assemblies to assess the success of the colonial project—but also in terms of creating new colonial controls.[92] The archive is not a disinterested organizing of the past and present; it is a site through which colonialism attempts to gain control over the future of human relations and knowledge production. Thus, if the colonial archive functions to measure and assign place to the colonial subject, then the postcolonial archive has the double duty of unmooring and unsettling colonial common sense and making the future an a priori, contested project. Colonialism functions in part by not enabling the colonized to keep or maintain an archive.[93] This means that decolonization efforts have had to turn to the perpetrator's archive, what Rosanne Kennedy calls "perverse archives," in order to fill in gaps and produce evidence to support the reconstitution and rehumanization of the colonized.

The reconstituted dossier imagined by Fanon is an example of such a perverse archive and practice.[94] Fanon describes *Toward the African Revolution* as a dossier that emphasizes the "rottenness of man, of his dreadful failure" against which even the dead are exhorted to speak:

> I offer you this dossier so that no one will die, neither yesterday's dead, nor the resuscitated of today.
>
> I want my voice to be harsh, I don't want it to be beautiful, I don't want it to be pure, and I don't want it to have all dimensions.
>
> I want it to be torn through and through, I don't want it to be enticing, for I am speaking of man and his refusal, of the day-to-day rottenness of man, of his dreadful failure.
>
> I want you to tell.[95]

The dossier is a key component to state surveillance archives against insurgents and revolutionaries—a record that, in the case of the Algerian rebellion against the French (the context in which Fanon was writing), meant that a subject of a dossier was also someone likely marked for death or disappearance. While the surveillance and record may be detailed, they are not publicly available.[96] Fanon imagines the dossier as a record of the dead who sustain the living. Fanon's reconstituted dossier tells the stories of those who are supposed to be annihilated and only represented through the state's narrative. To tell is a dangerous refusal against the state injunction to look away from disappearances and violence. To tell is also a reminder of the responsibility of those who witnessed the event, those who might be considered bystanders to the "day-to-day rottenness of man, of his dreadful failure." Fanon describes insurrection as facing and managing death. His is an ethics of death that comes out of conditions of occupation and decolonization and challenges the legitimacy of a state grounded in genocide and ongoing occupation. The reconstituted dossier is an archive of insurrection that may prevent the future return of violence "so that no one will die, neither yesterday's dead, nor the resuscitated of today."

The Japanese and Korean diasporas in the texts I study seek to tell the violence of Japanese and American militarism in the Pacific Arena. Each chapter of *Postcolonial Grief* becomes progressively more transnational in its scope, moving outward from Los Angeles to Japan, Peru, and South Korea. Chapters 1 and 2 focus on Los Angeles. Chapter 1 argues that the cultural politics around redress for WWII-era Japanese American internment reveals who is considered redressible and who is not given the right to bear grievance. I start this chapter with a close reading of Fanon's "Colonial Wars and Mental Disorders" from *Wretched of the Earth*, to understand how melancholia becomes pathologized by the colonial state. I continue with an analysis of Hisaye Yamamoto's singular short story and memoir, "A Fire in Fontana," published in 1985 at the height of the Japanese American fight for reparations, to rethink the relationship between violence and postcolonial grief within a neoliberal context in which the state seeks to co-opt narratives of racialized injury.

Chapter 2 maps postcolonial grief through the Los Angeles Riots of 1992 and reveals the intersections of American military violence and neocolonialism in Guatemala and South Korea with Black struggles against deindustrialization and segregation in Los Angeles. Creative engagements with the

1992 LA Riots imagine the kind of political transformation enabled by melancholy violence that arises during an interregnum, when normal law and social order cease to exist. Through analysis of *Sa-I-Gu* and *The Tattooed Soldier* this chapter argues that making sense of the violence of colonialism and militarism in the Pacific Arena through the LA Riots requires racial cognitive remapping and a rethinking of Los Angeles's place in the world.

Chapters 3 and 4 focus on and illustrate afterlives as abject ghosts and conjured spirits. Chapter 3 turns to disruptive Koreans, who highlight the continuity between Japanese colonial domination and American military occupation of Korea. The grief and resentment they carry—their *han*—not only impact the Korean landscape, but also haunt the American popular imaginary. I focus on the margins, border zones, and minor subjects of noir—one of the most enduring and popular American genres—to reveal and remap the anxieties of modern noir and exhume the figures of colonial conflicts at the heart of the genre and its ordering of the world.

Following *Antigone* along the Pacific Rim, chapter 4 discusses the attempts to produce a "Pacific Rim imaginary" which positions the United States and Japan as psychic and economic centers of a transpacific partnership. This imaginary is contested by transnational feminist aesthetic projects that link this history to the genocidal history and decimation of Indigenous cultures connected to the colonialization of the Americas. Through analysis of Teresa Ralli and José Watanabe's *Antígona* (1999), set in the aftermath of Alberto Fujimori's right-wing terrorist Peru, this chapter considers how U.S. neoliberal regimes colluded and created conditions abetting the refusal to see state terrorisms in the Pacific Arena. In doing so, this chapter contributes to attempts at destabilizing the colonial grounds on which Asia, the Americas, and the Pacific are produced as sites to be known and studied.

The epilogue posits "watery graves" as a geopolitical and aesthetic challenge to militarist neoliberal accountings that have arisen to deal with hauntings. I moor the book's theoretical reach to a twenty-first-century context where U.S. militarization across the Pacific is expanding, occurring at the same time as a transpacific decolonial imaginary and aesthetic challenges this military dominion. My conceptual framework of watery graves is developed by considering how the protests against Barack Obama's historic visit to Hiroshima as well as accounts of bones that rise from the seas between Japan and Korea are parts of an unsettling and insurgent cultural force that is the undercurrent across the transpacific.

A new critical analytic is necessary for exposing and addressing how liberal nation-states silence the violent past and enable the return of violence in the future. However, this is not the only way this violence is silenced—there is a policing of speaking of loss that criticizes the colonial past and postcolonial present within diasporic communities.[97] I came to understand the idea of loss on multiple levels when I was an undergraduate English major at Columbia University in the 1990s. After a vigorous student-led strike to establish an Ethnic Studies Program, the university had a successful search for an Asian Americanist in literary studies, hiring David L. Eng. After the strike, one of the most public events that brought us together was when Eng spoke to a large room about what it meant that over a period of a year over six Asian and Asian American students and members of the community had died or committed suicide. No one in the administration or community reached out to us to recognize our collective pain or thought this was a problem to be addressed. The idea that for Asians there is no pain to overcome and that discussing our pain was ungrateful and unbefitting is what Eng has termed "racial scapegoating."[98] At the same time, liberal humanist models for reparations have made pain almost verboten to radical political positions because it brings up the positivist idea of recognition. American popular culture is replete with representations of dead Asians and Asian bodies in pain. That pain is sensationalized, aestheticized, and reproduced as a desired image in American popular culture and politics.

I wrote *Postcolonial Grief* because it is clear to me that death surrounds the Asian diasporas in the Americas and across the Pacific Arena. It is a past of deaths unaddressed and threatens a future of violence. However, this book is not for healing, at least not in the sense of closure. Grief and loss turned to melancholia challenge the idea that the past is closed, even as those who refuse to forget may be called crazy and unfit. If we refuse to deal with pain, then we are in danger of letting violence define our future relations with others. The temporality of pain—its recurring nature, resistance to being forgotten, the ways it takes over the body—should inform how we theorize political violence and transformation. Such a critical project means helping to ensure that all who died and disappeared have a name and identity.[99]

· ONE ·

MELANCHOLY VIOLENCE

Frantz Fanon's *The Wretched of the Earth* and Hisaye Yamamato's "A Fire in Fontana"

This chapter considers the cultural politics around redress for WWII-era Japanese American internment to ask who is considered redressible and who is not given the right to bear grievance. This requires learning "the very [premise] upon which such a line is made possible."[1] Frantz Fanon argues in *The Wretched of the Earth* that all insurgent violence becomes pathologized as melancholy and unmournable by the existing colonial architecture. As I consider through Hisaye Yamamoto's 1985 short story "A Fire in Fontana,"[2] by linking who is grievable to who is redressible in her story we can map a postcolonial melancholy that disrupts the "problematic 'boundary line between violence and post-violence"[3] that seeks to delegitimate WWII-era redress claims.

The fear that prolonged and unchecked grief will lead to violence is one of the reasons grief is pathologized and surveilled by the state. However, the state's fear of the relationship between violence and postcolonial grief is real, insofar as grief can fuel resistance and insurgency. Frantz Fanon has argued that the colonial process is one that is at its core constituted by racial violence.[4] Liberal nation-states' claims to right to violence is fundamental to postcolonial modes of control and constitutive of the U.S. liberal nation-state. Postcolonial grief threatens these linkages and highlights the connections among colonialism, the liberal nation-state, and postcolonialism.

I start this chapter with a close reading of Fanon's "Colonial Wars and Mental Disorders" from *Wretched of the Earth*, where he demonstrates how the diagnosis of melancholia against the Algerians paradoxically authorizes violence as the sole provenance of the colonial state and now the postcolonial liberal nation-state's domain.[5] In turning to Fanon's insights in "Colonial Wars," my primary goal is to understand how he puts forth a way for understanding the flexible, mutable, and unmoored nature of mourning as it develops within the context of insurgency and as he speculates how it may live on after formal colonialism ends.

I continue this chapter with an analysis of venerated Japanese American journalist and short story writer Hisaye Yamamoto's singular short story and memoir, "A Fire in Fontana." The story was published in 1985 at the height of the Japanese American fight for reparations and apology, which culminated in the landmark 1988 Civil Rights Act. Yet in the story she does not address internment nor reparations. Through such strategic absence the story enables a rethinking of the relationship between violence and postcolonial grief within a U.S. neoliberal context in which the state seeks to co-opt narratives of racialized injury. The revival and desire to use Japanese American internment as a model for President Donald Trump's proposed Muslim Registry, for example, highlights how, regardless of receiving redress, internment is always in danger of being repeated.[6] I argue that Yamamoto's story refuses a future over and over again, in the process enabling an interrogation of state violence against racialized bodies connecting Japanese Americans, Native Americans, African Americans, and whites. The story is framed as a recollection of grief over a Black family killed when their home is set on fire in the 1950s after moving into a white suburb—the murder is set between the end of internment and the start of the Watts Riots of 1965. In the story, internment, Jim Crow, and the fight for reparations are presented as a palimpsest: memories of loss due to state violence that arise unbidden to keep alive in the retelling of the related losses that structure as well as unmoor these relations. These memories not only perform an archival and witnessing function, but prevent forward movement in the narrative, forcing a living and rethinking with loss. This refusal toward closure challenges the state's desire to co-opt racialized injury toward imperial reconciliation.

Melancholy Violence

Few have fueled modern thought and practice about insurgent violence more than Fanon. He rarely differentiates between colonialist and anticolonial violence, using the same term, *violence*, to describe both. Nor does he distinguish among epistemic, structural, and material violence under colonialism. For Fanon, "violence is the form of relationality itself" between colonial powers and colonized subjects.[7] As Nigel Gibson writes, for Fanon "there must be revolt" for Algerians "because life cannot be conceived otherwise than as a kind of combat . . . a combat breathing."[8]

Although much is written about Fanon's theorizations on violence, the relationship between mourning, melancholia and violence as offered in "Colonial Wars and Mental Disorders," the last chapter of *Wretched of the Earth* has received relatively little scholarly attention.[9] Published in 1961, this chapter is based on his practice as the chief psychiatrist at the French military hospital, Blida-Joinville, in Algeria between 1951 and 1957 during the height of violence in the Algerian revolt against French colonialism. What is central to his insights in Blida-Joinville is the recognition that there is rationality in the permeability between mourning and melancholia. Not only are Algerians pathologized by French colonialists for being Black and Muslim, but they are criminalized when they refuse to assimilate to colonial control. In that context the idea that subjects under colonialism can be healed is itself a colonizing idea. To be healed is to accept colonialism as a regular state of being for the colonized. Healing prepares the colonizer to wield violence for the state, and for the colonized to accept being terrorized as a regular state of being. When scholars turn to this chapter it is generally to understand how Fanon describes new psychological disorders raised by colonialism.[10] But Fanon is doing more than writing about how colonialism produces new pathologies. Here he is demonstrating how insurgency becomes criminalized by the French medical establishment and is one of the insidious and powerful ways that colonialism continues to influence the postcolonial condition.

Fanon was not only a strategist and ambassador for the Algerian revolution, he was foremost a doctor and healing the individual was indivisible from decolonization from Europe. Until Fanon the dominant consensus about war trauma within the medical field focused on the occupying soldier as the center for diagnosis.[11] In difference from the earliest period of his professional writings he has focused on how the colonized suffers differently from the colonizer. His thinking about psychiatry fundamentally changes from working in Blida-Joinville, where he treated both French occupiers and Algerian rebels.[12]

At Blida-Joinville, he worked with patients who were previously diagnosed with "reactionary psychoses." However, he disagreed with this diagnoses, which tended to emphasize the need to address the traumatic *event belonging to the past*, instead arguing that "according to all available evidence, the future of such patients is mortgaged."[13] Recognizing how dread mortgages the future of the colonized is a part of Fanon's complex theorization of colonial violence and the legitimacy of insurgent violence to end it. Within the context of decolonization, loss of life becomes the norm and threatens to never end. As he writes, "But the war goes on; and we will have to bind up for years to come the many, sometimes ineffaceable, wounds that the colonialist onslaught has inflicted on our people . . . which we must search out and mercilessly expel from our land and our spirits."[14]

This last chapter of the *Wretched of the Earth* is remarkable for the ways it describes the gendered violence of colonial occupation and war. For the soldiers and Algerians he treats, the trauma is physically manifested, and the violence they seek to keep at bay returns in dreams, through voices only they hear, and repeated in their violence toward themselves, their wives, and their children. Domestic violence and violence within the family arising from the Algerian war is a lingering concern for Fanon, leading him to conclude that "the hitherto unemphasized characteristics of certain psychiatric descriptions here given," "confirm, if confirmation were necessary, that this colonial war is singular even in the pathology that it gives rise to."[15]

It is in this context that Fanon warns of how the colonial medical establishment changes the diagnosis for melancholia to refuse to recognize the violent pathology of French colonialism: "They [the Algerian colonial medical establishment] were accustomed when dealing with a patient subject to melancholia to fear that he would commit suicide. Now the melancholic Algerian takes to killing." He continues, "How does the Algerian school respond to such an anomaly? . . . Killing oneself is turning into and against oneself; it means practicing introspection. There is no inner life where the North African is concerned."[16] Because they kill others they have no personhood, nor is there a history to which their action can be moored. Lacking "introspection" enables the medical establishment to recategorize the melancholic Algerian as a criminal, not a medical patient.[17] Adriana Cavarero demonstrates how this same pathologization continues in the twenty-first-century European context, where the Muslim female suicide bomber is continually represented as an empty vassal evacuated of thought and conscience and thus undeserving of mourning.[18] Fanon's medical knowledge enables him to see that the discussion over mourning and melancholia are always political in the colonial setting. The melancholic, like the mourner, can claim dangerous grievances against the state. Thus pathologized, Algerian melancholia becomes equated with a "zone of none being," a body without "inner life" and whose acts have no meaning and rationality. Diagnosed in retrospect, all Algerians lack inner life and being, whether they turn their melancholia inward to suicide or outward to kill others. The colonial medical establishment quickly disassociates all possibility of rationality from violence of any kind, spanning from suicide to killing, connected to Algerian actors. It is a circular ontology; any act of violence by the colonized that critiques the colonial system is melancholic, even when it severely contradicts the principles of psychoanalysis itself.

In the face of evidence that challenges their precepts, the colonial medical establishment refuses to acknowledge resistance against colonialism by pathologizing and diminishing the mind of the Algerian until they are nothing more than simply a cipher for criminality. This method of keeping violence the provenance of the state continues from the colonial state to the liberal nation-state form and is one of the ways colonialism continues to live on and threaten the project of decolonization and anticolonial nationalism.[19] Fanon quotes a doyen of the judges of a court in Algeria to demonstrate how this pathologization spans psychiatry to the legal terrain: "We are wrong in believing this whole revolt to be political. From time to time that love of a scrimmage that they have has to come out!"[20] The basis for this is misrecognition—it is wrong to recognize insurgency as having a political basis, and the insurgents misrecognize their revolt as political and legitimate. Under these terms, violence in the hands of the insurgents, even when it appeared rational and sympathetic, could not be considered to have been enacted by a mind with conscience, and can never be legal. Although violence was not considered completely irrational (as we can see in the distinction between melancholia pre and during the Algerian War), it can never be a rational option for colonialized subjects to use to create a new state.

This discussion over who gets to legitimately wield violence becomes central to the emerging global liberal human rights architecture in the 1950s and 1960s following the wave of decolonization globally.[21] For example, Amnesty International is established in 1961, the same year that the *Wretched of the Earth* is published. However, liberal nation-states, like the colonial state, have refused to recognize the rational basis of armed struggle against state violence. Randall Williams in *The Divided World* further offers a powerful critique that places this pathologization of non-state violence as bedrock to the liberal humanism that rises as a replacement for global relations in wake of colonialism's formal end.[22] Williams argues that with decolonization and the dissolution of European empires in Asia and Africa in the 1940s and 1950s, "new military humanism gains substantial ideological cover against the rhetoric of human rights." He suggests that "we need to look for less problematic forms of emancipatory politics."[23] The newly constituted liberal nation-state form does not create a new human society against the colonial state. Rather, it extends colonialism, particularly by endowing the nation-state with the sole power to use violence.[24] Amnesty International first creates the category of conscientious prisoners, but takes Nelson Mandela, imprisoned for his fight against apartheid, off their lists because in 1964 he was a part of an armed struggle against the apartheid state. In the context of an apartheid South Africa, where white supremacists increasingly turned toward targeted and random acts of violence to suppress the growing insurgency, even advocates for nonviolence like Desmond Tutu recognized that they were alive to be able to advocate for nonviolence because members of the insurgency were willing to kill and die—keeping the war against colonialism alive and deflecting the violence away from them. For Williams, the case of Amnesty International removing Mandela from the list of conscientious prisoners is important to remember as a constitutive act forming the bedrock of liberal human rights, as it demonstrates that violence is now legitimated as the sole provenance of the nation-state.[25]

Fanon writes that "Colonial Wars and Mental Disorders" seems out of place in a book concerned with modern revolutionary theory. However, given the extent to which colonialism and independence struggles shaped his understanding of alienation and subordination, it makes sense for him to return to the psychological impact of anticolonialism and insurgency as a way to prepare for decolonization and to consider how to address colonialism in the newly emerging and reconstituted states. While the state has the power of violence through its military and arsenal, postcolonial grief is an affective source of insurgency that includes both violent and nonviolent responses to colonialism: it shapes bodies' movements and the ways they connect with others in a manner that the state sees as a threat and something to be managed.

The Bloated Dead in Hisaye Yamamoto's "Fire in Fontana"

I turn to Yamamoto's short story "A Fire in Fontana" in order to discuss melancholy violence within the context of Jim Crow and the late twentieth-century fight for redress for Japanese American internment. My discussion of Yamamoto begins by developing the idea of "bloated dead" as a theoretical working through of the concept of postcolonial grief which is in dialectic with a history of dispersal, incarceration, and silencing that connects Japanese American internment to Black dispossession during Jim Crow. I then situate her work within a broader critique of Japanese American fight for redress and the limitations of the 1988 Civil Rights Act as it unfolded within Japanese diasporas.

Hisaye Yamamoto is a venerated Asian American writer and intellectual whose work is a part of the Third World feminist U.S. collective, a political-intellectual formation that emerges in the late 1970s.[26] At the same time they fought against white supremacy, U.S. Third World feminism also diagnosed the unfinished nature of radical transformation by highlighting the need for an internal critique, advocating for an intersectional understanding of power that contests multiple axes of oppression. Push back against liberal and radical antiracist gains was violent—epistemically, economically, and materially—by 1985, when "A Fire in Fontana," Yamamoto's loosely autobiographical short story, was published.[27] Grace Kyungwon Hong argues that given when and where it is published, we need to think about this story within the context of the battle for Japanese American reparations, despite the fact that Yamamoto begins with the end of internment and writes during the height of the reparation period without explicitly mentioning either.[28] Originally published in the Christmas issue of the *Rafu Shimpo*, Los Angeles's English-language Japanese American newspaper, the story later became included in the reprint of her canonical short story collection, *Seventeen Syllables*.[29]

Yamamoto's story points repeatedly to incarceration, surveillance, and use of militarized police violence in upholding white supremacy since World War II. Told in the first person, the unnamed narrator's recollections begin with her return as a young woman to the Poston Internment Camp in Arizona after leaving Chicago during World War II and continues to her first postinternment job at a Black newspaper in Los Angeles. Her subsequent travels throughout the country begin the new phase of her story before concluding with the protagonist, in her living room in a suburb of Los Angeles, watching with "an undercurrent of exultation" the 1965 Watts Riots unfold.[30] "A Fire in Fontana" spans more historical time than the other stories in *Seventeen Syllables*, but her economy with words and her skill at building allegorical structures of dual narratives—wherein the internal narrative and the external narrative unfold together—enable her to tell a story of many decades in relatively few pages. Central to "A Fire in Fontana" is the murder of a Black family, the Shorts, who are killed when their home (in Fontana, a segregated white suburb of Los Angeles in the late 1940s) is set on fire. The protagonist feels implicated in their deaths because as a journalist she did not believe them. She failed to advocate for them and did not expose the threats against them.[31]

Yamamoto's story twins her discussion of transformative politics not only to violence, but also to grief. The news of the death of the Shorts is one of two pivotal moments in the short story, the other being a brief recollection of the protagonist's mother's funeral as the story's second and parallel apex. Remembering her mother's death propels a physical journey across a segregated America from the early to mid-1950s that also begins the process of recalling the violence that is the condition of possibility for the present neoliberal nation-state. Yamamoto features grief and violence as sometimes cohabiting, sometimes existing in parallel spheres, and sometimes constitutive to racial formations in the United States. Grief and violence appear in the story in both themes of death, which cannot be forgotten, and as a history of returns that shapes the story's temporal drive and spatial organization. She describes a fear of memories coming at the wrong time and of transformation that never manifests, the temporality of grief turned into violent melancholy.

Yamamoto continually turns to metaphors of slow burning and warmed bodies to express this melancholy, a burning that is concerned with timing and fear of incompletion or lack of transformation. And yet this is not a story of futility.[32] This anxiety over lack of transformation is replayed throughout the story with recollections of a past of deaths, which constantly reappear in the protagonist's life and with which she does not let go. The story opens with this muted declaration: "Something weird happened to me not long after the end of World War II. I wouldn't go so far as to say that I, a Japanese American, became Black, because that's a pretty melodramatic statement. But some kind of transformation did take place, the effects of which are with me still . . . sometimes I see it as my inward self being burnt black in a certain fire."[33] Her use of fire connects both the burning down of the family in their home and the police cover-up of the murder. The story opens with this muted declaration and is followed by a story about a white jazz player who becomes a pastor in a Black church in Watts, Los Angeles, a life that "as I see it, represents a triumph."[34] However, we soon learn to mistrust the phrase "as I see it," as the protagonist is often misrecognizing or doubting what she sees. She continues with a statement of uncertainty about her own transformation, proclaiming in comparison, "I don't know whether mine is or not."[35] This tone of uncertainty dogs her throughout the story—an awareness of transformation yet a sense that this transformation is inadequate, comes too late, or is not recognizable:

"And that was the last time I heard mention of the conflagration. It was around this time that I felt something happening to me, but I couldn't put my finger on it. It was something like an itch I couldn't locate, or like food not being cooked enough, or something undone which should have been done, or something forgotten which should have been remembered."[36]

An "itch I couldn't locate" and "something which should have been remembered" describe the tactile quality of being haunted by the dead. The idea of burnt food also connects to the idea of improper mourning as traditionally mourning rituals have involved the (figurative) eating of the dead.[37] The past is always remembered by the narrator as one of bad choices—like eating undercooked food. Because the temporality of the story is driven by belatedness the story also refuses a future over and over again.

The melancholy violence that structures Yamamoto's story describes a past and present filled with violence that cannot be addressed by existing legal, political, and cultural frameworks. As Yamamoto's story makes clear, internment and postwar relocation of Japanese Americans into U.S. cities blend with Jim Crow laws that legitimate racial covenants, segregation, and denial of rights to property ownership, anti-Black edicts that were upheld by violence imprinted into law and maintained as often by white mob violence as by police collusion.[38] While white flight from urban areas to the suburbs is made possible by the GI Bill, bank loans, and state subsidies, racist banking policies made it nearly impossible for Blacks to get loans so they could not purchase property, particularly in the suburbs, effectively stunting the growth of a Black middle class.[39] As the 1968 Kerner Commission Report found, the concurrent state practices of divestment of state services from the urban core, leading to poor housing, schools, and lack of opportunities for Blacks leads to mounting frustrations that culminated in large-scale protests like the Watts Riots of 1965 with which the story ends.[40]

This grief bloats and permeates an American nation-state fundamentally shaped by segregation and internal colonization and upheld by violence. Yamamoto's story repeatedly turns toward and presents memories of burning and fire evoking not only lynching and segregation in the Jim Crow era, but also an alternative temporality of transformation.[41] Like Yamamoto Fanon also turns to fire as a metaphor for transformation and temporality. In the introduction to *Black Skin, White Masks* he writes, "This book should have been written three years ago. . . . But these truths were a fire in me then. Now I can tell them without being burned. These truths do not need to be hurled in men's faces. They are not intended to ignite fervor. I do not trust fervor. Every time it has burst somewhere it has brought fire, famine, misery [and] contempt for man."[42] Fanon advocates for strategically holding back, so that revolution does not "ignite fervor." This requires belated insurgent action so that the colonized subject becomes their own engine of transformation: "of those who heat the iron in order to shape it at once. I should prefer to warm man's body and leave him. We might reach this result; mankind retaining this fire through self-combustion . . . to dig into its own flesh to find a meaning."[43] The narrator's horror and disquiet become overwhelming when she sees signs of covering up the murder by criminalizing Short—all official sources claim the fire, defying all logic, was accidently set by Short himself. This knowledge, and that she failed the Shorts, "warms" her body and "digs into its own flesh to find a meaning." The repetition of provisional phrases such as "something weird happened to me," "something forgotten which should have been remembered," and "it seems" describes a slow process of self-combustion. The different ways that the state legitimated its own violence is brought to the present through the memories of deaths that should not be forgotten, even if remembering them also interrupts forward movement and mires the individual in melancholy violence. This hesitation also reminds us that the work of transformation is never done.

Soon after the murder of the Shorts, there is passing mention of the death of the narrator's mother. This occurs while the narrator is witnessing a racist rant by a motorist against a Black bus driver. After this point the narrator begins a journey eastward across the continent, mirroring the opening of the story when she is on a bus moving west from Chicago to Arizona, returning to her incarceration in the Poston Internment Camp: "Not long after, going to work one morning, I found myself wishing that the streetcar would rattle on and on and never stop. I'd felt the sensation before, on the way to my mother's funeral. If I could somehow manage to stay on the automobile forever, I thought, I would never have to face the fact of my mother's death. A few weeks later after this incident on the street, I mumbled some excuse about planning to go back to school and left the paper."[44]

This passage marks an important turning point in the story, as it comes when the narrator is about to quit working at the newspaper. She equates her feelings about her mother's death, which are both about denial, refusal, and prolonging of mourning as well as acceptance — with the desire to keep rolling and rattling past the office. The death of the mother is a significant break for the self in psychoanalysis, as she is the first Other the ego is supposed to kill in order for the self to emerge as an autonomous being.[45] Here, as opposed to "resolving" her grief for her mother, she "mumbles an excuse." She denies her grief coherency. On the level of narrative form then, the story pulls back again and again to moments of unresolved and unresolvable losses and forces a reengagement with this violence.

While "A Fire in Fontana" begins with the protagonist's return to incarceration, it does not discuss her experience in the Poston Internment Camp. In many powerful narratives about Japanese American internment, the experience of internment remains an inference, a rarely mentioned but pervasive presence. This strategy engages with a historical reality in which internment was heavily silenced after it ended, and has created fertile conditions for an intergenerational engagement with "postmemory."[46] In addition to haunting absence, internment also emerges through the dispossession of Blacks in the story, which brings the past to the present, forcing a coexisting of the two groups in the space of the urban city. Historical narratives might privilege a teleological telling of history, but the turn toward postcolonial grief means a turn toward the spatiality of imperialism. This allows us to see how spaces carry sedimented histories, how they are haunted not only by memories of events in the past, but also by memories that refuse to stop being lived.

The sedimented nature of space can be seen in a scene between the protagonist and her interactions with a white woman and a Black woman on her journey back to Poston. Soon after the opening lines, the story moves back in time to 1942, when the narrator was interned during World War II. Our introduction to World War II–era racial politics in the story arrives via public transportation. While traveling by bus across Texas to go back to Poston, the narrator is implicated in the glee of a young white woman enjoying the sight of a Black man turned away from a "whites only" water fountain. The white woman assumed that the narrator would share in her anti-Black racism and is disappointed by her reaction of disgust. Later, on the same bus trip, the narrator trespasses into a whites-only accommodation, as much testing the racial rules as conforming to white supremacist racial hierarchy: "I dared to try White first, and no one challenged me, so I continued this presumptuous practice at all the way stations of Texas. After I got back on the bus the first time, I was haunted by the long look given me by a cleaning woman in the restroom. I decided, for the sake of my conscience, that the Negro woman had never seen a Japanese before."[47]

During her exchanges with the women above, the "I" is separated from the body. She positions herself through the eyes of the Black woman and recalls the earlier scene in the bus back to Poston, where she herself had looked at a white woman with disgust. The story opens with the narrator describing her middle-aged self as outfitted with glasses for "myopia," pointing to a lifetime of engagement and difficulty with seeing. In this scene, she doubly distances herself by imagining herself as something peculiar to the Black woman, whose "long look" interpolates her, but now as an unknown subject. It is as an unknown that the internee subject exits the scene, and the "long look" is an interrogative exchange into which the reader is invited.

The kind of complex and unsettling looking relations enabled here recalls bell hooks's powerful formulation of the oppositional gaze: "The attempt to control the right to gaze [means] one learns to look a certain way in order to resist."[48] The gaze not only defines looking relations, but also directs the body's orientation. This scene exemplifies the internalization of surveillance as well as the materiality of white supremacist architecture externally enforcing Jim Crow laws. The passage that ends "A Fire in Fontana" reflects this negotiation and engagement with surveillance, and violence. This moment adds fuel to the fire that had as yet cooked the narrator incompletely:

> Appalled, inwardly cowering, I watched the burning and looting on the screen and heard the reports of the dead and wounded. But

beneath my distress, I felt something else, a tiny trickle of warmth which I finally recognized as an undercurrent of exultation. To me the tumult in the city was the long-awaited, gratifying next chapter of an old movie that had flickered about in the back of my mind for years . . . suddenly the house was in flames . . . then there could be heard the voices of a man and woman screaming, and the voices of two small children as well.[49]

This is a macabre scene, wherein her own metaphorical burning recalls the real screaming and "voices of two small children as well." Here, the narrator "finally recognizes . . . an undercurrent of exultation," in contrast to the opening passage, which is typified by passive language. The warmth in her progresses to the memory of the Shorts's deaths, which ignites her, and to which she connects to the anger in the city.

However, the distance she shows in the beginning — not really being Black but being burnt Black inside — is still present. She is mediated in many ways from the scene of violence. She is sitting at home watching the event unfold on television, living in a white suburb much like Fontana, which murdered the Short family just two decades prior. She gets there on the "coattails of a paler husband."[50] Surveillance emerges in the distance as she shows in her claim to feeling exultation from the violence as well as her feeling not-quite Black. The oppositional gaze here is also an act of subveillance — that is, surveilling and documenting state violence itself.[51] Here, as well as in the ongoing discussion of the arson killing of the Shorts, Yamamoto represents the narrator's individual trauma reflecting both a racial distance from and momentary confrontation with the long genealogy of state-condoned anti-Black bodily violence via lynching in which burning often played a role. Throughout the story, Japanese American raciality unfolds not only within the internment experience, but also, crucially, in distinction from American apartheid and its protogenocidal logics, a distinction and difference that the story is both invested in and seeks to bridge.

Reparations, Memorialization, Settler Colonial Violence

When asked during an interview for *MELUS* if she had ever gone back to the Poston Internment Camp, Yamamoto replies, "No. A friend went to the Grand Canyon once, and on the way back she and her husband and child visited Poston, where we were, and she said that the camp and grounds had all been taken back by the Indians, and they were growing alfalfa on it, and they were living in the adobe school building that we all built *with our own hands*, and cooking in them, and about all that remains of us was the little plaque that dedicated the school, and told how it had been built."[52]

The "little plaque" is the only trace of Poston's forced labor of Japanese Americans who were incarcerated there between 1942 and 1944.[53] Poston was the largest geographical area three miles west of the Colorado River and was built on the Colorado River Indian Reservation against the Gila River Tribal Council's objections. At one point, with 17,000 residents, it was the third-largest city in Arizona. Considering the little plaque more deeply reveals this scene instructing us how settler colonialism consistently and regularly incorporates racialized U.S. subjects into dominating and managing native lands.[54] Additionally, in recommending the end of internment, the War Relocation Authority (WRA) declared that the internment of the Nisei had increased the likelihood of the country "having a second American Indian problem."[55] Unlike other internment camps, Poston was also a work camp, as internees were made to build structures that would house them during their stay and later would be used by Native Americans. The building's most recent history recalls the dispossession of Native Americans and breaking of treaties, conscription of Japanese American labor, and long and bloody battles over the sovereignty of native peoples.

Poston and the forcible takeover of the Gila River people's land makes clear how Japanese Americans were compelled into acting in ongoing settler colonialism in the United States, at the same time that it reveals the violence that compels their participation as settlers. On the basic level, the renaming of the Gila River people's land as Poston (named after Charles Debrille Poston, a government engineer who established the Reservation in 1865) establishes how Japanese Americans settle on conquered land. Ikyo Day argues that the settler colonies of the United States and Canada were defined by "the diminishing role of an imperial metropole that facilitated successive stages of Indigenous conquest that involved invasion, removal, relocation, reservation, assimilation, termination, co-optation, and self-determination. This renders a paradoxical situation where 'the postcolonial operates simultaneously as the colonial.'"[56]

The little plaque is inadequate to explain the intertwined histories of occupation, displacement, and incarceration and the cycles of imperialism and its concomitant violence, loss, impermanence, and dispossession in the history of internment. Battles over memorialization, like redress, create momentum for friction and the revelation of contestatory histories. Such was the case with the first significant national level event in Japanese American redress for WWII-era internment—the passing of the landmark 1988 Civil Rights Act. The bill is landmark because both the apology from President Reagan, which acknowledges wrongdoing, and the financial redress of nearly $20,000 to 89,000 internees and their heirs, are historical and was nearly inconceivable.[57] For example, like the Blacks who are dispossessed in "A Fire in Fontana," the Gila River people also never receive any compensation or apology for the seized lands for Poston internment camp.

The limits of the 1988 civil rights act emerges around questions of settler colonialism and for subjects whose citizenship was revoked. The act names the redressible subject as a person who is of "Japanese ancestry" and "a citizen or a legal resident" during the period of internment. In practice it also required that internees demonstrate their property loss to be able to claim the financial compensation.[58] Japanese from Latin America and U.S. Nisei and Issei who were stripped of citizenship have still not been offered reparations by the United States.[59] In addition, non-Japanese peoples who were put into internment camps—like Carolinians and Chamorro peoples in the Northern Mariana Islands—have also not received an apology. As Congressman Gregorio Kilili Camacho Sablan of the Commonwealth of the Northern Mariana Islands stated in 2013, during the occasion of the twenty-fifth anniversary of the 1988 Civil Rights Act: "military internment is unfortunately not foreign to the history of the people of the Northern Mariana Islands, as thousands of Chamorros and Carolinians were also confined in camps after American forces captured Saipan during WWII." The imperial nation-state seeks to settle redress in national terms in order to assert the power of the nation's law. However, those left out of the possibility of redress by the 1998 Civil Rights Act challenged this national framing and revealed the ways that the "national is always global and local."[60] Because of how it is placed at the intersections of settler colonialism, expanding military imperialism across the transpacific, and white supremacy, who the Civil Rights Act does not see as subjects for redress for WWII-era internment point to the "presence of excess in the hegemonic post–World War II/Cold War epistemic and material formations."[61]

Such excess is not only found within extra-national spaces and subjects but was produced in the nation as well. In addition to incarceration and dispossession, there was a wartime fervor to renounce Japanese American citizenship. All Japanese Americans were reclassified as "alien citizens" during World War II, but some in Tule Lake were forced to give up their U.S. citizenship and live as a "Native American alien" for nearly twenty years.[62] Tule Lake was the only one of the ten internment camps that was also a maximum security segregation camp holding "potential enemies of America" like "no-no boys."[63] Between November 1943 and January 1944 Tule Lake came under even more extraordinary military force when it came under martial law. The internees were angered when on October 15, 1943, an internee was killed when a truck carrying these agricultural workers flipped over. They held an unauthorized funeral and soon began a strike. Military police occupied the camp, in turn creating severe hardships and widespread anger toward "the occupying army, the War Relocation Authority, and any person or group that cooperated with them, radicalizing many of the unjustly imprisoned inmates."[64]

This military control of Tule Lake ended January 15, 1944, but Public Law 405, or the Renunciation Act of 1944, passed by Congress and signed by President Roosevelt on July 1, 1944, was directed at these Japanese Americans at Tule Lake with the goal of coercing them to illegally renounce their citizenship and occupy a new position as a "Native American Alien." The senate hearings on the Renunciation Act reveal the racism and desire to deport Japanese Americans that drove the will to institute this into law.[65] It took twenty-four years for some to successfully argue that they were coerced into signing it. Compounding the uphill battle of their fight, Japanese, as "aliens ineligible for citizenship" "once stripped of citizenship, they were ineligible, under naturalization laws then in force, to again become citizens in the United States of America" [66] until after the Nationalization Act of 1952. On March 6, 1968, 4,978 stateless Nisei and Kibei were finally given their citizenship back.[67] However, portions of this law are still valid and the ability of Congress to demand the renunciation of citizens considered an enemy of the state is an alarming legal and sociopolitical precedent in the post-9/11 era.[68]

As the contests over the meaning of redress for Japanese American internment demonstrate, there can be no single reparative act for internment.[69] Such histories of racism against which many Nisei at Tule Lake fought against would not only be potentially silenced by the Civil Rights Act, but this silence may perpetuate a self-damaging performance of Japanese American "superpatriotism." As Chris Iijima stated during a community event held around the signing of the Civil Rights Act in 1990, "those who, at the time of the internment, saw it for the injustice and outrage that it was and chose to dissent continue to be silenced and unheralded even during the process of acknowledging their prescience. In essence, what Americans were being told by Congress to celebrate, by giving redress to Japanese Americans, was that patriotism—the kind of patriotism that does not resist injustice—gets rewarded."[70] As Iijima warns above reparations always carry with them the force for imperial demands of reconciliation, where significant compromise is forced to be made for the promise of visibility. Those critical of the neoliberal premise behind Japanese American reparations were concerned about healing the community, especially as the compulsion to remain silent about dissenting histories within Japanese American internment history is profoundly damaging.[71]

This is why Yamamoto's turn to grief, mourning, and melancholic temporality at this particular political junctures is so productive. By refusing to declare the past resolved and finished, and by linking Black dispossession with Japanese American internment, she links histories of loss.[72] As Sara Clarke Kaplan has argued, an "*articulation* of loss can reconstitute the remnants of violence . . . as 'a world of new representations and alternative meanings.'"[73] The Japanese American critique of reparations, like "A Fire in Fontana," may showcase how new systems of meaning can be crafted by recouping such losses.

Conclusion

Fanon's insights into the pathologization of melancholia, and Yamamoto's bloated temporality, enable imagining the kinds of transformations we can seek outside of those mandated by the liberal nation-state and international frameworks for rights and redress.[74] Japanese American redress culture intersects with a rising 1990s transpacific redress culture, like that which has arisen around "comfort women" and Cambodian refugees deported from the U.S., who had sought redress and justice mainly from the U.S. and Japan for war violence and military crimes since the WWII era. They have gained momentum not only through legal and political means, but as a result of making impact on cultural and social realities.[75] This confluence of demands for redress occurs in a neoliberal context where the U.S. seeks greater alliance across the transpacific, leading to racial and economic reorganization of global cities like Los Angeles to become a better engine for global capitalism and integration.[76] In such a twenty-first-century militarized neoliberal context, narratives of racialized injuries related to World War II–era U.S. militarism in the Pacific Arena, such as Japanese American internment, are in danger of being co-opted, requiring monitoring and interventions into how to challenge imperial reconciliation.

· TWO ·

HAUNTING ABSENCE

Racial Cognitive Mapping, Interregnum, and the Los Angeles Riots of 1992

Creative engagements with the 1992 Los Angeles Riots provide an opportunity to imagine the kind of political transformation that can be enabled by melancholy violence that arises during an interregnum, when normal law and social order cease to exist.[1] The absence of state protection and breakdown of social order during the riots enabled the resurgence of memories of related trauma and the production of new critique, not only by African Americans, but also among others with grievances related to U.S. militarism, including Korean and Guatemalan immigrants. Making sense of the violence of colonialism and militarism in the Pacific Arena through the LA Riots does the work of racial cognitive remapping: that is, it is a rethinking of Los Angeles's place in the world. While chapter 1 explores memories of loss that rise intermittently and unbidden, this chapter describes a world and worldview steeped in losses that seem impossible to overcome and leave behind, regardless of will.

By 1992, Los Angeles was the first city in the continental United States that was majority nonwhite.[2] A generalized anxiety that the erosion of white control would unravel the city's social fabric wrote the LA Riots as representing the inevitability of a dystopic future that awaits the United States. To further complicate this association of multiracial Los Angeles with unsurvivable futures, I turn to two canonical texts of the LA Riots — the 1993 documentary *Sa-I-Gu*, by Dai Sil Kim-Gibson, and the 2000 novel *The Tattooed Soldier*, by Héctor Tobar.[3] These narratives capture the riots through uncommon historical lenses: they critique the American militarism that emerged from these violent times when it became clear to the immigrants living through the riots that the U.S. government had abandoned them. The breakdown of social order accompanied by memories and unresolved/unresolvable grief that structure the everyday in these two works twin a critique of U.S. racism with antimilitarism. These texts are permeated with loss and mourning through which the LA Riots — and state abandonment and U.S. white supremacy more broadly — are racially cognitively mapped onto U.S. military-backed modernity projects in the Korean peninsula and Central America. The riots are not merely a backdrop on which these other, hidden narratives appear. Rather, the riots and military violence become interconnected.

The LA Riots are not only a historical and political event, but also a cultural-literary one.[4] As Min Hyoung Song has argued, the LA Riots and the deep anxiety they produced in the cultural imaginary became a locus for new symbols and meanings that gave shape to a pessimism and fear that were the result of the dramatically changing racial landscape in the United States. The vitality of the riots for fueling a critical imaginary was seen in the twenty-fifth anniversary of the LA Riots in April 29, 2017 — an anniversary that inspired great reflection, especially given the clear connections between the treatment of Rodney King and the crisis in violence and murder of Black people by the police and the lack of judicial justice in the twenty-first century. The feature film *Gook* (2017), by Justin Chon, which opened in the context of this anniversary makes evident the significance of the LA Riots not only for understanding Black–Korean relations but also for decoding intergenerational tensions between members of the Korean diaspora in the United States.[5] In a brief scene he showcases an intergenerational conversation between a Korean immigrant liquor storeowner who discusses his experience as a soldier for the Korean army, something the film's second-generation Korean American male protagonist cannot relate to. The unresolved impact of U.S. occupation and subsequent militarism of civilian life on the Korean continent on Korean American lives is also central in the documentary *Sa-I-Gu*, made nearly twenty-five years earlier. These repetitions and variations found in texts about the LA Riots help mine the imaginary produced within the context of the absence of the state and the breakdown of the social order. The particular focus of this chapter is how these creative engagements enable a way to deal with multiple levels of incommensurability and seeming intractability. An attempt to make commensurabilities out of incommensurabilities does not have to be defined solely by what was lost—in this case, faith in the U.S. nation-state.

My engagement with the idea of interregnum to consider the riots as a sociopolitical break and as a fount for creative engagement seeks to reignite the significance of politicized and insurgent mourning to state management and challenges to state claims to power. The term *interregnum*, or *justititium*, originates in the Roman period (late 500s) and defines a period in which absolute power may become absent due to the death of the sovereign. Much like the modern liberal nation-states in the West, in the Roman period, power was split between the executive (sovereign) and legislative (senate and magistrates). While the senate and magistrates made and administered the law, only the sovereign was imagined to possess actual power invested by God. The call *The King is dead, long live the King* captures the urgent need to secure a new sovereign to ensure peaceful transition. In order to ensure that the republic did not devolve into anarchy the senate was allowed to temporarily yield sovereign power. Thus, this was a dangerous period where power could be grabbed not only by an illegitimate ruler but by senators, magistrates, or citizens.

Since the Roman period, "interregnum" has been interpreted more broadly to mean a cessation or break in normal political power and social order. Most scholars deploying the idea of interregnum to explain twentieth- and twenty-first-century crisis in politics and rise in military dictatorships and far-right politics tend to take a variation on Agamben's argument of a state of exception—that the population is being governed by those who are holding illegitimate power, grabbed during periods of war or social upheaval. The power holders are not truly beholden to the republic that it dominates and rules but does not serve. However, Agamben also reminds us that the interregnum was managed in part by a politicized and public mourning period that sought to cover and legitimate the absence of sovereign power. Gramsci's writings in the *Prison Notebooks* also allude to both the broader definition based on illegitimacy and how the interregnum can lead to a reactionary state-centered mourning in terms that are alarmingly resonant with the neoliberal interregnum represented by the LA Riots and the histories of U.S. military empire that I seek to illuminate. He states, "The crisis consists precisely of the fact that the old is dying and the new cannot be born; in this interregnum a great variety of morbid symptoms appear."[6] These morbid symptoms manifest themselves "physically (depression), epistemologically (skepticism with regard to all theories), economically (poverty), and politically (cynicism)."[7]

The lingering anti-Black political affect that intersects with anti-immigrant Los Angeles demands recognizing that the multiple layers of abandonment central to the operation of neoliberalism and white supremacy extend temporally and spatially beyond the crisis in Los Angeles itself and necessitate a twinning of critiques of militarism and racial capitalism. Initial protests after a Simi Valley jury acquitted police officers of excessive violence against Black motorist Rodney King on April 29, 1992, quickly led to a six-day unrest that immobilized Los Angeles. The video of the beating showed graphic police attacks, and there was global shock that these police were acquitted.[8] The severity of the riots, including burning down entire sections of South Central and Koreatown, areas that were cordoned off and that in the absence of state protection—particularly the police and the national reserves—absorbed most of the violence, loss, and damages from the uprising. The recognition that the state does not value all bodies equally was already apparent from the treatment of King, whose subjection to extraordinary brutality was televised and unforgettable. Insurgent anti-state mourning, loss, and melancholia threaten to reveal and unravel these linkages and produce the possibilities for new political affiliations.

Los Angeles is a fallen figure in these narratives, offering a way to racially cognitively remap Los Angeles as symbolizing the end of the promise of the United States as a location of recovery from the violence of colonialism and premodernity. My development of the term *racial cognitive mapping* draws on Fredric Jameson's definition of cognitive mapping as "the imaginary representations of the subject's relationship to his or her Real conditions of existence."[9] I identify repeated representations of bodily suffering to represent the traumas of the past that are dangerous to speak and remember.

The works explored here describe Los Angeles in tactile terms, a place these immigrants felt they knew, a feeling that became reordered after their experience of living there. No longer the repository of images and meaning for futurity and survivability, Los Angeles is a repository for shared traumas across the Pacific Arena and the Americas. These texts describe walking through Los Angeles and being made to feel crazy with the bloatedness of past traumas that make claims on their everyday lives. Brought together with existing nationalist readings of the LA Riots, these texts enable an understanding of how U.S. militarism shapes our collective imaginaries and our (in)ability to imagine humane survival in a time of immense vulnerability and violence.

Dai Sil Kim-Gibson's *Sa-I-Gu* is set during and soon after the LA Riots of 1992. Following the Korean tradition of naming events for the day on which they occurred, *Sa-I-Gu* (4–2–9, for April 29) centers the voices of Korean women who, Kim-Gibson argues, were silenced during the coverage and assessment of the events.[10] It is framed by the funeral of Edward Jaesong Lee, whose death is recounted by his mother and sister. Lee had been inspired by the story playing on Korean radio of Korean women hiding rocks in their aprons to attack foreign invaders and had decided to go out into the riots to defend his people. Another Korean mistook Lee for a looter and shot him. Against the unfolding story of a mother's grief for her dead son, the documentary features Korean women shopkeepers who lived through the LA Riots seeking to understand why they were targeted for attack and then left abandoned by the U.S. state.

Pulitzer Prize–winning journalist and novelist Héctor Tobar's first novel, *The Tattooed Soldier*, links the brutality of Guatemala's civil war between the military state and insurgents to Los Angeles in the 1990s, where those displaced from this violence remain unsettled. During the civil war in Guatemala, Mayan Indians, caught in the battle between the military state and insurgents, were particularly targeted for genocide. It is estimated that over 200,000 people were "disappeared" and murdered beginning in 1960 in a situation that is still ongoing.[11] The novel has a unique narrative structure, a chiastic form told through the twinned perspectives of the protagonist (Antonio Bernal) and the antagonist (Guillermo Longoria, the soldier who murdered Antonio's wife and baby).[12] Competing claims come together during the LA Riots, or *quemazones*, as the Riots were referred in Spanish-language media, a term that means both fire and simmering resentment, including revenge.

Fleeing for his life and living undocumented in Los Angeles, Antonio cannot escape his grief for his wife, Elena, and baby son, Carlos. By chance he discovers their murderer, the tattooed soldier, is also living in Los Angeles. Kidnapped by the Guatemalan military as a youth and trained by U.S. special operations, the tattooed soldier became a sergeant in the battalion nicknamed "The Jaguars" during the height of military control over Guatemalan life in the mid-1980s. The novel ends with Antonio's revenge-killing of Guillermo Longoria, which was enabled by the chaos and state absence during the LA Riots.

There is no way for these subjects to displace their resentment or attach to new places or new bodies within the U.S. nation-state, and they are suspended in a state of morass, underwritten by the mandate to forget losses that implicate the U.S. military state across the Pacific Arena. David L. Eng and David Kazanjian's *Loss* theorizes how melancholia is fundamentally a structural condition within white supremacy that pathologizes and criminalizes raciality and thus places colonized subjects within what Frantz Fanon calls "zones of non-being" — zones structured by surveillance and violence from the state. Accounting for the overlapping dimensions of loss represented here makes reimagining other losses possible.[13] The creative imaginative work around the LA Riots, as these texts exemplify, is prescient in light of the fullness with which the confluences of U.S. white supremacy and military colonialism define human sociality in the twenty-first century.

In the first part of the chapter, I offer a historical overview of the shared legacies of U.S. militarism in Guatemala and Korea. I continue by analyzing the misrecognitions that lead to death in the midst of the riots documented in *Sa-I-Gu*. In the conclusion section of the chapter, I read *The Tattooed Soldier* to theorize how the military violence and history thematized in the book enables a racial cognitive remapping of the relationship between the United States and others within the Pacific Arena.

Comparative Politics and the Neoliberal Interregnum

In the 1990s, nearly three million Asians and Latinos immigrated to Los Angeles seeking refuge, fueled by neocolonial discourses that equated life in the United States with the height of civilization. Although these discourses unfolded differently in South Korea and Guatemala, these states are both part of U.S. Cold War military actions, neoliberal governance, and developing economic dominion in the Pacific Arena.

Given the importance of American military intervention, occupation, and presence in the Korean peninsula since World War II, Ji-Yeon Yuh describes Koreans in the United States as "refuge migrants": "Post-1945 Korean migration has been shaped by the division and militarization of the Korean peninsula. The Korean War in particular has had a dramatic and profound impact. Most, if not all, of Korean migration since 1950 can be traced to the war and its consequences."[14]

The formation of South Korea into a U.S. "pawn" of the Cold War is rooted in the Korean War, which solidified U.S. dominion over the Korean Peninsula. Since the end of World War II, U.S. dominance over the Koreas has been rooted in several treaties and moves involving the dissolution and dispersal of Japan's empire, including the International Military Tribunal of the Far East (1946–48), which tried the Japanese Empire for war crimes, and the San Francisco Peace Treaty (1951), which prioritized developing Japan into a U.S. ally and engine for capitalist development in the region. These precedents, along with the Republic of Korea–Japan Basic Treaty (1965)—which took over fourteen years to establish—ensured, as Akira Iriye argues, that the U.S.-led Cold War political economy had been grafted onto the region's prewar Japanese colonial order.[15]

The Cold War architecture upholding Japanese colonial order in Korea is evident, for example, during the San Francisco Peace Treaty, negotiations for which began one year into the Korean War.[16] The United States first invited the South Korean regime led by Syngman Rhee in order to bolster South Korea's legitimacy, but he was later disinvited. As historian John Price documents, "On July 9, [John Foster] Dulles met with the South Korean ambassador to the United States, Yang Yu Chan, to inform him that the South Korean government would not be permitted to be a signatory to the peace treaty since 'only those nations in a state of war with Japan and which were signatories of the United Nations Declaration of 1942 would sign the treaty.'"[17] This is certainly historical revision, since "a division of Korean troops had fought against Japan in China and . . . the Korean Provisional Government (KPG) had issued a declaration of war," but the U.S. delegation refused to recognize this provisional government.[18] This reversal in position, was because "Dulles mistrusted Korean nationalism and worried that South Korean delegates might upset his carefully planned conference by attacking Japanese imperialism. Second, Dulles was determined to exclude Korean nationals in Japan in order not to grant them Allied national status, an issue on which the Yoshida government had insisted."[19] This is how "Japan was allowed to preserve—and resume under the Cold War sanction of the United States—its presumption of superiority over other Asians. Also, Japan's racist wartime ideology, which had propelled atrocities against Asian soldiers and civilians alike, escaped scrutiny and condemnation."[20]

But the military roots and continued ties of the Korean diaspora to the United States, like the Korean War itself, are rendered forgotten. Forgotten because of an inconclusive, ongoing armistice and because the civil war is often seen as a conclusion to Japanese colonialism. Yet the war in the Korean peninsula is sandwiched between American self-regard in World War II and in Vietnam. As Jodi Kim has argued, "To label an event a 'forgotten war' paradoxically inaugurates an attempt to retrieve that which has been forgotten. Post-1945, and especially post-1965, Korean migration to the United States, then, is at once a significant trace of the erasure and its retrieval . . . it also signals a broader problem of Cold War knowledge that saturates both American nationalist discourse and Korean America's public, or 'admitted' knowledge, about the conditions of possibility for its very formation in the post-1945 conjuncture."[21]

The most powerful of these discursive formations called for the subject position of gratefulness to the United States from a besieged disciple. Thus, South Korean "independence," first from Japan and second from Communism, is remembered as a "gift" from the United States until the 1990s and the burden borne by these postcolonial immigrants.[22] Twenty-first-century South Korea rebels against this narrative, as seen in the overthrow of Park Geun-hye and the anti-U.S. base movements, which also dovetail with anticolonial movements. The threat to the Pacific Century as a psychic anchor between Japan and the United States is threatened by South Korea because of its position as dually colonized by the two countries.

Even as U.S. military projection in Asia metastasized from Korea to Vietnam, U.S. investment in Central America deepened starting in the 1960s and was connected to developing new markets and conditions favorable to American trade by installing military dictatorships in Guatemala, El Salvador, and Nicaragua. The Central Intelligence Agency supported and gave weapons and training to rightist regimes run by the military or to Contras, insurgent right-wing militias fighting leftist democracy spanning roughly 1954 to 1989.[23] This period also marks the height of brutality against Mayan people, who were targeted for persecution and execution by disindianization and modernization projects carried out by both the state and Marxist rebels. In the 1970s and 1980s, for example, when *The Tattooed Soldier* is set, violence defined everyday life for most indigenous peoples in Guatemala.[24] U.S. support of military dictatorships across Central America since the mid-twentieth century is similarly willed into invisibility through cover-ups and deception as with the Korean War. For instance, the Historical Clarification Commission (La Comisión para el Esclarecimiento Histórico [CEH]) was charged with reckoning with the aftermath of the violence in Guatemala (1994–96)—a historic event finally signaling an end to the period of brutal violence. The commission came into being after the United Nations-facilitated peace accords ended the decades-long violence there. The CEH condemned the United States' complicity in establishing a series of military dictatorships to create capitalist and military surrogates throughout the Americas.[25] Guatemala remains in essence a divided country at war with itself, although not split into separate entities as in the Korean context.

The increased size of the Salvadoran and Guatemalan community in Los Angeles in this period is not only economically driven, but also a direct outcome of President Reagan's policies of intervention in the civil wars in these two countries.[26] Denied refugee status (which would indict U.S. support of anti-Communist soldiers in Central America), those who settled in Los Angeles were left in a zone of legal limbo, receiving Temporary Protected Status with the passing of the Immigration Act of 1990 ("IMMACT"), PL 101–649, much like the limbo of the Deferred Action for Childhood Arrivals in the twenty-first century (2012–17). To this day many Salvadorans and Guatemalans with legal residency still have Temporary Protective Status rather than full permanent (or "green card") residency.

This is not to say that Central Americans and Korean Americans are naturally allies solely because of a shared military history. As we see in both *Sa-I-Gu* and *The Tattooed Soldier*, such an alliance is represented in neoliberal discourse and culture as nearly impossible. However, it is important to see their histories as linked in a way that contrasts the tendency in political and academic discourses to see Latinos and Asians as within a temporal spectrum, never occupying the same space or time. For example, Christopher L. Connery reminds us that "it is virtually impossible to find a conference on Latin American development that does not incorporate comparative research on East Asia."[27] But this comparison occurs to position Latin America and East Asia on a temporal spectrum, with Central and South America figured to be following East Asia, which is then imagined to be a latecomer to the United States. This developmental comparison continues in the 1990s and the twenty-first century. I have argued elsewhere that the encounters among Euro-Americans, Asians, and Latinos in the Pacific Rim are circumscribed by neoliberalism's demand for the opening of borders and reorganization of national economies that, in the U.S. context, has depended on the United States' particular post–World War II relationship to Asia and Latin America.[28] This differential dependence on Asian and Latino labor, market, and production capacity imagines essential differences among Euro-Americans, Asians, and Latinos. Euro-American/Asian/Latin American subjects are expected to inhabit exclusive states such as: free/indentured/slave; interiority/exteriority/primal; creative/hardworking/criminal; native born/immigrant/undocumented; and owner/manager/worker.[29]

In contrast to representations that celebrate Asia's emergence out of premodernity, Africa and Latin America are represented as mired and bogged down by their (essential) premodernity. Manthia Diawara argues that "there is a globalized information network that characterizes Africa as a continent sitting on top of infectious diseases, strangled by corruption and tribal vengeance, and populated by people with mouths and hands open to receive international aid."[30] She critiques the prevalent African nationalist and neoliberal perceptions that devaluation can help Africans "repeat the economic success of the 'Asian Dragons'"[31] and highlights how "there is much admiration for Japanese and Chinese leaders, and regrets that African leaders did not follow their example. The saying goes that the West respects Japan, Hong Kong, China and Taiwan today because these countries did not wait for the advice of the white man to jump into their own style of modernity. Africans, too, must find their own way in the modern world."[32] Some Latin Americanist economists and political theorists have similarly pointed to Asian success as a model for Latin American development that can bypass First World intervention. This admiration for Asian success is accompanied by a growing critique of Asian economic participation in Latin America and Africa that reproduces neocolonialism.[33]

Thus, necessary to understanding the LA Riots is not only the recognition that neoliberal capitalism is based on making abandonment a policy by defining and structuring urban spaces, but that this abandonment works in tandem with a global economic structure in which immigrants and citizens are recruited into racializing each other in dangerous and sometimes deadly ways.[34] In Los Angeles, the uprisings were mostly confined to Koreatown and South Central, where Korean and Latino businesses were targeted for looting and destruction.[35] The National Guard did not shut down the violence and looting, instead cordoning off the riot zones and protecting the wealthier adjacent communities. This cordoning off exemplified and made visible how the neoliberal disinvestment is rooted to a longer and deeper state practice of abandonment in the urban core as a structural practice and racial mode of state control.[36]

Jodi Melamed and Denise Ferreira da Silva have argued that within the U.S. national space neoliberal capitalism is predicated on "racial utopia"—that is, the total destruction of racial categories. This racial utopia seeks to reproduce a white supremacist-centered world economy. The propensity of racial capitalism to produce and benefit from racial and gendered hierarchies requires a racial critique, and the classical revolutionary proletariat who has been uncritically figured as a white male working-class figure needs to be challenged particularly within a post-Fordist and deindustrialized world economy as I have been describing.[37] Like the cognate term *postracial*, neoliberal capitalism's *racial utopia* seeks to create a new universal *homo oeconomicus* who is regulated to be self-invested in vitalizing the state.[38] However, the LA Riots revealed how neoliberal multiculturalism manages and orders these subjects of U.S. nation and empire by pitting refugee migrants, refugees, immigrants, and U.S. racial Others against each other, undermining the universalizing tendencies of neoliberal capitalism.[39] In particular the formation of racial power and racist state violence prior to, during, and after the riots demonstrates the lasting presence of anti-Black state violence as a paradigm for racial power relations even and especially in the multiculturalist emergence of Los Angeles.[40] This is an important juxtaposition to the Korean and Central American political affect that is under examination in this chapter.

Mourning in the Interregnum

One of the ways *Sa-I-Gu* and *The Tattooed Soldier* represent the specific way that U.S. military presence shaped colonized consciousness and impacted Korean women is through the repeated idea that living in Los Angeles *feels* wrong and different, at complete odds from what they had imagined. In *Sa-I-Gu*, Mrs. Choon Ah Song—an owner of a small corner store that burned down on April 29—said, "We dreamed about America like we saw in the movies. The streets would be clean. People in America would all have big noses, their faces would be white, their hair blond. It was more like Mexico.

It made more sense to call it Mexico. We hardly came in contact with white people. Even in the schools most teachers were second generation Japanese and Mexican."

Her sentiment is affirmed by the other women interviewed in the documentary, all of whom speak of an America they imagined from their youth, a fairytale place where their dreams would come true. This sense of America is not only dissonant to them, but also to American exceptionalism.[41] The description of America that Mrs. Choon remembers evokes recollections of a classic era of Cold War U.S. television and popular culture such as *The Wizard of Oz* and *Amos and Andy*, a period when the representational field was full of Orientalist tropes and desires.[42]

This understanding of Los Angeles is as a specifically racial space. Chungmoo Choi has argued that in the context of South Korea, "colonial double discourse has created for colonized people an illusion of living in the same social and cultural sphere as that of the metropolis, while it ruthlessly exercises a discriminatory politics of hierarchy."[43] Mrs. Choon breaks down the white body: big noses, white faces, blond hair—these are the important parts to be remembered, connected both to cleanliness and dreams and to the symbols of the racial hierarchy. This is the process of erasure and retrieval that Jodi Kim is describing, the process through which the devastation of the Korean peninsula during and since occupation refuses to be forgotten.[44] For Mrs. Choon, this discourse ingrained into the value given to spaces occupied by whiteness. She describes Los Angeles in racial terms that place whiteness as the height of modernity achievable through contact. However, that contact is made impossible in neoliberal Los Angeles by keeping them with "second generation Japanese and Mexican[s]" who were also unable to become white or access the privilege of whiteness despite their hyphenated citizenship status.

Los Angeles as experienced by these refuge migrants and displaced subjects intersects with decades of state violence and abandonment of Black communities, particularly in South Los Angeles. The shock at the LA Riots meets a sense of inevitability by the end of *Sa-I-Gu*, when the documentary concludes with the signs of a multiculturalist Korean American subject formation.[45] A large group marches down major thoroughfares in Koreatown demanding restitution and acknowledgments of wrongs committed not only against Koreans, but against all people of color. The documentary offers a powerful lesson on how colonized subjects unlearn not only whiteness, but also Blackness, a knowledge that emerges simultaneously.

In *Sa-I-Gu*, understanding the injustice experienced by African Americans is expressed and ruminated over as the women try to comprehend it. One of the shopkeepers articulates the claims that African Americans used to describe them: "Mrs. Kim, you were educated over in Korea," to explain why Koreans had preconceived notions of Black criminality based on Hollywood and U.S. military culture's racist stereotypes that shaped their treatment of Blacks in the United States. But of course, Blacks have also served in American wars in the Pacific Arena, where they developed complex and intimate relationships with Asian bodies and cultures overseas.[46] This becomes a common reference in popular culture representing the riots and Korean–Black relations—that Koreans and Blacks came to know each other first through the conditions of war and U.S. military expansion in Asia.[47]

The women interviewed in *Sa-I-Gu* consistently emphasize how they focus on working so hard they hardly sleep, socialize, or keep up with the news. In other words, they were willing to sublimate an initial desire and fantasy (inclusion in a white America) with another American myth (hard work for a just reward). However, the looting of their businesses, the lack of police protection, and the denial of reparations by the state shatter any possibility of sublimation. If the immigrants were willing to suffer the deferment of their dreams by investing their faith in the economic sphere, then the loss of their property, unfair representation in the media, and betrayal by the state devastated and made legible the impossibility of that dream. As a Korean shopkeeper interviewed in *Sa-I-Gu* laments, "It is a crazy country. Crazy country. This is not a beautiful country. In Korean, American means beautiful country. This is not a beautiful country. All my childhood dreams have been turned upside down." The women all describe the LA Riots in terms of misrecognitions, misrepresentations, and cognitive dissonance—forces that create will and questioning of colonial knowledge.

The loss of their oft-repeated "dreams" demonstrates the depth of their loss, but this loss is complicated because it also speaks of a desire for whiteness that they imagined *was* America. As these women express a sense of loss for a white America to which they imagined they would be kin, they also critique their own colonial history. Near the middle of the documentary, two Korean women shopkeepers articulate their thoughts about the events of April 29, 1992. One states, "All night I was thinking, where is the police? Where is the police?" She then continues, "But no! We Koreans were sacrificial lambs. This is how I like to think about it. We were sacrificial lambs," while her friend slowly nods. Her statement that "this is how I like to think about it" reveals a powerful critique of dominant representations of the LA Riots, one that spurred Kim-Gibson to make *Sa-I-Gu*. While dominant analysis sees the event as a hopeless fight between immigrants who only care about money and property and an African American "underclass" who only knows how to resort to violence, she instead comes to consider what it means to be a lamb led to slaughter.

When the shopkeeper recognizes that the state would not intervene on her behalf and in fact would be willing to allow her to take the blame, she identifies her position as a "sacrificial lamb," which is also a kind of scapegoat.[48] This is a powerful statement because it indicates her ability and willingness to locate herself within the U.S. racial spectrum and criticizes the position of "middle-man" or "middle-woman" Korean storeowner. This middle position is paradigmatic of Gramsci's Marxist interpretation of the petit bourgeoisie as monsters lurking within the interregnum prohibiting a Communist revolution. But in this case anticolonial knowledge intersects with class stratification as the shopkeeper moves from "middle-woman" to "sacrificial lamb."

These women resist being co-opted into a narrative and schematic power relation in which the destruction of their property is inevitably linked to lurking criminal Blacks. Much of what was happening in Black Los Angeles during the riots entailed an expression of grief without closure over the terror and loss at the hands of the U.S. state. As opposed to the police, for example, King and Black masculinity were put on trial. The brutal treatment of King and the ways the police were set free confirmed the sentiment among African American communities that the legal system overall does not accord Black bodies any value.[49] In *Sa-I-Gu*, the transition from this mainstream discourse to recognition of the long history of state violence against Black and immigrant communities requires a postcolonial understanding and resituating of positionality vis-à-vis U.S. racial order. For these Korean women, the LA Riots revealed the impossibility of ever really aligning with the colonizer and brought forth the desire and impossibility of aspiring to whiteness.

To close this section, I turn to the series of misrecognitions that surround the narrative of the death of Edward Lee as another moment of what Jodi Kim has described as "erasure and attempt at retrieval,"[50] of how American militarism seeks to silence Korean American dissidence. *Sa-I-Gu* begins and ends with moving scenes showing Edward's funeral and a close-up of his mother, father, and sister sobbing and in pain as they lay his body to rest.

This funeral frames the LA Riots first and foremost as a tragedy grounded in the death of human lives and argues that such violence should not be repeated. The documentary closes with a haunting scene, inviting thinking on what comes after loss for the survivors. The final scene zooms in on a painting that hangs above the fireplace of the Lees's home, a family portrait that includes Edward, his mother, father, and sister. The next shot outside of their home frames the remaining three Lees as they stand still, as though posing for another painting. We hear Mrs. Lee say, "People think it's crazy but I think he will come back. I wait for him." For the second time, someone in the documentary describes her experience in Los Angeles as crazy. This is an instance in which the ghosts of injustice and the dead of the transpacific refuse to disappear.

According to his mother, Edward is inspired by a narrative of Koreans fighting against Japanese imperialism, which he hears on the radio and has his mother explain to him. Min Jung Kim argues that Mrs. Lee is mistaken in her retelling of the story on the radio. Mrs. Lee interprets it as Korean women throwing rocks at Japanese imperialists, whereas the founding narrative more broadly connects it to the protection of Korea under siege. War crimes during the Japanese colonial period of Korea is a continued and pressing concern. However, within the Korean diaspora and in the U.S. national space, what also occupied concern was the period of disappearances and state violence under dictator Park Chung Hee who was installed in 1962 with the support of the U.S. military.[51] The Kwangju Massacre (May 18–27, 1980), in which over 606 people were killed, was part of a slowly emerging public discourse in the 1980s and 1990s, describing a Korean politics that criticized the right wing military state, as well as fueled a growing anti-occupation movement against the U.S. military.[52] The Korean diaspora in the United States stayed deeply connected to politics in Korea, but were relatively disconnected from local politics and surprised when the LA Riots erupted.[53] Mrs. Lee's choice to focus on anti-Japanese imperialism may describe a broader difficulty of translation between generations—those of the first generation find it difficult to describe the brutality of American military occupation of the Korean peninsula to their Korean American children.

The retelling of Edward's death throughout *Sa-I-Gu* invites deeper understanding and meaning that can be gained from rehearsing his life and by ruminating on his death. He was one of sixty-three people who were killed that day. These women mourn Edward, and in renarrating his story they resist the hero-victim binary. Mrs. Lee says, "People think it's crazy but I wait for him to come back." This is a statement layered with not only multiple temporalities, but also spatialities in which loss lives on. To return to the image at the end of the documentary, the camera frames the three members of the family as they stand in front of a well-manicured home. All three smile politely, giving a sense that life continues on even while living with devastating losses. This is preceded by what Edward's sister says of her brother's death: "My brother was killed by mistake. They mistook him for a looter." This is a difficult truth to express because it is hard to identify a specific actor. The case remains unsolved, and there is no trial at which they can testify or receive an apology and retribution. Mistakes make things messy, and here Edward's sister condemns the conditions that led to the riots, not an individual pathology. Instead, her story about her brother's death takes us beyond ethnic and nationalist frameworks and into the conditions of neoliberal abandonment wherein mistakes between racialized men become deadly.

Racial Cognitive Mapping in *The Tattooed Soldier*

As *Sa-I-Gu* suggests, neoliberal Los Angeles can make people feel crazy. Complex militarized global interconnections simultaneously force a renewed engagement and understanding, driven by this sense of craziness, to reorient how the neoliberal subject stands in relation to the world and others. Similarly, *The Tattooed Soldier* is remarkable in the ways it navigates neoliberal and postcolonial Los Angeles. Central to my analysis of the novel is the focus on how it offers a redrawn racial cognitive map of neoliberal modernity rooted in the perspective of the multiply constituted displaced people of Guatemala's thirty-six-year internal war between 1960 and 1996. As with chapter 1's discussion of how Japanese Americans living on Poston Internment Camp become unwitting settler colonialists on Native American land, the displacement of Guatemalans to Los Angeles and within Los Angeles also call forth how settler colonialism is constitutive even in the neoliberal present.

The Los Angeles of 1992 described in Tobar's *The Tattooed Soldier* is at the immediate outskirts of the setting for *Sa-I-Gu*, in the heavily Central American immigrant neighborhood of MacArthur Park, and downtown Los Angeles's homeless encampments. Educated, light-skinned, uncritical of his Euro-Spanish roots and from his nation's middle class, in the 1980s Antonio flees the violence of Guatemala City with his pregnant wife, Elena, when death squads target their friends and other university students as subversives and communists. Antonio works as a civil servant in a small outpost of San Cristobal, Acatapan, in the highlands, where they go to hide. They become targets of renewed scrutiny when Elena, despite Antonio's urging, refuses to stop her investigation into the pollution that is killing Mayan and other indigenous people in the slum Colonia La Joya (Jewel Settlement), precariously settled in a ravine near their home. After Elena, in Antonio's loving memory, "recklessly" writes a letter to public health administrators complaining about pollution, they are targeted, and Antonio comes home to find that Elena and their infant son have been assassinated. He is forced to leave before he can mourn or bury their bodies, but not before he sees their murderer eating ice cream in a nearby park, as though nothing had happened. Antonio imprints in his memory the image of a tattoo of a jaguar on the man's arm. Desire for revenge drives Antonio and gives him a sense of mission after he becomes homeless in Los Angeles and by chance encounters the tattooed soldier, retired sergeant Guillermo Longoria, playing chess in MacArthur Park.

Antonio is dominated by a strong spatial drive. That is, Antonio's own negotiation of his grief and desire for vengeance is tied to his forced and constant movement as a homeless person, which makes him acutely aware of space and his connection to it. This drive is notable for a character like Antonio, whom the novel describes as prone to melancholia when he inexplicably becomes mean, withdrawn, and immobile. Living in Los Angeles after becoming homeless, he begins to see Los Angeles as a melancholic space itself, defined by connections and ties that demand to be understood. Antonio reads it as fate to reencounter Longoria in a park in Guatemala and a park in Los Angeles.

As a homeless person, he settles in an empty lot in Crown Hill, near downtown Los Angeles. Here he discovers old street signs, such as that of Diamond Street, and other evidence of the city's layered histories, which can be razed but not erased. The novel's connection to colonial La Joya in Guatemala is not only in terms of shared symbolism; it also tries to force a recognition between the kinds of sovereignties that enable such human degradation and continued settler colonialism. This cognitive mapping of Los Angeles divines what Achille Mbembe has called the "third zone": "Sovereignty meant occupation, and occupation meant relegating the colonized into a third zone between subjecthood and objecthood."[54] There is an uncanny awareness in the novel of a racial cognitive mapping intimately connected to death: "From the grave, Carlos and Elena had given Antonio the power to see these differences, another layer of truth near the surface but invisible to so many."[55] This third zone, between subjecthood and objecthood, is one in the novel in which grief and loss transform how neoliberal spaces are apprehended and can be challenged.

The novel begins with Antonio's eviction. A Korean-immigrant building manager named Hwang evicts Antonio from his apartment because he cannot pay rent: "Neither man could claim English as his mother tongue, but it was the only language they shared.... Through the narrow opening of a door pushed slightly ajar, he was speaking to the building manager who was about to evict him from his apartment.... After several minutes of mumbled exchanges, they began to toss night-school phrases back and forth like life preservers: "Repeat, please." "Speak slower." "I don't understand."[56]

This passage paints an image of a Los Angeles where meetings between Koreans and Central Americans are often circumscribed by the emergency of their encounter—eviction, meeting on sweatshop floors as employee and employer, building manager and evictee. English, the only language they share, does not allow these men to understand each other better—instead, by the end of the passage, they only use English to ask the other to explain himself.

In *Black Skin, White Masks*, Fanon critiques how learning to master the colonizer's language is a constitutive part of learning to internalize white supremacy. Everything from pronunciation to the tone of speech matters, as the colonial subject "will practice not only rolling his *R* but embroidering it."[57] If the Creole middle class and elites seek to embroider, then here the petit bourgeoisie and undocumented find that their tongues become "mumbled," thick, and that they are increasingly prevented from forming coherent speech. In this scene, Hwang and Antonio's failed attempt at communication in English demonstrates how night school failed to teach them how to master the colonial tongue. They "squint" at one another as each finds himself confused by the other's diction and mispronunciation, even as they use English as a "life preserver." English forces them to measure themselves against an Other and a Self that seem increasingly alien.

As the novel progresses beyond his eviction, Antonio learns to build new affinities with a Los Angeles space that is simultaneously becoming unfamiliar to him: "Years ago, when Antonio lived in Guatemala, he had an electric idea of Los Angeles.... Long before he set foot in this country, Antonio felt that he knew California because he had seen it come to life over and over again in his television set."[58]

The internal monologue continues: "If his own mind were not clouded with so much pain, they would not exist. *They are what I feel.* Somehow he had tainted the prosperous Americanos with his condition. . . . As soon as Antonio went away, they would slip back into their fit American bodies."[59]

This passage exemplifies the privatized nature of melancholia, the will to drive ever inward. This privatized narcissism, despite the reality of his claim against the soldier, shapes Antonio's revenge. After he encounters the soldier at MacArthur Park, Antonio follows him, developing a dossier on his habits and schedule. Significantly, the scene in which Antonio decides to kill the tattooed soldier is mired in deep melancholia and violence. After a week of following the soldier, Antonio tells his friends about his chance encounter with the killer. After he shares this story, he looks for a photo of Elena and Carlos, digging through the contents of his black garbage bag, only to discover that he lost this photo in the confusion of his eviction from the apartment. He finds instead unopened letters from his mother; inside one is a new photo: a gravestone of Elena and Carlos. She writes that she has had new gravestones installed for Elena and Carlos. She tells him he should come home and get psychiatric help. He becomes angry and mean, unreasonably blaming her for their deaths by sending them away to the country.[60]

We learn that being melancholic defines Antonio's essential being. Elena describes him as mean and unmovable, like a "stone."[61] Driven to fury by his mother's letter and unable to acknowledge his own sense of guilt, Antonio finds a metal pipe—his first weapon against Longoria—and repeats the mantra "Mr. Hwang, my mother, the tattooed soldier" as he forms his resolve to murder the tattooed soldier. Antonio connects his grief to his mother, but this time in unreasonable anger. This scene dramatizes his arrested state due to his melancholia. Antonio believes he has disappointed as a man, husband, and father, feeling infantilized that he continuously fails in taking care of his family. He hopes "this mission [will cleanse] him of sorrow and guilt,"[62] but the novel suggests that absolution for vengeance is unavailable to Antonio. When Antonio's friend Frank decides to help him, Antonio promises lifelong loyalty, to become a "rock" for Frank. However, given the novel's symbolic repertoire, Antonio as a rock is mired in melancholia, unable to move or act for others. Antonio kills Longoria by shooting him twice and leaves him for dead. Mortally wounded but not yet dead, Longoria follows Antonio to an abandoned tunnel in the outskirts of downtown Los Angeles. Later, as Antonio watches Longoria die, he wonders whether Longoria's girlfriend will mourn him, but has to remind himself, "Enough. Forget him."[63]

What further complicates Antonio's claim against Longoria is that he seeks vengeance in Elena's name. Would Elena have wanted Antonio to avenge her life in this way? How does Antonio's individual act account for the needs of those who also seek justice from Longoria and to hear what happened to their loved ones? Early in the novel, a Native Guatemalan woman who recognizes Longoria's tattoo while at Longoria's place of work demands to know what Longoria did with her son, her agony and loss indicating the freshness of her pain. This scene puts Elena and Carlos's death in a larger perspective and requires an understanding of the countless bodies that demand to be named, found, and mourned. They become caught in the midst of the hundreds of thousands of indigenous people who were the primary victims of Guatemala's civil war. The selfish and privatized melancholia that defines Antonio's being becomes the central drive that enables him to act against Longoria. He is not moved by justice, but by melancholy violence. Given the context of the LA Riots and the failures of the judicial system, his desire for vengeance appears reasonable and is even made possible.

My extended reading seeks to map the transnational geography Antonio negotiates through his memory and grief. This constitutes parts of a new symbolic order and ontological ordering within the novel that displace Antonio's former colonized sense and knowledge of Los Angeles. It is not within the realm of the juridical, but within that of the spatial, that Antonio approximates a subjectivity that privileges shared survivability: "The vacant property, the plastic shelters, the ruined homes. The more he thought about it, the more Antonio began to feel a kinship with the flattened earth around him."[64] This is a racial cognitive mapping of Mbembe's third space, a symbolic and material order to which colonized Others are relegated. In formulating this concept of racial cognitive mapping, I extend Kevin Lynch's formulation of cognitive mapping, in which he describes how the new, deindustrialized city (Jersey City in the 1970s) offered no national cognitive point for the deindustrialized worker.[65] As Fredric Jameson writes, "Kevin Lynch taught us that the alienated city is above all a space in which people are unable to map (in their minds) either their own positions or the urban totality in which they find themselves: grids such as those of Jersey City, in which none of the traditional markers (monuments, nodes, natural boundaries, built perspectives) obtain, are the most obvious examples.[66]

Racial cognitive mapping is at once a description of new social relations as well as something incredibly familiar. Tobar describes Antonio walking among Los Angeles's homeless as him finding "so many of his countrymen transported, as if by some dark magic, to this freeway-covered plain, wandering about Los Angeles in an amnesiac daze, far from even the memory of the soil."[67] Tobar's racial cognitive map of Los Angeles describes an unstable space built on top of previous layers, the remnants of which refuse to disappear.

The killing of Longoria occurs on a day the novel represents as "the municipal day of settling accounts, a day for all vendettas, private and public."[68] In the novel, this is possible because "the police were staying home,"[69] not acting to save South Central or Koreatown. Like the Korean women interviewed in *Sa-I-Gu*, Antonio did not follow the police brutality case, nor did he anticipate the anger the not-guilty verdict would incite for his friends Frank and Larry, two African American homeless men with whom he has built a community. Driven as much by the horror of Longoria's act as his desire to be a part of history, Frank helps Antonio strategize to kill Longoria and to find a gun. As Antonio sits with Frank and Larry while they learn of the not-guilty verdict, his friends "looked like people who had pinned great hopes on something and suddenly those hopes shattered."[70] He learns what it means to be an American racial subject as he watches their shock and anger unfold over the refusal to accord value to Black bodies. By the end of the novel, they form a strong class and race solidarity rooted in their understanding of each other's different histories and shared predicament. These layers are sustained by their connections to sites across the Americas at different moments in history—connections at once melancholic and enlivening.

The racial cognitive map of Los Angeles presented here is not a geography of lament, despite the melancholia underwriting it. Instead, it offers a new lens for understanding mobility across immense scales—that is, jumping scales. Spatial mechanisms to create ever more subservient bodies for capitalism is in scalar relation with the displacement of bodies across the Americas and Asia due to American militarism that works in consort with the continuing project of colonizing the Americas and killing native populations. From downtown Los Angeles's homeless encampments, filled with formerly working-class African Americans and indigenous populations, to remittance centers, these are the new spatial anchors that cognitively delink from nationalist narratives. Racial cognitive mapping expands on this classic analysis of urban alienation to link the neoliberal economy and the structure of global cities such as Los Angeles to U.S. military domination across the Pacific Arena.

Building on this map, I conclude my reading of *The Tattooed Soldier* to observe the revenge with which the novel ends. Despite the horror of his acts, the narrative offers many points through which to absolve Antonio's antagonist, the peasant soldier Longoria. By the novel's end, he dies having recognized his lost humanity as a forced soldier. While killing Longoria does not bring closure for Antonio, the novel offers absolution for Longoria at death. Through flashbacks, we learn Longoria's story: born into a peasant Mayan family, he was forced to join the Guatemalan military at age seventeen. Longoria represents the historical reality of peasants and Indios who were forced to fratricide and Tobar repeatedly turns to the Holocaust and Nazis to explain what happened in Guatemala. As the novel puts it, soldiers like Longorio "had carried out a holocaust in the mountains."[71] Both the insurgency and the state used peasants as cannon fodder in their war against each other, justified by a racial construction that represents peasants and the indigenous population as atavistic and diseased bodies in need of eradication.

Much of Longoria's life before his capture is made unavailable in the novel, symbolizing the ways his soldier self can only survive by shutting off his indigenous self. This division is represented by an unforgettable fetish, a jaguar tattoo on his arm. He received his tattoo after completing his training with the U.S. military at the School of the Americas in the Panama Canal Zone and at the military base in Fort Bragg, North Carolina. The U.S. military training and the military base itself are formative for Longoria's colonization, as the order, cleanliness, plentitude, and might of the U.S. military form the image of what Guatemala could become. He carries certificates from these schools that are simultaneously his most prized possession and something that can never be shown, hidden in plain sight, in one of his dresser drawers.

Arriving in Los Angeles in the late 1980s after retiring from the Guatemalan paramilitary, Longoria creates a new life and has a stable job working as a clerk for a remittance center. Even if on the surface he has resettled successfully, it is clear that the horrors of what he did remain close to him.

Although he refuses to feel guilt for his actions, he cannot silence and must forever live "with the voices of boys and girls, their last words, the calling out to their mothers. That was the biggest sacrifice. It took a lot of out of a soldier to see this and hear this and live with it. You were never the same again."[72]

After Longoria describes the certificates from military training in the United States, he offhandedly describes the rest of the album as filled with battle scenes. When Antonio breaks into Longoria's apartment, he finds the album, and we discover it contains photos of Longoria and his peers posing with corpses they had killed: photos their superiors had given all soldiers as a reminder of the horrors that tie them together and as a continued threat of the violence they could face if they ever tell. Longoria's inability to bring the two realities together, that being a soldier is also being a murderer, is tied not only to his individual desire, but also to a forced mandate by the state he served as a murderer. Longoria manages to keep the horror at a distance through obsessive ritual and cleanliness, as well as through his fixation on his jaguar tattoo. After he encounters Antonio, however, he is forced to see himself as a monster, a cognition that he tries to refuse until the moment of death.

Longoria's being is tied to actions that he cannot acknowledge, and this inability to acknowledge what he has done means he is alienated from himself. Thus, the novel makes it clear that even though he is no longer a soldier, his life does not belong to him, opening him up for violence. One of the most powerful scenes in *The Tattooed Soldier* details Longoria's capture and conscription into the Guatemalan military, told in the third person with Longoria's voice. He was seventeen, still a child, but at the cusp of adulthood, one year away from required national service. His mother had sent him to town to buy soap for his family. Having finished his errand, he could not resist the allure of the movie theater and stopped to watch *ET*. He marvels at the wealth and luxury of American life.[73] Before the movie is over, the theater is overrun by soldiers who separate and take the young men into the military.

This scene is rich in symbols that ground Longoria's character, particularly soap. Soap represents his guilt as well as names the horror of the state seeking to "disinfect" and "cleanse" itself of native people. When cleaning his body is not enough, Longoria tries to silence his head by remembering that everything was "a virus. A plague. An infection spread by ideas, a disease carried on the spoken word."[74] This was central to his training and his ideology, as both sides of the war increasingly turned to metaphors of disease and sanitation to justify genocide. As Longoria lies dying, he recalls playing with his mother and remembers his love for his family. Like a child, he wishes he could have been a good boy and come home directly with the soap like his mother had asked.

Longoria's capture at a movie theater showing Hollywood films dramatizes how U.S. militarism supported and upheld the depletion of the land, the people, and the life forces of land — body and people. Colonialism creates, encourages, and fosters the idea of disease and sickness infecting a healthy body. Words like nurture, support, feed, and health — not available to Antonio and Longoria — mean the refusal to die and imply insurgency in a colonized land. Thus, despite the compelling desire for vengeance, the novel never fully condones the murder, instead allowing both Antonio and Longoria the possibility of finding absolution. As he dies, Longoria has a vision of a smiling Mayan woman beckoning him to his death, calling *balam* (jaguar), suggesting absolution for some soldiers in death. The jaguar on his arm is resignified from representing his affiliation to American military might to recalling his Mayan heritage. His last moments are not memories of those he killed, but memories of his mother, returning to the land, and embracing his peasant self.

Conclusion

The confluence of militarism and white supremacy expressed and discussed in *Sa-I-Gu* and *The Tattooed Soldier* serve as both a parable and an expression of the living ruins to which present-day Los Angeles is still connected. On the most immediate level, the LA Riots were an important wakeup call for immigrant communities living close to African Americans whom they had not bothered to know, did not know *how* to know, or thought had nothing to do with their American dreams. It spurred the start of what Edward J. W. Park has argued is the birth of a Korean American consciousness[75] and challenged Latinos in Los Angeles — who were now poised to be the racial majority — to consider their relationship to the history of white supremacy that continues to structure the global city landscape.

These representations of refugees and immigrants and of a crazy and melancholy city offer a provocative reorientation of Los Angeles, as well as showing how postcolonial grief and the afterlives of the Pacific wars are at once both local and global, erupting in neighborhoods that were constructed through transnational conflict and decades of U.S. imperialism.

Though the LA Riots are commonly read as a moment of tragic racial rupture — a discontinuity in the story of U.S. multiculturalism — this chapter examined the afterlives of the LA Riots as an opening for something more. These moments in *Sa-I-Gu* and *The Tattooed Soldier* are read not to erase the immense interracial violence of the LA Riots, but to highlight the potential of resultant attempts at recognition. Unlike mainstream accounts of the LA Riots, African Americans become the focus of these narratives only insofar as their relationships to the nation-state — which claims to be a modern, multicultural utopia — is called into question, just as the relationship of the nation-state to immigrant populations is interrogated. These representations of racial recognition are an interregnum between anti-Black racism and a not-yet-arrived-at future free from violent state persecution.

· THREE ·

TRANSPACIFIC NOIR, DYING COLONIALISM

To expand the conceptualization of postcolonial grief by connecting it to the nature of the unhealed, to the zone rendered unhealable, this chapter turns to the literary and film genre of noir. I argue that the anxiety caused by the inability or refusal of former colonial subjects to heal is maintained and alive in the genre of noir, especially in a subgenre I call "transpacific noir," which keeps a record of the unease created by the histories of military violence across the Pacific Arena. In this chapter I look at how hidden Koreans, colonized by Japan and silenced by U.S. geopolitical dominance over the Korean peninsula, disrupt narrative coherence and attempts at closure.

Noir has a constitutive relationship with the cultural and visual imaginaries associated with atomic modernity. The United States dropped the atomic bomb "Little Boy" on Hiroshima on August 6, 1945, immediately killing nearly 80,000 people and incinerating close to two-thirds of the city.

More than 240,000 people ultimately died as a result of the atomic bomb in Hiroshima. Approximately 70,000 Hiroshima victims were Korean—one in seven of the total *hibakushas*—and likely 20,000 Koreans were killed by the atomic bomb. They were first tethered to their colonizer and then died through that tie. The survivors of atomic holocaust, Japanese and Korean hibakushas, live with the debris and decay of nuclear fallout, which includes cancer, radiation poisoning, and social alienation. This genocidal act operated under an ontological field that positioned American lives as threatened by the existence of a militaristic and imperialist Japan.[1] Iconic images of the mushroom cloud caused by the second bomb, "Fat Man"—along with the buried knowledge of American society's implicit consent to genocide—gave birth to an apocalyptic, anxious global structure of feeling, ideal for the genre of noir.[2]

The imaginative field found in noir and evoked by figures such as hibakushas, which figure more frequently in noir's margins than might be assumed, also demonstrates the broadened field of U.S. imperium resulting from the Asia-Pacific wars. The dropping of atomic bombs over Hiroshima and Nagasaki effectively stopped the imperial ambitions of Japan in Asia and in the Pacific Arena, only to create the conditions under which the United States could militarily dominate the region, including the devastating Korean War, which led to the division of the peninsula and the redevelopment of South Korea under U.S. auspices. The continued dropping of 105 more atomic bombs by the United States over the Pacific Ocean, bodies, and life caused annihilation and displacement. This is a constant reminder of the United States' power to enact genocide. In the twenty-first century the Korean peninsula is radioactive with U.S. and North Korean nuclear ambitions.[3] The broader American nuclear history in the Pacific is about the assault on the Pacific Arena as a whole, land and water, all connected along "the sharp edge of a killing machine."[4]

As an imaginative zone in which colonialism refuses to be scabbed over, transpacific noir is defined by a melancholic temporality. In other words, transpacific noir is a constant point of return, both in terms of its generic innovations and because it is a zone that society often returns to and reflects on. I would liken the popularity and enduring relevance of noir in contemporary American society to an unhealed wound to which one returns, to worry over again and again. This is a wound formed and maintained by silence around colonial complicities. This is a return full of meaning and implications, the synchronic temporality of which functions like Mikhail

Bakhtin's dialogic, wherein every utterance carries on a continual dialogue with its previous iterations and opens to the future. As Bakhtin writes in *Speech Genres*, "Dialogic expression is unfinalizable, always incomplete, and productive of further chains of responses: meaning is never closed and always oriented toward the future."[5] What offends common sense about the refusal to heal is the belief that it is selfish, that it is a melancholic attachment to a wound, a process that is seen as unproductive, morbid, and moribund. However, the wound tells how conditions for healing have not been met.

This chapter turns specifically to the margins, border zones, and minor subjects of noir to remap and reveal the anxieties of modern noir and exhume the figures of colonial conflicts at the heart of the genre and its ordering of the world. What I identify in transpacific noir is a genre full of broken and degraded bodies, which makes visible the necropolitic that structures U.S. military dominance in the Pacific arena during and after the World War II era. These bodies haunt noir and may enable what Avery Gordon has called a "transformative recognition": "Haunting describes that which appears to be not there [but] is often a seething presence, acting on and often meddling with taken-for-granted realities."[6] It requires hard work not to see this. The noir genre gave shape to a specific alienation emerging from the genocidal conditions of the World War II era and the wars in the Asia-Pacific that followed.[7] In transpacific noir this existential crisis is not only represented through the characteristic chiaroscuro lighting and bleak subject matter found in noir, but is a material expression found in the representations of degraded bodies of the victims of U.S. militarism.

Bartov's analyses of industrial killing and the practice of mass murder that arises during World War II have been influential in the fields of Holocaust studies and memory studies. He offers a powerful formulation of "necessary victimhood" to explain the ways industrial killing has become a normalized function of war: "This is not a world of sacrifice but of victimhood, and perhaps its most terrifying aspect is that it is based on the assumption that the victim is necessary. The victim is not a sinner; he does not go to hell for his actions but in order to make it possible for others not to end up in hell flames. Therefore he is a modern figure, in a modern, man-made hell, where industrial murder is perpetrated by those who want to be saved from it."[8]

For Bartov, genocidal modernity is enabled by the creation and simultaneous disavowal of a category of people who are necessary victims, exemplified by the Jews who experienced mass murder in Europe. These subjects occupy zones of bare life, and the sovereign has almost complete control over whether they live or die.[9] This power is intimately linked to technologies of war that made industrial and indiscriminate killings possible. This includes the gas chamber, the atomic bomb, and napalm used in Korea and Southeast Asia.

In this chapter I look for and follow Korean colonial subjects and hibakushas in the U.S. cultural sphere and examine how they refuse the invitation and interpellation to forget their stories. In doing so I excavate the "remnants of trauma so that they can be pieced together to tell a story about the Korean colonial subjects as figures of loss and creativity."[10] The complicity between Japanese colonialism and American military imperialism in the Koreas lives on as a recurring wound and as a fear of a future return of violence. This is a site of unhealing that is the locus of both loss and creativity.[11] Thus, transpacific noir is as much about orientation and reading practice as it is about recuperating the influence that the wars in the Pacific have had on constituting noir's absent field.

There are powerful interests in co-opting the figure and legacy of hibakushas into a biopolitical narrative of healing and evidence of human resiliency. This reifies the progress narratives of World War II as an era in which liberal nation-states become newly born in the Pacific, to flourish under U.S. tutelage. Such co-optation seeks to silence the dissenting narratives of colonialism and ongoing military occupation. However, an against-the-grain reading of the genre of noir demonstrates that such silencing is incomplete. The dissident narratives of figures such as Korean hibakusha, who in political and cultural spheres are rendered beyond healing, are silenced and erased in the wake of Japan's surrender. Although they are silenced, they exert pressure and make themselves felt within popular culture.

Most Koreans in Japan during World War II were coerced or kidnapped laborers and subjects of Japanese empire. Japan formally colonized Korea in 1910, consolidating control the empire had had over the peninsula since the late 1800s.[12] By the end of the war there were close to two million Korean immigrants and forced workers in Japan. During World War II, Hiroshima had the highest number of Korean colonial subjects in Japan, many of whom worked in its munitions plants and shipyards.

Their disavowal and invisibilization translate into a cultural practice and geopolitics of "proxy" that prevent Korean subjects of Japanese colonialism to speak for/in/of themselves. Both Japan and the United States have spoken for the Korean nation and people at crucial junctures in its postcolonial history. A key tool of Japanese colonial governance involved taking control over Korean names, an effective and powerful way to gain control over lives defined by family lineage. *Soshi-kamei* was a policy enacted by the Japanese colonial government in 1939 that forced Koreans to adopt Japanese surnames. This was meant to encourage assimilation into the Japanese colonial presence, which reflected a change in official policy—just twenty years before, Koreans were banned from taking surnames that were too close to Japanese names. Even after Japan's formal surrender to U.S. forces in 1945 and its relinquishing of dominion over most of its colonies, including Korea as a result of the San Francisco Peace Treaty of 1951, naming as a vestige of colonial control and a tool of erasure would continue to affect Korean attempts to gain restorative justice.[13] The Japanese government demanded from all claimants proof of their original Korean names in order to gain the right to access their wartime records. As all the Koreans who were in Japan during the war were forced to relinquish their Korean surnames, this strategy derailed all but the most persistent inquiries well into the 1980s.[14]

Shades of soshi-kamei and the compulsion to eliminate Korea's colonial status exist throughout post–World War II transpacific geopolitics and the global economy. For example, the San Francisco Peace Treaty, which formally ended U.S. occupation of Japan at the end of World War II and dismantled Japan's empire, was signed without either of the Koreas present.[15] It is a significant moment in the formalization of U.S. dominance over what will become the newly formed liberal nation-state of the Republic of Korea in 1953. The United States negotiated the treaty language, even while the Korean peninsula was in the midst of a brutal civil war, which effectively voided any future claims toward Japan for war crimes on behalf of Koreans who were not invited to the deliberations or signing of the treaties. Similarly, the Republic of Korea–Japan Basic Treaty of 1965, which creates a geopolitical blueprint for the normalization of ROK relations with Japan for the first time since the end of Japanese colonialism, is crafted in terms to make conditions favorable to the United States.[16]

Japanese imperialism in Korea was made to disappear just as Korean names were erased from the official record. Nation-states challenge claimants based on the grounds that if you are unclaimed, or if no one remembers you and your family or friends, you have no actionable claims, no basis for reparation. These unrecognized claimants are susceptible to Wendy Brown's argument that the citizenry depends on our identities from the state, but that means that we are also subject to the state's arbitrary domination.[17] These conditions make more salient the ways literature and film become critical alternative archives for the recuperation of the forgotten, the unseen, and the unhealed. My analysis spans the language of treaties and policies and literary and filmic archives because ruptures and abject subjects can only be seen and heard when disciplinary constraints are transgressed.

Noir's sense of place is generally the urban and gritty city, with Los Angeles as its icon.[18] This chapter demonstrates that representations of that gritty urban locale are directly related to our anxieties about transpacific relations. In the following sections, I turn to noir texts separated by nearly fifty years: Sam Fuller's film *The Crimson Kimono* (1959) and Naomi Hirahara's novel *Summer of the Big Bachi* (2004).[19] We can recuperate the noir genre from its nationalist boundaries toward the transpacific and consider how that which is erased and silenced from geopolitics when the United States steps into the places that Japan used to occupy is mediated and visualized in popular culture. I draw on Bakhtin's notions of the dialogic to develop and give shape to the analytic I call "transpacific noir." This is a symbolic and affective repertoire that, like an unhealed wound, one returns to in order to worry over the genre again and again.

Beyond the Narrative: Transpacific Noir

Noir is replete with narratives that involve the people and islands of the Pacific and Asia, and yet the genre is still defined primarily by its relationship to European cinema and arts.[20] These Asian figures are ubiquitous and marginalized in popular noir as gardeners, maids, and houseboys.[21] To render the cultural exchanges across the Pacific Arena meaningful is to engage in a collective acknowledgment of American empire. The richest sites to animate these discussions are found in the margins, border zones, and minor subjects of noir.

More popularly known as hardboiled fiction, literary noir begins to saturate the pulp presses from the end of the nineteenth century. Hardboiled fiction mediated the conditions of urban industrialization at the turn of the century, and the violent and morally ambiguous world described by noir authors spoke to the conditions of economic depression in the 1930s and global anxiety after World War II. As Lee Horsley has argued, "In the noir fiction of this period, the anxious sense of fatality is usually attached to a pessimistic conviction that economic and socio-political circumstances will deprive people of control over their lives by destroying their hopes and by creating in them the weaknesses of character that mark them out as victims."[22]

Their style is defined by a harsh realism, "but their focus on the real conditions and problems of interwar society is repeatedly joined to the fantastic and the symbolic," a trait that makes the genre so ideally suited to film.[23] Film and literary noir are intimately related to each other, with popular authors such as James Cain (*Double Indemnity*, 1943) and Raymond Chandler (*The Big Sleep*, 1939) leaving their marks on both spheres. The hard-boiled noir protagonist is also notable for the morally unsavory physical violence to which they often resort.[24] The two fields share obvious and subtle elements, such as film noir's distinguishing stylistic element of voiceover narration by the hardboiled protagonist, which is clearly linked to the first-person perspective and voice found in the novel form.

Film noir adds a change in the visual experience with on-location shooting and a stark, high-contrast visual style that is made possible by the advances in lighting technology necessitated both by the austerity and the opportunities of World War II.[25] The designation "film noir," or "black cinema," comes from French reception of American Hollywood films such as *Stranger on the Third Floor* (1940), *The Maltese Falcon* (1941), and *The Big Sleep* (1946). In summer 1946, watching American films for the first time since German occupation, French viewers were surprised and impressed by these stylish crime dramas and saw in them a significant departure in ethos from the previous period of the American style of filmmaking; the noir period embraced bleakness, the ugliness of humanity, and the erotic lure of power. This was captured by a new style that heightened the viewers' sense of unease and discomfort. The stark, black-and-white chiaroscuro (Italian for "light-dark") lighting style, low-key lighting,[26] and unbalanced composition resonated with the dark German Expressionism films such as Fritz Lang's *Metropolis* (1927), *Hollywood Like Fury* (1936), and *You Only Live Once* (1937) — an echo accentuated by the fact that many German filmmakers fled to Hollywood to escape Nazism. Paul Schrader explains the consequences of such a style: "Compositional tension is preferred to physical action. A typical film noir would rather move the scene cinematographically around the actor than have the actor control the scene by physical action."[27]

The visual makes the anxiety over race explicit and central to the film genre. Manthia Diawara sees racial borders as invoked and implicated in Hollywood lighting conventions.[28] Richard Dyer has pointed to how big-screen female icons of the early film era, such as Lillian Gish, were brightly lit to make it appear that they had a halo and seemed to be a "source of light"[29] — a rare innocent in an industrializing First World rapidly changing as a result of racialized Others from across the Pacific as well as domestic racial others.[30] In this sense, noir's characteristic look and sound are what Eric Lott has called "a sort of whiteface dream-work of social anxieties with explicitly racial sources, condensed on film into the criminal undertakings of abjected whites."[31]

The constant references to the "Chinaman" in the Coen brothers' homage to noir, *The Big Lebowski* (1998) — set during the first Gulf War in the early 1990s and featuring Korean and Vietnam War veterans — are clearly a nod to Roman Polanski's *Chinatown* (1974), as well as to Howard Hawks's classic noir film *The Big Sleep* (1946), which was based on Chandler's 1939 novel. Sam Fuller wanted *House of Bamboo* (1955) to be the first American noir to be set in Japan because he saw in American noir elements present in the styles of Japanese filmmakers like Akira Kurosawa and Yasujirô Ozu.[32] Orson Welles's *The Lady from Shanghai* (1948) and its famous mirror scene — influenced by Josef von Sternberg's *Shanghai Express* (1932) — is also in conversation with Kurosawa's room of mirrors in *Drunken Angels* (1948), which was released later the same year.[33]

I offer this catalogue as a genealogy of transpacific connections in noir to demonstrate how systematic and thorough the representations of Asian bodies and symbols have been to noir, from its most classic to more avant-garde elements. Yet it is surprising how little this orientation has been mentioned in noir scholarship. Impeding knowledge and discussion of the Pacific in noir is the silence around American imperialism in the Pacific Arena. Marc Vernet best encapsulates the dominant representation of the genre as a romance between the United States and Europe: "The stories it tells are both shocking and sentimental, because it is a great example of co-operation — the Americans made it and then the French invented it."[34] In other words, "noir is like a Harley-Davidson: you know right away what it is, the object only the synecdoche of a continent, a history and a civilization, or more precisely of their presentation for non-natives."[35]

However, this version of noir history is a strategic erasure of the genre's history: it was under occupation and the Marshall Plan that Japan and Germany become acquainted with Hollywood and American noir and, in return, influenced the genre.[36] Rather than the Harley-Davidson, it would be more appropriate to point toward a different machine — the atomic bomb —

and how it creates intense and universal human anxiety, tailor-made for noir. The atomic bomb was officially born on July 16, 1945, after the first successful testing of the bomb technology in the White Sands Desert near Alamogordo, New Mexico. The detonation was given the code name *Trinity*. The code names *Little Boy* and *Fat Man*, credited to Robert Serber, a member of J. Robert Oppenheimer's group, are themselves likely rooted in noir. Originally named "Thin Man" and "Fat Man," these names are influenced by Dashiell Hammett's *The Thin Man*.[37] The dropping of the atomic bombs on Hiroshima and Nagasaki and the visual culture these events inspired were central to creating and sustaining anxiety and a feeling of imminent crisis.

These bombings caused an ontological and epistemological shift within Western modernity, and, unlike the Harley-Davidson, this shift threatened U.S. imperialist knowledge production and geopolitics. Rey Chow describes the impact of the atomic bomb as creating a state of knowledge production and geopolitics in which the symbolic order no longer refers to any meaning and its only responsibility is to name things: "War after the atomic bomb would no longer be the physical, mechanical struggle between combative oppositional groups, it would more and more come to resemble collaborations in the logics of perceptions between partners who occupy relative, but always mutually related, positions."[38]

Despite the seemingly evident nature of the claim that the atomic bomb is a machine of genocidal modernity, it actually requires a great deal of work to recognize its essential nature as a machine of industrial killing for the American popular and geopolitical imaginary. During the Cold War, the mushroom cloud dominated how the atomic bomb was conceived and represented in the United States. Iconized and fetishized, the cloud dominates the frame (sometimes taking up the entire frame), representing a completed and successful act—the mass annihilation and destruction of its target. This is an origin narrative that functions both to obliterate and to establish itself as always already, augmenting a new moment in the symbolic order in which nothing comes before this realized image of American military might.[39] In this way, the destruction caused by atomic modernity goes "from being [a] negative blockade to being normal routine, war becomes the positive mechanism, momentum, and condition of possibility."[40]

Even texts that self-consciously attempt to address the blind spots in noir scholarship and the unconscious of noir do not recognize the constitutive effect of imperial ambitions and expansion in the Pacific Arena in their analyses of the Asian figures of noir. For example, in the introduction to the reissue of *Women in Film Noir* (first published in 1978), editor E. Ann Kaplan discusses how the groundbreaking original collection's lack of attention to race inspired her to invite new essays for the 1998 edition.[41] However, her own contribution, a chapter on the meaning of race in Welles's *The Lady from Shanghai*, manages to make evident how imperialism over the Pacific Arena is erased from American history and culture. Kaplan argues, "But as colonialism began to wane under the challenges made effectively by subaltern groups in the [19]40s, so white culture's unconscious search for other "*dark continents*" to fill the gap left by Africa. One such *continent* was the psyche of women now coming into consciousness as [Sigmund] Freud's theories spread in the wake of World War II. But this *dark continent* of the female psyche never quite lost its links to displaced reference to racial *darkness*."[42]

The growth of American military empire over the Pacific Arena is missing in this account of waning colonialism. The repetition of "darkness" as a naturalized term to explain a host of ideas related to degradation and brutality also reveals colonial residues in First World white feminist thinking, which may be inherent to orthodox Freudian psychoanalysis.[43] We could treat this as an isolated tendency if not for the fact that *Shades of Noir*, another collection seeking to render noir criticism more complex and rich, does not take seriously the provocation of its title and surprisingly does not address the topic of race in any way in the introduction to the volume, despite the provocation offered by the opening chapter's analysis of Delmer Dave's *Dark Passages* (1947).[44] Lott's analysis of Diawara's use of darkness and lightness as metaphors to describe noir demonstrates his concern about how noir scholars unreflexively amplify in their own texts the racial symbolic order they are trying to critique.[45]

This nationalist and Euro-American-centric notion of noir has made it difficult to recognize how "noir lends itself to domestication in different national contexts, in part because it is concerned with the local and for this reason travels well and endures historically. Indeed, noir's international circulation has been historically linked to the problem of national culture and the status of national cinema in an era of increasing global interconnectedness."[46] The renationalization of noir may not lead to a decolonial understanding of noir, but it does unsettle the idea that it is only oriented toward Europe.

Exceptions to such blindness to white supremacy and imperialism come from scholars such as Rachel Adams, Donald E. Pease, Lott, and Diawara, whose primary work is not in noir.[47] However, even in their work the presence of American empire in the Pacific Arena is addressed obliquely. The invisibility of Asians in noir analysis also mirrors the invisibility of Koreans as never seen/never healed, and the situation of the Korean survivor parallels the racial position of Asians in America. For example, Lott's thesis on the whiteness of film noir opens with an insightful and deep reading of Billy Wilder's film *Double Indemnity* (1944) that does not address how the replacement of the Filipino houseboy of James Cain's novel with the Black woman housekeeper of the film complicates and nuances Lott's own black-and-white framing and could potentially link white supremacy to U.S. imperialism in the Pacific Arena.[48]

Imagining transpacific histories of colonialism forces recognition of ongoing occupation, struggles for decolonization, and the fight to regain sovereignty. This requires interrogating the existing spatial language and orientation with which we imagine the nation. Challenging the primacy of the term, Amy Kaplan argues that "frontier implies a model of center and periphery, which confront one another most often in a one-way imposition of power," while "borderlands not only lie at the geographic and political margins of national identity but as often traverse the center as the metropolis."[49] Building on Gloria E. Anzaldúa's original conception, Kaplan's notion of borderlands helps to reimagine sites of American empire across the Pacific Arena as a locus of "decentered cosmopolitanism," such as the inspiration drawn by the Rapa Nui from their Polynesian neighbors.[50] The margins of transpacific noir resemble these borderlands, existing within noir yet also offering alternative, even if unintentional, archives and histories of connection centered on American imperialism in the Pacific Arena. These are sites where wounds lurk, reside, and find their homes.

The Return of the Korean War and Dialectic Temporality in *The Crimson Kimono*

Sam Fuller's *The Crimson Kimono* (1959) exemplifies the tendency of transpacific noir to return to wounds resulting from the wars in the Pacific. Featuring Japanese American detective Joe Kojaku (James Shigeta) and his best friend and partner, Charlie Fuller (Glenn Corbett), much of the film was shot in actual locations throughout Los Angeles, including Little Tokyo and Evergreen Cemetery.[51] *The Crimson Kimono* is not highly regarded within noir scholarship, which tends to focus primarily on stylistic elements. When critics do focus on the film, it tends to be because of the unique representation of interracial love between a Japanese American man and a white woman, made more exceptional because of the competition between him and his white best friend for her love.[52] Scholars also note that Fuller's late noir deviates from the norm in its representation of Asian ethnic ghettos, which tended, as in Polanski's *Chinatown* and Welles's *The Lady from Shanghai*, to situate the location as a point of condensation for the film's racial anxieties.

Joe and Charlie's fraternity due to their time together in a foxhole in Korea is established offscreen as part of the film's backstory, but we are able to see the violence that shapes that fraternity when they attack a Korean man, Shuto, they suspect of committing the principal murder of the film. Shuto represents not only a manifestation and return rooted in the anxieties over the unfinished nature of the war between Communist North and South in Korea; he also embodies the unresolved/unresolvable contradictions and fissures in the transition between Japanese imperialism and American military occupation. This joint attack is the last moment of unity between the two men before their competitive pursuit of the film's white femme fatale breaks apart their brotherhood. *The Crimson Kimono* begins with the murder of a burlesque dancer. The first suspect in the investigation is Shuto, a Korean with a Japanese name who lives in Little Tokyo.[53] Shuto is presented as an enigma, a Korean who lives as Japanese and whose history is deliberately left unexplained. Two sympathetic Japanese American nuns that Joe and Charlie interview as they try to find Shuto describe him as "beastly, ill, and inarticulate. It's just pitiful." Shuto is likely tied up with Japanese empire as a *Zainichi* Korean.[54] While "zainichi" translates as "foreigner," it is used as shorthand to refer more generally to Koreans in Japan who are of the colonial generation.

On the level of the film, Shuto represents the kind of overtaking challenge that establishes fraternity between Joe and Charlie, especially now that they are civilians. The scene where they beat him up brutally is notable for its violence and its long duration. Charlie and Joe's interracial fraternity is in danger of falling apart, a precarity managed in part by continuously reproducing and destroying enemy Others in East Asia beyond and after the Korean War.[55] Charlie was Joe's commanding officer during the Korean War, where they both exceeded expectations and acted with extreme heroism. Although the Korean War is the genesis of Charlie and Joe's kinship, this fraternity must be reestablished in the context of a late-1950s U.S. domestic, racial, and imperial terrain. This includes the march toward full-scale U.S. involvement in Southeast Asia as well as the civil rights movement, which threatened to dismantle U.S. imperialist and white supremacist architecture.

The fact that Shuto is zainichi makes Joe particularly important to the case because Joe is an insider in Little Tokyo. However, to all Japanese Americans (Nisei) in the film, Shuto is indecipherable and inarticulate. He is a racial Other whose lack of civilization reaffirms Joe and Charlie's position of power over him and, by extension, a premodern Korea. However, that Shuto is inarticulate to Joe and other Nisei takes on added meaning if we consider Japanese American internment and the repatriation of the Issei generation and the demand that Nisei perform their patriotism in every way, including renouncing their Japanese language. This prohibits and silences the Nisei in the film, which also then silences Shuto. Even if Shuto spoke, he would be neither heard nor repeated. Shuto represents the will of Japanese imperialism in Korea to remain unintelligible, a will in which the white supremacist and imperialist U.S. nation-state invests and is complicit. This unintelligibility manifests as Shuto's incomprehensibly sweaty and ill body—his illness has no cure, and he is a subject who cannot seek a cure. This is what I mean when I say that transpacific noir is replete with broken and degraded bodies, where the traumas of war unable to be spoken become physically manifested on the body. Thus, Shuto's body symbolizes the unhealed and unhealable, a site where that which is supposed to be erased remains.[56]

Shuto's body is not the only one in danger. So was Japanese American Joe's. Charlie donated his blood to Joe after he was critically injured in their foxhole during the war in Korea. After Joe receives Charlie's blood transfusion, he rejoins the front with a renewed vigor, winning the Silver Star for his valor. The reference to the donation of blood is another instance, like the beating up of Shuto in the film, where the violence over the Korean peninsula is sought to be covered over by a narrative of American heroism and interracial fraternity. However, the reference to the danger Americans faced always already threatens to reveal the violence they perpetrated.

While the violence and mass killings of World War II are well documented, even if the history is contested, unacknowledged and actively hidden is then new military technology of napalm practiced on the Korean people by the U.S. military. Much of the attack on the Korean land and bodies was perpetrated by air assault, and "between 1950–1953, U.S. bombers dumped as much as 600,000 tons of napalm over the Korean peninsula. . . . This was more napalm than had been used against Japan in World War II and more than would be later dropped in Vietnam."[57] Historians have detailed how the destruction of civilians was indiscriminate in the Korean War, structured in part by the inability and unwillingness to distinguish between civilians and North Korean combatants. Like the firebombing in Japan that almost completely decimated all the major cities even before the atomic bomb was dropped, in Korea the U.S. military practiced a "scorched-earth policy," burning down entire villages and indiscriminately bombing nonmilitary and nonindustrial targets like hospitals and schools. These accumulated practices were deployed in Vietnam just a few years later. This entire history was deliberately concealed when it was occurring, and the subsequent geopolitical dominance that the United States has in rebuilding the South Korean nation it devastated made this history verboten.[58]

When the Korean War is represented in U.S. popular culture (e.g., *The Crimson Kimono*, *M*A*S*H*), the war is represented as a proxy for another war, such as World War II or Vietnam. As I have been arguing what contributes to the seeming fungibility of the Korean War is Korea's postcolonial status—colonized under Japan, treated by the United States as de facto Japanese subjects during the imperial period, and brought under U.S. geopolitical dominance after the San Francisco Peace Treaty of 1951 and as a result of the Korean War.[59]

In *Haunting the Korean Diaspora*, Grace M. Cho argues that what haunts the living is not the trauma or the event itself but the accumulated silence around the trauma.[60] She formulates the idea of trauma as "dread forwarding," asserting that "just as a new trauma can trigger an older one, inducing a flashback, it can also flash forward, projecting itself into a future haunting."[61] Dread forwarding is a temporality of trauma driven by an anxiety due to a fear of a traumatic and painful future; it is an experience of multichronicity in the present.[62] Looking at the nearly four hundred civilians massacred by the American military at Nogeun-ri in 1950 during the earliest days of the outbreak of the Korean War and comparing them to the My Lai civilian massacres in Vietnam 1968, Cho argues that such a comparison "speaks to the ways in which the trauma of militarized violence can traverse boundaries of time and space" and "illustrates how one occurrence can evoke another moment that has not yet happened."[63] She continues, "A temporality in which past and future collide is the temporality both of an unconscious haunted by trauma and of the affective experience of traumatic event, in which the past opens directly onto the future because the present moment happens too quickly to be perceived. Events and their contexts are folded into the body as potentialities, and the present moment is accessible to conscious experience only through its traces."[64] One of the survivors of the Nogeun-ri massacre in Korea, then sixteen-year-old Hee-sook, recalls wading through the waters surrounding her village, shifting through hundreds of dead bodies to look for her dead father. Cho quotes her saying, "It seemed that the bones and flesh moved separately. . . . I virtually scooped up the remains of my father — like mucus — with the cup of my bare hands."[65]

The contradictions of U.S. involvement in Korea, which includes the unresolved nature of Japanese colonialism in Korea, is materially manifest in the broken apart, viscous body of Hee-sook's murdered father. It lives on every day in the Demilitarized Zone that separates the two Koreas. Symbolically, this makes the war impossible to incorporate into a narrative of closure. The Korean diaspora in the United States, which Shuto is clearly a part of, is especially dangerous to this attempt at closure. Analyzed using the lens of the dialogic temporality of transpacific noir reorganizes Shuto, Charlie, and Joe's relationship and hierarchy. Their interactions defy the conventions of the interracial buddy film, formed and consolidated against an uncivilized Other. Instead, Joe and Shuto are variously colonized and silenced. In addition to serving as the manifestation and return rooted in the anxieties over the unfinished nature of the war in Korea, Shuto haunts the fraternity between Joe and Charlie. He represents an afterlife of imperialism, keeps alive the record of the links between Japanese and American colonialisms, and refuses to allow this interracial fraternity to heal itself. We can see this when we read texts not only for the ways they offer continuity, but also for the ways they rupture, revealing places where the narrative no longer coheres or wounds refuse to heal. This is the work of transpacific noir.

The classic noir period ends in 1958 with Welles's *Touch of Evil*. It would reemerge in the late 1960s as neo-noir — with self-assuredness and known references to the original noir style, which was initially less self-conscious about meeting the rules of the genre. It is in the neo-noir period that the anxious affect produced by the wars in the Pacific Arena emerges more obviously, and disavowal of it requires more active work and management. The country is no longer simply sutured to the narrative of heroism rooted in World War II, but to new wars in the Pacific, including Korea, Vietnam, Cambodia, and Laos, and an increasing awareness is deeply situated in American cinema and its revitalization. Genre represents a kind of "social contract between a writer and a specific public"[66] and is an ideal site to stage a narrative about anxieties of an unknown present, anxieties caused by the refusal of the past to remain dead and buried. This means a living of the present as a state of anxiety, as it is still uncertain who the Pacific will serve in the Pacific Century: American or Asian dominance.

This flourishing of the transpacific space of noir is also the result of creative activity in the Pacific Arena itself. New presses (e.g., Pacific Noir Pulp Press) and authors (e.g., Graeme Kent and his series set in the Solomon Islands and Hawaiian authors Kiana Davenport and Victoria Kneubuhl) demonstrate the growth in the field in all directions. Naomi Hirahara's novel *Summer of the Big Bachi*'s transnational reorientation of the genre across the Pacific joins these Pacific Islander authors as well as U.S. mainlanders Leonard Chang, Chang Rae Lee, and Dale Furutani, who refigure and animate the transpacific against the histories of erasure and proxies I have been arguing against.

What Goes around Comes around in *Summer of the Big Bachi*

Referencing a history of racial borders that thrive in noir, Naomi Hirahara describes her work in relation to the African American literary noir tradition: "I've definitely been inspired by Chester Himes's Coffin Ed Johnson and Grave Digger Jones series and, of course, books by Walter Mosley." She credits Black writers for "leading the way" on using the mystery as a "vehicle to explore social issues and cultural themes."[67] Hirahara's well-regarded and award-winning seven-novel Mas Arais Mystery Series features a *kibei* and hibakusha hardboiled protagonist and gardener—sixty-nine-year-old Mas Arai. Kibeis are Japanese Americans who traveled to Japan as young children for education there. During World War II they were unable to return to the United States and thus became marooned in Japan, not claimed by Japan, but no longer certain of their American citizenship. Hirahara was an editor for the *Rafu Shimpo*, the longest-running English-language Japanese American newspaper in Los Angeles. By linking her work to the Black cultural sphere, Hirahara highlights an important counterpublic within the genre of noir—authors who and narratives that center protagonists of color in a genre otherwise renowned for its fraught relationship to race.[68]

Any Asian American detective figure is racialized in relationship to the legacy of Charlie Chan, the "honorable" detective from Hawai'i. Popularized as a character serialized in the *Saturday Evening Post* by Earl Derr Digger starting in 1924, Charlie Chan became an international sensation and profoundly profitable for Paramount Pictures, who put Werner Oland in yellowface to become Charlie Chan.[69] Chandler's novel *The Big Sleep* demonstrates the emasculating terms under which Charlie Chan has become ingrained in American popular cultural consciousness: "Fat face, Charlie Chan moustache, thick soft neck. Soft all over"[70]—this describing a murdered pornographer accused of kidnapping the film's young white heiress.

Charlie Chan has become a floating signifier for a particular type of emasculated Asian American masculinity, so much so that his backstory no longer needs to be narrated. He is reviled by Asian Americans because he is seen as "a pernicious example of a racist stereotype, a Yellow Uncle Tom, if you will; the type of Chinaman, passive and unsavory, who conveys himself in broken English."[71] Charlie Chan is not only an important American cultural figure; he is also referenced over and over again in Asian American culture—from Wayne Wang's *Chan Is Missing* (1982) to Jessica Hagedorn's *Charlie Chan Is Dead*[72]—to fuel criticism of this white supremacist repertoire. I interpret Mas Arai's accented English and turn toward the seedy outskirts of ethnic enclaves that clearly reference iconic noir as well as opposition to the racial architecture of the genre.

Summer of the Big Bachi is set in Los Angeles in 1995 and in flashbacks to Mas's youth in Hiroshima in the midst of war with the United States. Like the accented and slight Japanese gardener in *Chinatown* who inadvertently helps J. J. Gittes (Jack Nicholson) solve the crime, Mas Arai has gardened for the Los Angeles elite only to see them fall from glory. The novel holds back on his recollections of the day the atomic bomb was dropped on Hiroshima until near the middle of the narrative, as this moment is also shrouded by his deepest guilt—letting his friend Joji Haneda die alone in the initial hours after the bomb fell. He has never talked about Joji's death until this point in his life. Mas is forced to face this buried memory when people from Hiroshima descend on Los Angeles looking for a Joji Haneda who stands next in line to inherit land worth over ten million dollars. Like many hardboiled heroes, Mas is not officially a detective. His willingness to get involved stems from his own need to follow through on Joji's legacy, although that drive changes as the story develops and he becomes aware of the vast and powerful consortium invested in keeping Joji's death silent in order to cover up a larger crime committed against Korean hibakusha and conscripted workers, evidence for which lies buried within Joji's inheritance.

My reading of *Summer of the Big Bachi* considers its focus on *bachi*—an alternative juridical, ethical, and religious model the novel uses to think about the afterlives of the atomic bomb. The motivating factor driving the criminal activity in the novel—hidden evidence of crimes against Koreans by the Japanese government during the colonial period—suggests a festering wound connecting the people and the land that can only heal if uncovered. Translated as "what goes around comes around," bachi is tied to the novel's overall concern with the inheritance the atomic generation leaves for the next, which not only brings up questions of reparations, redistribution, and atomic radiation, but also dread as it "forwards," threatening to return violence from the past in the future. What is notable about Hirahara's story is that, unlike *The Crimson Kimono*, it seeks a way to represent Japanese and Korean histories during and after the Japanese colonial era as inextricably interlinked. The pain of one cannot be resolved without addressing that of the other.

Bachi, like "karma," refers to a spirit of retribution that makes sense in this context, wherein the overwhelming pressures of uncountable wounds inevitably will action. Bachi is an everyday invocation of an ethical and spiritual realm that metes out justice to those whom unwieldy institutions and fallible humans cannot. However, bachi is a proxy for immediate and just punishment and, in that way, always already reveals the impossibility of equal return for loss. In the novel, living with the fear of bachi is not just about waiting for punishment long deferred, it is also about anticipating a future pain that is rooted in resistant and elastic wounds caused by the dropping of the atomic bomb.

There are three manifestations of bachi in the novel, ranging from quotidian to life-changing: "In Japanese, bachi was when you snapped at your wife, and then tripped on a rock in the driveway. You didn't suffer your punishment in another lifetime, but within the same life, even within the next few minutes."[73] The other bachi in the novel is cancer: "This other trouble was more familiar. It chased him through the corridors of his life, turned when he turned, flew over ocean and land. Mas, in fact, had gotten used to it, like a pebble in his work boot. Soon the sole of his foot would get so callused and blistered that he couldn't feel a thing."[74]

The fact that someone close died of cancer unexpectedly is repeated often and throughout the novel like a mantra and is a constant reminder that the hibakushas are a cancer cluster.[75] Mas's personal and third form of bachi comes as the result of abandoning a friend and fellow kibei, Joji, to die alone in the immediate moments after the atomic bomb was dropped on Hiroshima. Mas let their friend and another survivor, Riki Kimura, steal Joji's

American citizenship papers, which were stuffed inside Joji's boots: "So I stole Joji's foot. I found a piece of metal and tore open the boot. The papers were right there. His birth certificate, everything."[76] Riki confesses as he lies dying, now also nearly seventy years old like Mas. Desperate, Riki stole Joji's papers so he could escape Japan and start over in the United States. This scene is one of many desecrations of the human body we encounter in the novel.

Like Joji's body in the novel, Nisei bodies have become degraded, broken, and remade, and this symbolic repertoire indicates a living of life in the shadow of atomic modernity. Nisei gardener Stinky Yamamoto's eyes are described as being "bloodshot and milky yellow like a stirred raw egg"; his friend Tug has a missing forefinger; and "Mas's best friend, if he could call him that, was Haruo Mukai. He was scrawny and a little shriveled, like a piece of fat that you couldn't quite chew through."[77] In addition to this general description, Haruo's face is deformed, due to the right side melting after the bomb dropped. Mas is described for the first time in similar terms: "His cheek looked bad, like someone had tried to hull out a piece of flesh with a spoon."[78] The Nisei generation have had to face their bachi but have had neither their luck replenished nor their bachi reciprocated.

Mas fears that the potential for vulnerability and permeability will be passed on to his daughter, Mari. But his inability to mourn Joji's death and his silence around what happens also ensure that Mari may inherit his trauma. The initial descriptions of Mari offered in the novel are suggestive of how trauma can be manifested physically and can be passed on to the next generation. The first one we have of her is at age one: "[Sitting] in her booster chair, her silver-capped front teeth shining as she chewed a piece of liver. Like always, she remained quiet, her eyes focused on a large crack on the wall. Soon the argument would escalate; plates shattered against the wall and ceiling, soy sauce dripping over the crack like black blood."[79]

"Silver-capped front teeth" is hard to imagine on such a young infant. In the context of a silencing fight between her parents, the silver cap suggests she needs protection and that it functions as an outward manifestation of her internalized trauma. Postmemory scholars argue that the silence within families about unspoken war trauma can manifest as depression, disconnection, and sometimes as violence. The next generation or those who did not live through the same violence fill in the gaps between silence themselves. This makes the memories of these others feel like they were generated from the self. Cho connects this silencing not only spatially but temporally, to a fear of a future of violence: "As noted in research on transgenerational trauma, it is often the act of not speaking that generates trauma's capacity to move across boundaries of time and space. Yael Danieli describes the unspeakable traumas of a family or collective history as an 'audible void' (1988). It is precisely this void, according to Abraham and Torok, that 'transgenerational haunting begins.'"[80] The traumas Mas experiences but cannot speak of, the deaths he cannot mourn, feed other silences, which in the novel deforms bodies.

This silence, both personally and structurally enforced, ensures that the past can never be grasped as a whole, but only in parts. Traumatic events are remembered partially because the "present moment happens too quickly to be perceived."[81] Later in the novel, as a teenager, Mari is described as having a mouth full of teeth that are "tightened," "stretched," and "capped" from braces and dental work meant to straighten and beautify her teeth. This is a ritual for American middle-class teenagers, a normalization of neoliberal biopolitics that encourages "care of the self, integral to a neoliberal regime in which the health of the body becomes an enterprise one must invest in to maximize health and vitality."[82] In that context the silver cap simultaneously suggests something else — that Mari's body is worth investing in, fixing, and improving.

The novel's symbolic repertoire forces a comparison between the death evaded that surrounds the Nisei and the care for the body — demonstrated by Mari's braces — as necessary for the prevention of a future return of violence. The fear of an atomic inheritance for his daughter constitutes a key part of "dread forwarding" for Mas, wherein he dreams and fears his daughter and grandchild will melt and die because of cancer and radiation. Speaking his trauma and mourning Joji's death may mitigate some aspect of his dread. However, even efforts to recall his past trauma are hampered by the fact that language about certain kinds of trauma is lacking and when spoken may seem incomprehensible. In interviewing her mother about her experience having survived the Korean War, one of the things Cho returns to is how "there are ... no memory that she could speak."[83] Cho explains how her mother never recalls whether "she had been witness to her brother's death or to the deaths of neighbors or strangers traveling with her, if she was like the young people whose memories are documented here, who at every turn encountered bodies that were burned or ripped apart, who came to embody the ripped-apartness that was the Korean War."[84] What is notable to Cho is that her mother can remember with detail her horror at seeing North

Korean girl soldiers with guns — notable to her because "the vision of these girls with guns, she says, is the most horrifying image she can remember from the war. . . . It was terrible, she says, because women are not supposed to fight. A woman in combat was beyond her frame of reference . . . but so was consorting with American men in bars."[85] While her mother may recall this moment because she possessed language and knowledge about gendered expectations, she may not be able to speak about the deaths she saw around her because that is officially mandated as never having occurred. The official narrative is of an unwavering South Korean loyalty to the United States. Speaking against this imperial common sense means having to develop new language and metaphors. It is to risk being called crazy and incomprehensible.

In *Summer of the Big Bachi*, it is not only the next generation whose bodies are worth saving and investing in. Joji's bodily remains may finally be discovered, and evidence may soon surface that will help Korean hibakusha and forced workers win an apology and backpay from the Japanese government, perhaps also enabling the healing of the land itself.[86] This is a multilayered conception of a vulnerable body, diachronic and defined by simultaneity. There is no healing unless the living, the dead, the colonized, the colonizer, and the land on which they all reside are healed all at once.

Conclusion

Hirahara's conception of bachi is premised on the fallibility and limits of existing systems of moral and judicial accountability. This is certainly the case for the zainichi Shuto in *The Crimson Kimono*, who only exists so that his presence can become systematically negated. In a sense, bachi elucidates the myriad ways that justice produced by the colonizer has not and cannot recognize the claims of former colonized subjects willed into disappearance. Bachi also calls forth the need to recognize other modalities of accounting that can make the postcolonial feel alive, such as the Korean grief work *han*. Chungmoo Choi explains that han, as "the pent-up resentment that can bring destruction into human relationships, stems from a situation in which such repressed emotion is not allowed to emerge."[87] Grace M. Cho describes how in the years after the civilian massacres in Nogeun-ri there is a reported phenomenon called *honbul*, or "ghost flames," in which flickering lights rise up from the ground. "The survivors of the massacre were haunted by *honbul* that were stirred up each summer near Nogeun-ri. The ghost flames are perhaps a material expression of han (often translated as 'unresolved grief and rage')—han of the dead for having been murdered and of survivors for having been witness to their families' slaughter."[88] Han shares bachi's juridical concerns to address a wrong done in the past as well as to investigate how this past comes to occupy space in the present. Han's "ghost flames" are akin to bachi's "tripping on a rock"—in both, the past lingers beyond its time, growing, lingering, and exerting pressure.

Through Mas and his negotiation of his bachi, the novel offers a version of seeking justice that reveals a fundamental problem with current models for redress and reconciliation. One of the main venues for transpacific redress claims since the 1990s, the International Criminal Courts are structured around liberal democratic models that seek an "overcoming" on the part of the injured so that the nation can be defined by a narrative of overcoming, healing, accepting, forgiving, and creating.[89] This developmental narrative affirms a linear view of modernity, and the coming together of the nation represents a redeemed present. Once the apology has been given and then accepted, then, for the nation-state, the problem of power is imagined settled.[90] However, as my reading of transpacific noir cautions, "reconciliation may require for victims and their descendants recognition for the right not to forgive in order to keep the process open to their needs following from the injustices of the past."[91]

· FOUR ·

DESTINED FOR DEATH

Antigone along the Pacific Arena

This is the time of Antigone. Many in the Americas and along the Pacific Arena have turned to and revised Sophocles's *Antigone*, the story of a girl condemned to death by a cruel king, Creon, for trying to bury her brother Polynices, whose traitorous dead body is left to rot as a warning and to terrorize the populace. After King Oedipus is banished and killed, his sons Eteocles and Polynices battle for the kingdom of Thebes and end up killing each other. The first day of peace is also the first day of tyranny. Their uncle Creon has assumed the throne and, in declaring Polynices a traitor, has demanded the shaming and degradation of his dead body. Polynices is denied holy burial rites and his corpse is supposed to be left uncovered and left to rot to terrorize the populace. Teresa Ralli and José Watanabe's 1999 adaptation, *Antígona*, is set in Peru where the story of a sister's struggle to bury her brother under the edict of death speaks to Peru's recent history of disappearances and state terrorism under President Alberto Fujimori.[1]

Following *Antigone* along the Pacific Rim, this chapter discusses the attempts to produce a "Pacific Rim imaginary" which positions the United States and Japan as psychic and economic centers of a transpacific partnership.[2] This imaginary is contested by transnational feminist aesthetic projects that link this transpacific history to the genocidal history and decimation of Indigenous cultures connected to the colonialization of the Americas. Through analysis of Teresa Ralli and José Watanabe's *Antígona*, this chapter considers how U.S. neoliberal regimes colluded and created conditions abetting the refusal to see state terrorisms in the Pacific Arena. In doing so, this chapter contributes to attempts at destabilizing the colonial grounds on which Asia, the Americas, and the Pacific are produced as sites to be known and studied.

By "refusal to see" I am discussing the production of a kind of blinding that Diana Taylor calls "percepticide," or the blinding of the population.[3] Taylor describes how the Argentine and Peruvian state terrorist tactics of public and sudden "disappearances" forced people to turn a blind eye to state violence, a looking away that threatened to become instinctive.[4] It is the *hypervisibility* of violence that authorizes more violence and exemplifies the powerful point of percepticide. Making state violence seem quotidian, pervasive, and natural promotes looking away, but looking away does not prevent mourning. "Percepticide" describes the great deal of will it takes to stop thinking about the disappeared Antigone, murdered by the state for refusing to stop mourning her dead brother.

This chapter thinks expansively about the afterlives of the Pacific Wars in the Americas. It puts the previous chapters' work in comparison with mourning, transformative melancholia, and restorative justice within a broader Pacific Arena. Creating an alternative remapping of the Pacific Arena means starting over on new conceptual ground, with specific implications for critiquing the "percepticides" and looking away related to U.S. knowledge production about the role of the Asia-Pacific in the increasing violence and militarism in the Americas name of development and modernization. Studying the intersections between Asia and Latin America has the potential to offer a "radical appeal to an epistemic outside" where "the goal is to point attention not to knowledge that naturalizes itself but points to the material conditions of its own making."[5] Making the connections between how those in Peru mourn the nearly 80,000 Peruvians disappeared or murdered by the state certainly enriches the melancholia expressed by the Japanese and Korean diasporas I have discussed so far in the book. However, as I will argue in this chapter, the looking away from the violence that occurred in Peru promoted within U.S. cultural and political spheres is endemic to a U.S. knowledge production that has systematically elided the role that the United States has played in enabling state terrorism along the Pacific Rim in the name of economic modernization and capitalism. This elision is engaged by a growing hemispheric and transpacific anticolonial cultural imaginary which contests the terms on which this elision occurs.[6]

A long history and complex transnational network of dispersal and migration constitutes relations between the Latin America and the transpacific. Colonial inception of the Americas is "a *transpacific* as much as a transatlantic project, yet conventional history, even of the most elevated kind taught in the best history departments of the United States and Europe, has always framed the history of the Americas as part of the Atlantic, rarely if ever mentioning critical and enduring transpacific connections."[7] Because of a regulatory form of Cold War knowledge formation, Latin America, Asia, and the Asia-Pacific came to be constituted as different areas to be known and studied. This is because "for comparisons to be read as intelligible . . . Europe must serve as the universal point of reference."[8] The West is meant to be the universal subject, while Latin America, Asia, and Africa represent a particular, an "area study," which exists solely as a point for affirming or disproving a (Euro-American) rule. The Pacific Rim idea, which rises in the 1970s, connects the Americas and Asia but makes Japan and the U.S. the psychic and economic centers adapting this Cold War knowledge formation.[9] Thus scholarship that centers on Asia–Latin America, reveals uneven circuits of knowledge on the histories and cultures of Asians in the Americas and the occluded history of U.S. military and economic interventions, enabling "sharper resolution" and delineating comparative and overlapping constitutions within and across the Americas and the transpacific.[10]

I look at a specific event in the presidency of Alberto Fujimori, Peru's first Japanese Peruvian president (1990–2000), as a particularly fruitful way to think about how to conduct such hemispheric and transpacific work of recovery and remapping. A rebel group, members of Movimiento Revolucionario Túpac Amaru (MRTA) took control of the Japanese ambassador's home in Peru on December 17, 1996, making the country hypervisible to Americans throughout the entirety of the 126 days of the crisis, which ended when Peruvian military commandos entered the ambassador's home through underground tunnels it had dug secretly.[11] All fourteen hostage takers — twelve men and two women, indigenous from Peru's highlands — were killed. Initial approval of how President Fujimori had handled the hostage crisis became shrouded by scandal amid accusations that some of the hostage takers were murdered after they surrendered. The president refused to release the bodies of the dead MRTA members to their families or conduct autopsies on them. This situation then came to be understood not as a laudable end to terrorism against the state, but rather as an extension of the state's use of terrorist tactics against its citizens by killing and "disappearing" those it classifies as dissidents and insurgents. These tactics have been in use in Peru since the civil war between the state and Maoist insurgencies started in the late 1970s.

In the United States, although much of the aftermath of this hostage crisis was ignored, it revived memories and interest in American Lori Berenson. One of MRTA's demands was the release of political prisoners, including Berenson, who became a symbol for global human rights in 1996 after she was arrested for allegedly conspiring with MRTA in their ongoing attempts to overthrow the Peruvian state. Despite the attempts of several powerful presidents around the world to free her, Peruvian presidents (including Fujimori, Alejandro Toledo, and Alan Garcia) refused to release her from prison. By closely engaging the novel *Bel Canto* and *New York Times* article "The Liberation of Lori Berenson" focuses on how these narratives produce Lori Berenson as an maternal embodiment for feminized leadership, ideal for an atavistic Latin America. This production occurs through a narrative structure that promotes looking away from state terrorism and U.S. complicity.

Comparing U.S. and Peruvian representations of Fujimori's authoritarian regime in Peru is an opportunity to discuss a blind spot in knowledge production as well as how states and citizens learn to turn a blind eye. Peru under Fujimori was both neoliberal and authoritarian — that is, neoliberal reforms were only possible through state terrorism. Although it was no secret that the Fujimori regime used the military to terrorize its population into submitting to the denationalization of its economy, transpacific economic and political interests in Peru after Fujimori's election, particularly from the United States and Japan, continued to support him and his attempts to transform Peru into a Pacific Rim capitalist miracle.

The power of the Antigone narrative demonstrates feminist interventions against disappearances and state violence across a broad scale, from direct action against the state to challenging the erasure of this history from knowledge production. The various wars in Latin America were an important source of transformative politics and formation of anticolonial subjectivity for Latin Americans as well as U.S. Americans. Maoist rebels, like MRTA were the mirror on which U.S. American leftists cast their desires onto Latin America. Throughout the 1970s, 1980s, and 1990s, a small but significant subset of women leftists, radicals, and mercenaries from the U.S., like Berenson, were drawn to armed insurgency led by mainly Maoist factions in Latin American nations such as El Salvador, Nicaragua, Ecuador, and Peru. This desire to participate in liberation and freedom of Latin America makes twenty-first-century representations of Antigone fruitful for both imperial and decolonial feminist interventions. In this chapter, I start by addressing works by two popular and renowned novelists to map neoliberal feminist "anti-conquest narratives" of this state violence: Pulitzer Prize–winning author Jennifer Egan's coverage of Berenson's 2011 release from a Peruvian prison for the *New York Times* and Ann Patchett's 2001 novel, *Bel Canto*, set during the hostage crisis.[12] These texts, in different ways, render the historical conditions of Peru incomprehensible, a point of limitation we find over and over again in anti-conquest narratives when the Other becomes "excessive, disruptive, disturbing, in ways that damage us, rather than enhance our lives."[13] Unlike the Antigone figure in Ralli and Watanabe's *Antígona*, the anti-Antigone is invested in creating a personal and vindictive sphere of family and promoting privatized and silenced mourning.

Literature has always played a role in instructing the Self on how to care for an Other, to feel for an Other whose experience we do not share but whose difference with which we can empathize and sympathize.[14] However, this study of neoliberal and anti-Antigone narratives demonstrates not only a desire to expand contacts with the Third World Other, but the desire to set limits within what seems like an infinite and uncontrollable contact as a result of a world integrated through neoliberalism and war.[15] In this sense, neoliberal anti-Antigone narratives are essentially imperial and promote self-blinding.[16]

This obscene desire of imperial neoliberal feminism resonates within a 1990s Peru, where the state used the tactic of taking suspects suddenly and denying they had been taken, creating what Michael Taussig calls "death spaces."[17] The disappearances left a palpable void, and civil society was structured by "the reminder, constant and loud, that [they] were disappeared, lost to [their] world, without any hope of retrieval."[18] In addition to the ability to take bodies with impunity, the state enacted terror beyond the disappeared subject by withholding knowledge about what happened to the missing, thus sustaining an overall feeling of constant terror. For the state, the disappeared "do not have an entity, they are not there, neither dead nor alive."[19] The state agents of disappearances were anonymized, wearing masks and never identifying themselves, heightening the sense of hopelessness felt by survivors. It is in the context of percepticide that the narrative of Antigone enables representation and visibility on multiple stages.

If "The Liberation of Lori Berenson" and *Bel Canto* express the desire for limits and the incomprehensibility of nonenhancing difference as the Other living in death, the Peruvian play *Antígona* continually disrupts and pushes against limits, between life and death, survivor and disappeared, witnessing and complicity. *Antígona* was performed publicly across Peru as a part of the Peruvian Truth and Reconciliation Commission (TRC) gathering in 2002. The commission asked the political theater collective *Grupo Cultural Yuyachkani*, which Ralli is part of, to perform outreach works in communities where public hearings of testimonies of survivors and witnesses were to be convened. Given that the state was the culpable body, it was hard for survivors and witnesses to believe they should testify to the state or that it would matter. In the play *Antígona*, not only does Antígona speak her pain, she is always accompanied on stage with the dead Polynices's body, representing the disappeared. Focusing on the ways *Antígona*'s representations of the dead and disappeared of Peru's civil war reveal what remains incommensurable and what cannot be reconciled.

Destined for Death

Rather than an incidental moment in U.S. neoliberal cultural politics, the 1996 takeover of the Japanese ambassador's home in Lima would come to play an important role in shaping American consciousness and imaginations of terror. Berenson was arrested in 1995 in Lima, Peru, and charged with being a member of MRTA. In 1996, she was found guilty by a hooded military tribunal and not allowed to see the state's evidence against her. Her statement made to local broadcast media immediately after her arrest that MRTA is "not a terrorist group but [a] revolutionary group" brought her instant global celebrity and local infamy. At this point in Peru's history, the war between the insurgents and the state raged on for over twenty years, and the local populace's well of sympathy for insurgents had run dry.[20] Maoist insurgencies inaugurated the "largest insurgency on Peruvian soil since Túpac Amaru's rebellion two centuries before and [it was] one of the most violent in late twentieth century Latin America."[21] Both the Peruvian state and the insurgents used violence beyond any acceptability. In particular indigenous populations were targeted because of the idea that there are two Perus—which coexist simultaneously—a "deep," or "profundo," Peru that represents the country's historical roots and an "official" Peru, which represents the modern nation-state.[22] The indigenous are imagined to exist only within the sphere of the profundo—out of time and space with modernity—and thus a priori occupy the zone of social death.[23]

Although Maoist insurgents belonging to Sendero Luminoso (Shining Path) and MRTA did not have the power of the state, between the 1970s and 1990s, they were immensely effective in disrupting the operations of capitalism, by targeting local power stations and other utilities to disrupt everyday life and orchestrating bombings that paralyzed much of the state and civil society. In addition to the countryside, they deeply impacted the ability of Lima and Arequipa, Peru's centers of government, to effectively operate. For Peruvians, there was little sympathy for Berenson, who was seen as a solipsistic and callous young American adventurer who symbolized ongoing First World imperialism and American interference in Peru's domestic affairs.[24]

Berenson's arrest and the hostage crisis would be entwined in U.S. news coverage and the American imagination for the duration of the hostage crisis—December 17, 1996, to April 22, 1997, and in 1999, responding to public pressure, Amnesty International named Berenson a political prisoner. Lisa Duggan illustrates the importance of Latin America to the cultivation of American radical politics and sensibilities and helps clarify what might have drawn women like Berenson there, especially in a U.S. 1970s context in which revolutionary change seemed to have stalled: "When I said I wanted to be a 'revolutionary,' this was not received as ludicrous or sectarian, but as a declaration of affinity with those whose overlapping aspirations for equality—social, political, economic, and cultural equality in a global context—seemed both thrilling and attainable."[25] Berenson's work in a successful guerrilla war makes her an exciting figure for First World leftists and confirms the value of their (past) radicalism.

How little the U.S. public knows about Peru outside of sensationalized figures and moments such as Lori Berenson's imprisonment and the hostage takeover is the work of geopolitical percepticide. The depth of relationship between the two countries, as well as Peru's significant history within the Americas with Lima as the center of the former Spanish empire, makes it even more so. Within the geopolitical sphere of the United States, Peru is one of the few countries that interned Japanese Peruvians and sent them to the United States during World War II.[26] The United States also exerted great influence in Latin America's drug policies, with U.S. intervention in Peruvian coca growth reaching its height in the 1980s and decimating the economic and cultural base for Peru's indigenous population. U.S. American involvement in Latin America and the Caribbean in the late twentieth century was a twinning of development and military support aimed at stopping Communism and strengthening the United States' geopolitical and economic relationship with its neighbors in the Southern cone. U.S. representations of Peru during Fujimori's presidency depend deeply on perceptions of the United States as allied with Japan, a positionality that consistently references World War II and the "just" war fought then.[27]

In their demands, MRTA also singled out Japan's foreign aid to Peru, arguing that the terms of the aid exemplified the neocolonial aspects of neoliberalism, as it would only benefit wealthy and industrial classes. Decades of civil war had exacerbated and entrenched the neo-imperialism that structured Latin America. The nation's wealth and power were centrally held in Lima by the light-skinned and European-identified traditional elite. For the Maoist rebels, neoliberal economic reforms sweeping Latin America in the 1990s and championed by Fujimori would further align this long-established elite with a global elite, while Peru's poor and working classes would become a part of a newly constituted global Third World.[28]

Fujimori became president of Peru in 1990 and held the seat until 2000, when he attempted to resign by fax from Tokyo, a cowardly, bizarre, and attention-seeking act that characterizes his colorful persona.[29] Under his presidency, the Peruvian nation-state embodied both neoliberalism and authoritarianism.[30] Fujimori's success in bringing a decisive end to the Maoist insurgency earned him domestic and global popularity not accorded to any other modern president in Peru. For most of his presidency, Fujimori was intensely popular, as his economic doctrine of "Fujishock" appeared to propel this underdeveloped economy into a newly relevant position in the Pacific Arena.[31] Even when he dissolved Congress and reorganized the judicial branch with his auto-coup of April 5, 1992, giving himself almost limitless power to fight the Maoist insurgents, global leaders and elites in Peru supported him. These executive powers included extended periods of detentions, and the use of torture to gather information became the norm. For example, under the Law of Repentance (1993–94), thousands of innocent civilians were caught up in anti-terrorist witch trials.[32] It was under these conditions that Berenson was tried. Fujimori furthered the terrorizing power of disappearances by enacting amnesty laws and granting immunity to members of government death squads.[33] His justification for these acts was survival in the new world order—society must get rid of disruptions in order for neoliberal reforms to take place so Peru could place itself in a position to receive funding (from the International Monetary Fund, World Bank, and foreign investments) and participate in the global economy via affiliation with the Pacific Rim.

In his comments at the 1997 Inter-American Dialogue (Peru: Challenges for the 21st Century) in Washington, DC, Carlos Iván Degregori explains how Fujimori's brand of neoliberal reform and authoritarianism was seen as propelling Peru into futurity. These comments came only months after the hostage crisis was violently resolved: "I remember meetings in Washington in 1991–92, when we simply could not talk in terms beyond six months or one year. The future was closing, it continued closing, and seemed increasingly problematic. We always had to speak with reverence to the 'coyuntura' (particular moment). Today we can discuss and disagree about the future, and I believe this is a decisive change that should be recognized—and of course to which the entire country has contributed. It is not just the product of some recipe but a collective effort on the part of all Peruvians."[34]

Here Degregori describes the ways Fujimori is imagined to have enabled a future for Peru that was unimaginable just five years prior in a country ravaged by daily violence. This is a dynamic future in which everyone is "open to discuss and disagree." Thus the Peru of 1997 is described as inherently democratic and essentially Peruvian in nature because it is shaped by the will of the Peruvian people, and also represented by the multiracial nation represented by Fujimori's Japanese ancestry.[35] Degregori's comments exemplify how in the recent moments after the hostage crisis had ended Peruvians, including intellectuals and liberal leftists, saw Fujimori as a hero, someone who had done the difficult and ugly work necessary to give Peru a future it had been denied. Although Fujimori would proudly proclaim his Peruvian heritage, he also publically manipulated his Japanese ancestry as a comparative advantage against a Euro-centric Peruvian elite. This was perceived as particularly advantageous as Peru sought to enter the Pacific Rim economy.[36] As opposed to keeping Peru stuck to a melancholic present defined by "reverence" for failed modernization, Fujimori was characterized here as enabling Peru to join in these global neoliberal interactions.

Although seen as standing in for racial progress in a world defined by "ethnic cleansing," something dark underwrites Fujimori's success. Degregori continues, "In a world in which ethnic cleansing begins to be a risk—and whether one is in agreement or not with current policies—it is a source of pride that as Peruvians we elected as president a first generation migrant, who is racially 100% Japanese. . . . Racial politics played a central role in Fujimori's initial popularity by Peru's citizens and cements the support people have in him, despite the *darkness* surrounding his presidency."[37] Degregori's mention of "ethnic cleansing" and "darkness" is notable for the brevity with which he dismisses this historical reality. Fujimori's Japaneseness outweighs the darkness of Peru's desindianization. Conducted between 2001 and 2003, investigations by the Truth and Reconciliation Commission revealed that because of historical racism, Peru's indigenous populations and *campesinos* suffered most in the battle between the insurgents and the state.[38]

The report outlined the massacres, forced disappearances, acts of violence against women, human rights violations, and extrajudicial and lawless abuses enacted in collaboration by the justice system and the state as well as by the Maoists between 1980 and 2000. Both sides positioned the indigenous population as collateral damage, unworthy of concern, as they were "condemned to ultimately disappear in the name of progress, whether they like it or not."[39] The TRC report also forced recognition of the systemic racism and classism that had permitted such abuses to happen, noting that 75 percent of the victims who died during this internal conflict spoke Quechua or another native language.[40]

Much of the early period of killing evidenced the long and intractable racialization—and the genocidal violence that this racialization authorizes—rooted in Spanish colonialism and still existent in the modern nation-state of Peru. This genocidal history overlaps with a Pacific Rim imaginary in which Japan plays a central role in Peruvian capitalist imaginaries.

How melancholia can interrupt the formation of a Peruvian nationalism that situates its base as the tragic but unavoidable death of indigenous people has much significance to a U.S. knowledge formation also formulated on the genocide of native bodies and cultures. This genocidal violence against the indigenous is constitutive across the Americas. This process has been functioning in the New Worlds since "discovery" and as with Peru "in the [United States] the Indian is the original enemy combatant who cannot be grieved."[41]

Anti-Antigone: "The Liberation of Lori Berenson"

While a publicly reviled figure in Peru, Berenson received a reception in the West that could not be more different. As novelist Jennifer Egan writes in her interview and profile of Berenson for the *New York Times* after Berenson was provisionally released from Peruvian prison in 2010, "But what I heard most often, especially from women, was that Berenson had reminded them of themselves: young, passionate, risk-taking."[42] What interests me about Egan's account of Berenson is how Egan does not recognize the complexity of the political transformation Berenson experienced while being in prison. Instead, Egan focuses on how Berenson's maturity into motherhood is made to stand in contrast to Lima, a place stuck in a state of melancholy violence. Over and over, Egan points to American women who see in Berenson reminders of themselves in their early twenties and who are now also mothers.

During her thirteen-year stay in prison, Berenson gave birth to a son, Salvador, in 2008. Berenson's transition into motherhood is the change-over-time, the historical measure that dominates the narrative. Egan writes, "Such an outpouring of rage at a 40-year-old woman, mother to a toddler, who was convicted in her mid-20s of abetting a terrorist plot that never took place, is a measure of the degree to which Peruvians are still traumatized by the violence that convulsed their country during the years when the Shining Path warred with the military and nearly 70,000 Peruvians were killed. It also underscores the fact that terrorism, all but defunct in Peru for more than a decade, is still a hot political issue."[43]

In the time since Berenson became a mother, adding to and enhancing her life, the change over time in Lima is described in these ways—from surviving a "terrorist plot that never took place" to overly concerned about "terrorism [that is] all but defunct." Limeños are imagined as stagnant in a melancholic state and attached to an unworthy wound—*which was never inflicted*—and thus not deserving of mourning and should not be allowed to mature and coexist with Berenson and her toddler son.

Egan's narrative limits are found in her inability to describe and produce empathy for the deep anger raised by Berenson's provisional release in 2010. Her embrace of Berenson's motherhood narrative minimizes terrorism and its impact on the Peruvian nation-state, including the continued struggles by many mothers and family members, to force the state to account for the disappeared and dead and for communities to reconcile and learn to live together. Here, and throughout the article, a Berenson who has progressed and matured stands against an illogic of a Peru that cannot seem to let go. First World readers are led to interpret postcolonial grief as a kind of stasis and futility rather than the kind of grief that demands accounting and fuels a refusal to forget.

After detailing how the courts denied Berenson freedom to leave Peru, Egan describes that "carrying Salvador, she stepped from a car into an aggressive throng of cameras, all of which captured his panicked tears and Berenson's visible strain as she tried to shield him and push her way to the door."[44] The "aggression," though, threatens to break down Berenson, and even more alarmingly, it threatens her innocent son. Here again we see how Berenson's motherhood aligns her in the realm of life. Her protection is now extended toward her son, whose precarious situation heightens the sense that her motherhood is the only thing that stands between him and death.

The links among motherhood, ethicality, and life heighten: "[Berenson] seemed haunted by some particular ones. A woman said, both to Berenson and her father, on separate occasions when they were with Salvador: Watch after that kid. Something is going to happen to him. Another time, a woman with two dogs called Berenson 'garbage.' And the dogs were put on alert."[45]

Peruvian melancholia makes the unnamed Peruvians akin to animals, incapable of rational feeling and thinking. Again and again, Berenson's toddler symbolizes her participation in modern temporality, her maturity, and her progression. Robin Kirk, director of the Duke Human Rights Center, who worked in Peru as a journalist throughout the dangerous upheaval of the 1980s, said she identified with Berenson but also — as a mother — with Berenson's parents: "Your bright, adventurous child goes off, and you have to be supportive, of course, but what kind of things are going to happen to change their lives?"[46] The way that Egan develops the trope of the mother to connect the First and Third worlds operates as a central pivot in the production of a neoliberal "anti-conquest" narrative. Mary Louise Pratt argues that the production of the anti-conquest narrative served as a primary mean by which "European bourgeois subjects seek to secure their innocence in the same moment as they assert European hegemony."[47] Novels, travelogues, and other narratives enabled the production of a colonialist European planetary consciousness throughout the discovery of the New World, in which Europeans cognitively located themselves as the center of the world at the same time they rejected any recognition of their colonialism.

Egan's turn toward motherhood and maturity to describe Berenson's significance and transformation erases Peru's historical conditions altogether, which is paradoxical because the politics of motherhood have been central to bringing the state to account for the disappeared. Egan's lack of display of knowledge about the global radical work of motherhood in Latin America is evident in her treatment of Berenson's motherhood (and maternal feelings for her) as uniquely and individually possessed by American women and as an unrecognizable trait in Limeños. Thus Egan's focus places her analysis far from the critical perspective on mothering present in movements such as Tiananmen Mothers in China and Mourning Mothers in Iran, who stage public demonstrations to demand accountability from the state for the disappearances and deaths of their families.[48] Perhaps no other movement against state terrorism in the Americas has been as formative as Argentina's *Asocacíon Madres de Plaza Mayo* (*Madres*), particularly for highlighting the productive tensions in bringing never-ending mourning to bear on liberal human rights and struggles for restorative justice. During the Dirty Wars (1976–83), in which an estimated 11,000 were killed, "Aparicion con vida" (bring them back alive) was the rallying cry as they demanded that the state bring their disappeared loved ones back alive, despite the knowledge that they were most likely dead. As in Peru, Argentina's Dirty Wars were characterized by state terrorism and disappearances, tactics directly influenced by France's war against Algerian independence.[49] It is under the threat of death that the Madres occupied the plaza in front of the presidential palace and marched every Thursday around 3:30 p.m. from 1977 until 2016.

By holding on to the designation "disappeared" as opposed to asking for justice for their "murdered" loved ones, the Madres were demanding that the state be held accountable for an ongoing state of terror, not a completed act in the past. Looking at the activism of these Madres, Avery F. Gordon asserts, "Death exists in the past tense, disappearance in the present . . . [and to] insist that disappearance is not death but its own state of being *consolation enclosed*—because it exists and is living with us, doing things to us, scaring us, driving us from our homes into exile, making us inconsolably lonely, or crazy, or unable to see what is right in front of our faces, or because it is goading us to fight—is to pinpoint its haunting quality."[50]

The demand that the state "bring them back alive" meant that the mothers would not stop fighting until all those who were disappeared had been accounted for. This does not symbolize a refusal to accept death. Rather, it recognizes that disappearances call forth a larger constellation of the operations of power — and the subsequent reorganization of kinship and social structures — that deny the disappeared person had ever existed. We can see why the Madres and their insurgent melancholia were so dangerous to the nation-state: they were refusing the state's apology and pointing out the unrealizable aspects of reconciliation that demanded the dissolution of the state itself.[51] Gordon emphasizes that "the ghost is primarily a symptom of what is missing. . . [giving] notice not only to itself but also to what it represents."[52] Here she argues that dominant sociological thinking has invisibilized and elided histories of social injustice, rendering them "ghostly matters" that disrupt and emerge as inexplicable presences and ruptures. She turns toward literature and the affective qualities of terror found therein as an alternative archive. We are aware of the alternative knowledges, histories, and voices of the dead because these invisible experiences and histories haunt.[53]

Berenson appears to understand what Egan does not — that Peruvians are not destined for death: "I realized that behind suffering was politics. It wasn't just like, Oh, these people are poor and they're destined to suffer. No. There are interests behind that — political, economic — in having a social class be relegated to dying in misery, and being exploited, and being harmed, and suffering repression."[54] However, her knowledge is repeatedly silenced in the article. In the United States, Berenson represents a youthful American radicalism that has now politically matured and resonates with neoliberal tenets, including self-reliance and leadership over others.

Imperial Common Sense and the Pacific Rim Idea in Ann Patchett's *Bel Canto*

While Berenson is the focus of Egan's narrative, Patchett's *Bel Canto* zeroes in on the hostage crisis itself. Patchett watches the hostage crisis unfold on television and found herself compelled by what she saw unfold: "Usually it's hard to pin down the exact point at which you come up with an idea for a novel, but this one is easy: December 17, 1996, the night that the terrorist organization Tupac Amaru [*sic*] took over the Japanese embassy in Lima, Peru. I'm sure I didn't know that day that this story would turn into *Bel Canto*, but I was completely focused on it from the start. It had so many elements that were compelling to me: confinement, survival, the construction of family."[55] She continues in the interview describing how she imagines that the process of feeling for an Other will augment and add to her life: "For a long time I'd wanted to find a way to experience the things I read about in the paper, to grieve for disasters that had no immediate effect on my life. Turning a tragedy I knew nothing about into this novel was part of that process."[56] Unlike the women described in Egan's article, novelist Patchett does not desire to be a part of the war in Peru. Rather, she seeks to experience and feel moved by events happening far away. Her description of how she came to understand and desire to represent the crisis exemplifies Mary Louise Pratt's description of the anti-conquest narrative as "enabling the production of a planetary consciousness" rooted in imperial conquest. In this section, I discuss the "imperial common sense" about the Pacific Rim which structures the grammar of this neoliberal anti-conquest narrative through a reading of Patchett's *Bel Canto*.[57]

Bel Canto is set "somewhere in South America"[58] and centers on four characters—American soprano Roxane Coss; Japanese industrialist Katsumi Hosokawa; his young translator Gen Watanabe; and Carmen, a hostage taker who is Quechua, an indigenous people from the highlands of the unnamed country. The primary and constitutive condition of possibility for Roxane's survival is established early in the novel via the inevitable death of the hostage takers. Within the first chapter the reader is warned that "it was the unspoken belief of everyone who was familiar with this organization and with the host country that they were all as good as dead, when in fact it was the terrorists who would not survive the ordeal."[59] This is the only time in the novel that there is any foreshadowing of the end of the hostage crisis. The commonsense knowledge of violence against the captors' bodies, upheld by both fact and belief, suppresses mourning and grief for their deaths. This is how Patchett turns "a tragedy [she] knew nothing about into this novel,"[60] transforming imperial relations into imperial common sense.

By the end of the novel the massive differences among the characters are bridged by a shared love of opera. Each of the hostages and hostage takers participates in sustaining Roxane so that she can sing every day—including playing the piano and becoming her students—around which a peaceful domestic routine develops. Opera becomes the base of a new global Pacific Rim culture shared among Japanese, Americans, Europeans, and a crew of "South Americans" across the social and racial spectrum. Meanwhile Peru is constructed as a part of a nameless Third World.[61] While a space that is filled with violence and lacking civilization, the vice president's mansion where they are all held hostage becomes redeemed by entrance into global high culture and the Pacific Rim economy.

Although *Bel Canto* stays close to the facts of the hostage crisis — such as the duration, location, and outcome — it is not a historical drama. *Bel Canto* is an allegory for the commonsense understanding of the Pacific Rim as an extension of the U.S.[62] Common sense, as something that is assumed and rarely spoken, is integral to reifying and reinforcing white supremacist and colonial genocidal states as the status quo. Dylan Rodríguez defines common sense as "epistemological obstructions" and the base for an imperial common sense that functions to "preempt, displace, or render illegible a historical materialist mode of analysis."[63] Due to the general conditions of postmodern aesthetics under neoliberalism that enable the production, circulation, and exchange of global images to become dehistoricized and depoliticized, knowledge production has turned into "information retrieval" where common sense and what is already known drives the search for knowledge.[64] What replaces deep engagement and critique is a kind of imperial "common sense." This can be seen most fundamentally by the fact that Peru is identified as an "unnamed nation in South America" despite how clearly the novel is about Peru. This does not universalize Peru, rather disappearing it all together into a general "third world."[65]

This is the basis for neoliberal imperial common sense that creates and maintains an imperial grammar — namelessness as the condition for Peru entering universal global relations — that polices proper and insurgent utterances. Imperial common sense operates primarily by seeking to produce colonized subjects as ones who consent to their own subjugation. Any kind of insurgency is "postponed, absorbed, and expelled from the lexicon (words, expressions, meanings) and grammar (rules governing language)."[66]

As such, common sense is an "epistemological obstruction" that seeks to be the condition of impossibility for the decolonizing subject. Colonial logics and enterprises have drawn heavily from languages, symbols, and feelings attached to affect and affectivity to render the colonized subject out of time and space, with rationality and logic related to intelligence and ability to govern and thus, out of step with common sense. "Violently reiterated and fixed in their affectivity," colonialized subjects are seen as repeatedly reiterating their need and desire for colonial patronage and dominance.[67] The most important figures in *Bel Canto* are the American soprano, Japanese capitalist, and Japanese translator, each of whom develop a close relationship to a Quechua hostage taker in the role of a teacher or mentor. It is only by seeing the hostage takers as subjects willing to learn from the civilized West that empathy for their historical position is produced. Like the Limeños described in Egan's *New York Times* article, the hostage takers are "violently reiterated and fixed in their affectivity."[68] Denying the Limeños and hostage takers the right to be mourned and named in their deaths is central to upholding imperial common sense, central to reinforcing the fantasy of colonialism as mutual transformation.

Taken together, Egan's and Patchett's texts illustrate the broader terrain and strategies of representation that shape neoliberal anti-conquest narratives and fuel perceptide. Narratives that describe living in the war zone and that seek to bridge the distance between the First and Third worlds both depend on managing grief, loss, and mourning. Duggan has argued that neoliberalism is defined by an "emergent, multicultural, neoliberal 'equality' designed for global consumption."[69] This requires producing recognition of narrative "limits, their finitude and their historicity."[70] Anti-conquest narratives reveal that neoliberalism seeks to co-opt the voices and histories of the dead and only establish as legible and comprehensible the moments that show how global relations have improved upon First World lives to make it seem incontrovertible that the First World Self is enhanced and enriched by exchanges with global Others.

Seen from current imperial formations, the longing to identify with Berenson is not an outlier subject formation or an outlier desire within a 1990s or twenty-first-century cultural politics. A bellwether event for the rise of neoliberal feminism took place one year before the hostage crisis. The 1995 United Nations Conference on Women, which convened in Beijing, China, officially links women's rights to human rights and seeks to elevate it as a central concern on the global level. Then U.S. first lady Hillary Clinton's declaration that "women's rights are human rights" however, also gave voice to a geopolitical reality in which First World women were becoming more powerful in national politics and economy and in which Third World figures who became marked as "the final frontier—as [representing] our temporal and global end."[71] Within this symbolic and discursive sphere, Berenson emerges as a feminist hero in the United States, particularly in the ways she enables a framing of Peru's civil war between the Maoist insurgents and Peruvian military as a crisis of global human rights and atavistic nationalism in which women like her can participate.

Ralli, like Patchett, was witness to the seizing of the Japanese ambassador's home—she lived on the same block and remained gripped by the events "for four months and seventeen days."[72] She recounts watching from her balcony as a motley public—journalists, family members of the hostages, women selling T-shirts—formed outside the hostage scene. After Fujimori raided the home and had all the captors killed, one particular death haunts Ralli: "Above all else, the windows of the mansion, a young girl, a rifle at her side."[73] After the ambassador's home was invaded, she recalls that Fujimori himself stood beneath this girl's window, "his eyes welling with tears over the death of . . . two brave soldiers . . . without even mentioning that they had wiped out seventeen of the enemy (including the young girl with the rifle by the window)."[74] Watching the crowds gathering to hear Fujimori, Ralli wonders, "Was Antigone perhaps among them, a small woman, trying to discover if her young brother was among the dead bodies?"[75]

As a member of *Grupo Cultural Yuyachkani*, first formed in 1971, Ralli traveled the highlands of Peru with the TRC in 2002. They performed two plays, *Antígona* and *Adios Ayacucho*, often in outdoor public spaces, to inform and to help survivors and witnesses deal with the injustices committed and trauma caused during Peru's internal conflict.[76] During Fujimori's presidency, public speech was strictly controlled, and the private homes of the wealthy became compounds as Limeños hired armed guards to protect their homes. The fortressification of private spaces also dissolved the covenants of sanctuary and created symbolic and familial gaps that can never be sutured. Breaking this silence, Ralli, in collaboration with Watanabe, met with survivors and witnesses and integrated their testimonies into *Antígona*. Not only the narratives, but also the gestures, pauses, and tones of those bearing witness have been worked into the characters when performed by Ralli.[77]

Three figures inspired Ralli to think of *Antigone* as emblematic for Peru under Fujimori: the murdered young hostage taker, a sister in the crowd looking for her dead family, and a figure in a photograph. Ralli saw a photograph of an indigenous woman in mourning garb running across an empty public square, which invoked for her Antigone, hurrying across an empty battlefield in order to give her dead, exiled brother a proper burial. These three versions of Antigone name her as the disappeared, the sister who seeks, and the sister who defies all in the endeavor to give her brother a proper burial.[78]

Ralli and Watanabe's *Antígona* innovates the telling of Antigone most significantly in two ways, revealing what remains incommensurable, what cannot be healed, and what was always broken. First, *Antígona* ends with the revelation that the play's omniscient narrator has always been Ismene, the sister who refused to offer Antígona refuge and did not help her defy Creon's unjust rules. Antígona repudiates Ismene for her cowardice. As opposed to the tragic heroine, the play is sutured to the perspective of the survivor, who is a witness and must deal with the guilt of having been a bystander. Second, Ralli performs all seven of the play's roles in a spare production that emphasizes her solitary position. The transition from one character to the next is accomplished through a shift in voice and change of the dress, or *fustan* — a woman's white petticoat that she wears variously as a scarf, robe, or gown. Multiple subject positions and narratives in relation to the disappearances are singly bodied, highlighting that "Yuyachkani viewed Peru's many survivors, relatives of the disappeared and victims of state violence, as the country's own many Antigones."[79] This process of reconciling and cohering a broken human society into a single body, however, is also defined by excess, and illustrates what remains excess to the project of reconciliation and closure, what cannot be represented or brought back together, and what has always been broken. This excess is represented in *Antígona* by the dead bodies that make claims on the living.

In the play's penultimate scene, Antígona is caught by Creon's guards and banished to die slowly and alone, entombed in a cave. She recites her final lines:

> I want all the dead to have a funeral
> And then
> After that
> Forgetfulness.[80]

Immediately after this is the play's final scene. Ralli appears on the stage holding a box containing the mask she leaves on one side of the stage. Ralli has changed her costume to become the narrator, who reveals herself as Ismene:

> The dead in this story come to me not so that I can speak of distant sorrows.
> They come to me so vividly because they are my own sorrow:
> I am the sister whose hands were tied by fear.[81]

Ismene moves to complete the funeral rites for Polynices that Antígona was never able to perform. This final scene is significant because it is the only time there are two faces on stage—Ismene and a mask representing the dead Polynices. As she reveals the mask, Ismene turns her back to the audience and speaks: "Look, my sister: this is our brother's face before the dogs and vultures came, before rot set in. . . . And tell him how great my punishment is: to remember your act every day—a torture and shame for me."[82]

She turns, smashes the mask, and covers it with a shroud and sand to finish the funeral rites. The stage returns to a single face, and the play ends. These last two scenes mete out contradictory messages—one of dying Antígona asking to forget and one of Ismene proclaiming her burden of never forgetting. Visualized on stage via the mask, these scenes together speak of letting the dead body rest at the same time that it must live on to haunt the present. These scenes challenge us to think about what kind of accounting we must demand in the name of the dead and how to marshal their memories for future political transformation. Watanabe is known for his grace with naturalistic symbols, and his talent is well suited to describing the indignities of the human body left unprotected in the elements: "Oh gods, you could have created us as invisible beings, or from stone needing no burial, then why did you create us from matter that decomposes[?]. . . . How shameful, how obscene, to die and not be buried, exposing soft flesh and viscera to the eyes of the living."[83] This describes how Creon's punishment is meant for the living. Although seeing the fragility of the body—the pain and torture it can live through—may terrorize the living, it can also embolden; and so can the figure of the dead body that the play constantly evokes.

Antígona is produced and performed to aid the TRC's efforts to enable dialogue across the nation. Tending to work both juridically and symbolically to bring about truth within Peru's history, the TRC represents incidents and periods of injustice with the belief that such acknowledgment and recognition can produce genuine pledges to depart from the systemic and social order that enabled, allowed, and ignored such abuses. However, the TRC has been met with consistent criticism that it is hampered by liberal humanist frameworks for human rights that seek to situate past traumas in history and drive them toward closure. In *Antígona*, however, we have a public performance that refuses closure.

This refusal of closure works both on the level of performance and narrative. Like Polynices, Antígona is a product of incest between Oedipus and his mother, Jocasta. It is for the crimes of incest and patricide that Oedipus is exiled. Judith Butler has drawn on an epistemology of Antigone to mean "rejecting motherhood" or "against motherhood," arguing that Antigone "represents not kinship in its ideal form but its deformation and displacement."[84] Antigone does not live life in death only due to her incestuous devotion to a traitorous brother, but because she does not marry and not produce any children. Antigone names how nonnormative kinship is aligned with natural death, and subject to the punishment by the sovereign. Her life drive is toward burying her brother as opposed to motherhood. Antigone's choice not to become a mother is equated to a life lived in death: "That she has not lived, that she has not loved, and that she has not borne children. . . . Thus death signifies the unlived life."[85]

That Antigone symbolizes "mother as death" suggests another layer to the power of that figure to critique within the context of the neoliberal feminism with which I began this chapter. Although this suggestion of queerness and incest is not in *Antígona*, the pressure for reconciliation makes the play's implicit critique of normative kinship relations intensely productive and important to reading *Antígona* against the grain. Antigone names how state violence has created a society defined by an absence of relation and an inability to fulfill the normative duties of family (e.g., lineage and passing on of blood relations), anxieties that are clearly being negotiated in Egan's story of Berenson as in Ralli and Watanabe's *Antígona*.

While Peru's many survivors, relatives of the disappeared, and victims of state violence are the country's own many Antigones, they are also Ismenes and Polynices.[86] In the process of representing reconciliation and coherence, the play stages closure as impossible and resolution as constituted by excess and irreconcilability. The dead are buried but not disappeared, the disappeared may be dead but not buried, and they all exert their own pressures for justice beyond existing frameworks and imagined possibilities.

Conclusion

Following Antigone along the Pacific Arena has enabled me to reveal the complex links between and across the transpacific that demonstrate how "Asia, Americas, and Pacific Islands are themselves problematic terms, whose boundaries and locales have been shaped by competing histories of colonialism and militarism."[87] In the play *Mina*, by Kyoung H. Park the "competing histories of colonialism and militarism" is narrated by a female Korean

Peruvian immigrant protagonist. She recalls from her psychiatrist's office in New York that "during the nineties, my parents followed the Japanese, to live under the rule of Fujimori." But "ironically, my father would never say anything nice about the Japanese: 'No trust them! They took advantage of our people—we fermented cabbage, because we were poor. We made kimchi with onions, garlic and chili. We let the ingredients fester for months before we ate it. But the Japanese invaded our shores stole our fish, and they had raw, expensive sushi!"[88] By describing her family's migration as linked to Fujimori, she dramatizes how a Peru led by Japan is made attractive for Korean immigrants and capital. However, her father denies that their migration is the result a colonized mentality and seeks to disrupt the psychic centering of Japan in the narrative by educating her on Japan's colonial history over Koreans. The story of how the Japanese "stole our fish" also recalls Peruvian ceviche, which tends to be marinated in lime juice, and is not "raw, expensive" like sushi. [89] However critical they are of Japanese colonialism, they harbor racism against Peruvians. Her father and mother are horrified to learn that she is pregnant with a child from a mixed raced Japanese Peruvian man, a rift in the family that never heals before her father dies.

Mina is a counternarrative and a transpacific parable that shows how desire mediates "competing forces of colonialism and militarism" which is foundational to the history of the Asian diasporas in the Americas. Vijay Prashad had asked what histories and knowledge might we gain if we were to allow Third World intellectuals from Asia, Africa, and Latin America to speak to each other without the mediating presence of the West.[90] An emerging cultural imaginary has responded by connecting transpacific histories across Asia, Oceania, and the Americas within and against the genocidal history and cultural politics connected to the European colonialization and modern-nation building in the Americas.

· EPILOGUE ·

WATERY GRAVES

The theoretical reach of the book has been moored to late twentieth- and twenty-first-century contexts where U.S. militarization across the Pacific is expanding. In such a juncture, we need to be attuned to the (re)production of Asian bodies in pain across the transpacific and how they are produced to uphold the legitimacy of the garrison state.[1] As I have been arguing throughout, narrative limits that foreclose melancholia as a possibility for transformation seek closure, resolution, and promote looking away. This epilogue concludes the book by coming full circle, but not enacting closure. I address the historic occasion of Barack Obama's official visit to the Hiroshima Peace Memorial in May 2016. His plea for a U.S.-led "moral revolution" to rid the world of nuclear weapons was made unstable by a geopolitical pressures exerted by counternarratives and histories, particularly those that emerge from the "watery graves" in the straits between Korea and Japan.

President Obama's visit to the Hiroshima Memorial in May 2016 was historic because it was the first time that a sitting U.S. president visited Hiroshima since the atomic bomb decimated the city. Although he did not offer an apology, the visit is notable in that he acknowledged sadness for the loss of lives and met with Japanese hibakusha. Because he also revisited other sites of WWII-era war crimes, U.S. critics called this an "apology tour" indicative of his soft military position. Many in the Pacific Arena he visited, however, criticized how his visit occurred in the context of an increasing U.S. militarization of the Pacific.[2] They connected this expansion to his lack of discussion about Japanese-era war crimes. In addition to Korean hibakusha, Chinese expressed anger at Japan's revisionist history, which refuses to acknowledge the Rape of Nanking. Both groups argued that his visit threatened their fight for an official apology from the Japanese government.

Commemorative and redressive acts are always marked by limits, limits which the subaltern may exploit. Protesters argued that in visiting Hiroshima but not addressing Japan's revisionist history, Obama was privileging a colonizer's pain over that of unaddressed victims. While the visit of a sitting U.S. president to Hiroshima could never be neutral, recalling such protests ensures that the dominant narrative that the Obama administration sought—the visit of a victor to the loser of a war, now made into an ally—could never fully cohere. The attempts to manage these dissident claims reveals the potent militarized undercurrent that shapes U.S. relationships to the liberal nation-states of the Pacific Arena. U.S. military dominance over the Pacific must rely on constant ideological and cultural work to reframe histories of violence as relationships built on mutual security.[3]

One of the most vocal critics of the limits of Obama's visit to Hiroshima were Korean hibakusha.[4] Studying the Korean protests against such residues of World War II–era geopolitics opens up a broader understanding of how contemporary Korean society continues to be defined by the conditions of postcoloniality, which structure its emergence as a modern nation-state vis-à-vis the United States and Japan. The devastation of the Korean War includes destruction and lack of production of archives about the violence experienced by Koreans by the U.S. This lack of coherent archive requires, as Grace M. Cho advocates, a way of reading in a manner that is multichronic, focused on "the unconscious aspects of looking,"[5] that seeks to recognize how "the past seeps back into the present, as sensations rather than representations."[6]

I close by offering the space of the "watery graves" as a response to the devastated archive of the Korean war violence and how to formulate a "multichronic" mode of reading, seeing, and feeling. Around the Korean peninsula and the Pacific Arena are watery graves, full of unclaimed dead souls.[7] For example, in *Straits of Dead Souls*, Fukagawa Munetoshi recounts trying to locate the Korean forced laborers he worked with after the atomic bomb was dropped on Hiroshima.[8] Fukagawa is a celebrated Japanese hibakusha artist who has written poetry and music that explore hibakusha subjectivity and experiences. His crusade to find out what happened to his Korean coworkers has helped bring attention to their cause.

"Straits of Dead Souls" refers to the international waters surrounding Iki Island, which is between Japan and Pusan, a port city in the southern part of Korea. The Korean atomic bomb survivors fled Hiroshima in the aftermath of the chaos but drowned in these straits. Bodies of Korean hibakushas, such as the ones for which Munetoshi was searching, washed up on shore and were buried in unmarked graves by people living on Iki Island.

Long contested between Japan, North and South Korea, Russia, and China, the straits around the Korean Peninsula are a large, watery grave—a site where unclaimed bodies remain as a part of a "devastated archive." In 2014 the devastating sinking of the *Sewol* ferry killed 304 people, mainly high school children on a field trip near the southern part of the Korean peninsula. Nine bodies remain missing in the seas and "Sewol parents" refused to stop fighting until all their children are recovered from their watery graves and the guilty punished.[9] This was a man-made disaster and could have been prevented had there been any government oversight. Like the "Sewol parents" whose wait for the missing bodies of their children has come to equate a criticism of a corrupt state Fukagawa invites us to reimagine the straits where the hibakusha drowned as an interstitial space, filled with dead souls who have not disappeared and who still exert pressure.[10]

Asian diasporic literature and culture are fertile sites for the biopolitical regime of mourning and loss across time and space due to the ongoing state of war connecting the United States to Asia throughout the nineteenth, twentieth, and twenty-first centuries; to the militarized violence and disavowal of colonial atrocities (as well as the lingering effects of those atrocities) committed by both the United States and Japan; and to the racialization of Asian Americans as toxic immigrants who contaminate and traumatize the national body. Rooted in the diasporic and radical political and intellectual traditions of critical ethnic studies and feminist studies, *Postcolonial Grief* has expanded and challenged existing geographies and conceptual frameworks by arguing for a critical imaginative geography of the Pacific Arena.[11] Like the dead and unaccounted souls that exert pressure from their watery graves, I hope to have shown how melancholia and loss constitute an unsettling and insurgent cultural force across the transpacific.

· NOTES ·

INTRODUCTION. Mourning Empire

Epigraphs: Henry R. Luce, "The American Century," *Life*, February 17, 1941, 61; Teresa Ralli and José Watanabe, *Antígona*, Performance, 2000.

1. Lisa Yoneyama, *Cold War Ruins: Transpacific Critique of American Justice and Japanese War Crimes* (Durham, NC: Duke University Press, 2016), 23. See also Achille Mbembe, "Necropolitics," trans. Libby Meintjes, *Public Culture* 15, no. 1 (2003): 11–40; Yen Le Espiritu, *Body Counts: Vietnamese War and Militarized Refugees* (Oakland: University of California Press, 2016).

2. Leo T. S. Ching, quoted in Setsu Shigematsu and Keith L. Camacho, eds., *Militarized Currents: Towards a Decolonized Future in Asia and the Pacific* (Minneapolis: University of Minnesota Press, 2010), xvii.

3. Judith Butler, *Precarious Life: The Powers of Mourning and Violence* (New York: Verso, 2004), 33. The 1991 U.S. State Department banning photos of caskets of dead U.S. soldiers to be made publically available as they are repatriated to the United States from the first Gulf War exemplifies this prohibition to mourn. This is because the military was afraid that the caskets would be politicized for an unpopular war and sought to silence it. In 2009 the ban is lifted, but lifting the ban upholds the security state by encouraging the production of a public sphere that is invested in energizing and supporting ongoing aggression.

4. For more on how popular culture participates in the process of the production of the Asian body in pain see Christina Klein, *Cold War Orientalism: Asia in the Middlebrow Imagination, 1945–1961* (Berkeley: University of California Press, 2003); Melanie McAlister, *Epic Encounters: Culture, Media, and U.S. Interests in the Middle East Since 1945*, updated ed. (Berkeley: University of California Press, 2005); Karen Kuo, *East Is West and West Is East: Gender, Culture, and Interwar Encounters between Asia and America* (Philadelphia: Temple University Press, 2012); Marita Sturken, *Tangled Memories: The Vietnam War, the AIDS Epidemic, and the Politics of Remembering* (Berkeley: University of California Press, 1997). 5. Butler, *Precarious Life*, 33.

6. Butler, *Precarious Life*, 34.

7. Ann Laura Stoler, *Carnal Knowledge and Imperial Power: Race and the Intimate in Colonial Rule* (Berkeley: University of California Press, 2002), cited in Naoki Sakai, "On Romantic Love and Military Violence: Transpacific Imperialism and U.S.–Japan Complicity," in *Militarized Currents*, 205–31.

8. Luce was born in 1898 in a port city in the Shandong province in China to wealthy missionary parents. After World War II and the defeat of Japan, Luce would become increasingly aggressive in his lobbying for American intervention to stop the rise of Communist China. He lobbied heavily for Chiang Kai-Shek and established numerous other connections with China through charities and academic centers; see Alan Brinkley, *The Publisher: Henry Luce and His American Century* (New York: Knopf, 2010).

9. Luce, "American Century," 61.

10. Luce, "American Century," 61.

11. As with the United States, it is wrong to say that British, Dutch, and Japanese imperialism does not have an afterlife of its own. We see this in the 1997 turnover of Hong Kong to China from Britain, the ongoing civil wars in Indonesia and the Philippines, and the dominance of European and American culture across Asia.

12. For more on representations of the Pacific and Oceania in the nineteenth and twentieth centuries see Paul Lyons, *American Pacificism: Oceania in the U.S. Imagination* (New York: Routledge, 2005). For the role of Hawai'i in the U.S. imperial imaginary see Gary Y. Okihiro, *Island World: A History of Hawai'i and the United States* (Berkeley: University of California Press, 2009).

13. Haunani-Kay Trask historicizes the process through which native peoples in Hawai'i have continually resisted American occupation, despite the systematic silencing of this insurgent history. Trask, *A Native Daughter: Colonialism and Sovereignty in Hawai'i* (Honolulu: University of Hawai'i Press, 1999).

14. Ronald Reagan, during a presidential debate with Walter Mondale in 1984. "The Candidates Debate; Transcript of the Reagan–Mondale Debate on Foreign Policy," *nytimes.com*, October 22, 1984, accessed September 4, 2017, http://www.nytimes.com/1984/10/22/us/the-candidates-debate-transcript-of-the-reagan-mondale-debate-on-foreign-policy.html?pagewanted=all.

15. Hillary Clinton, "America's Pacific Century," Op-Ed for *Foreign Policy*, October 11, 2011, accessed January 28, 2012, http://foreignpolicy.com/2011/10/11/americas-pacific-century/. Similar to Reagan, nowhere in this thorough and thoughtful accounting of U.S. involvement in the Pacific does she mention the history of U.S. wars in Asia in the twentieth century.

16. Theodore Roosevelt, cited by Bernard K. Gordon, "Pacific Futures for the USA," in *Moving into the Pacific Century: The Changing Regional Order in the Asia-Pacific*, ed. Tiek Soon Lau and Leo Suryadinata (Singapore: National University of Singapore, 1988), 3.

17. Douglas MacArthur, cited by Arthur Herman, *Douglas MacArthur: American Warrior* (New York: Random House, 2016), 560. Similarly, Fujioka, president of the Asian Development Bank in 1982, declared "the Pacific is the ocean of tomorrow. . . . We are witnessing the dawn of the Asia-Pacific era"; "Dawn of the Pacific Era,"

library.cqpress.com, last modified July 5, 1985, http://library.cqpress.com/cq researcher/document.php?id=cqresrre1985070500.

18. This is what Fukuyama describes as the "end of history" as the free-market capitalism accompanied by the liberal nation-state that has defeated other historical possibilities, such as communism; see Francis Fukuyama, *The End of History and the Last Man* (New York: Avon, 1992).

19. Christopher L. Connery, "Pacific Rim Discourse: The U.S. Global Imaginary in the Late Cold War Years," *boundary 2* 21, no. 1 (1994): 37. He is drawing from Bruce Cumings, *The Origins of the Korean War* (Princeton, NJ: Princeton University Press, 1990).

20. Michel Foucault, *"Society Must Be Defended": Lectures at the Collège de France 1975–1976*, ed. Mauro Bertani and Alessandro Fontana, trans. David Macey (New York: Picador, 2003).

21. Luce, "American Century," 65.

22. Espiritu, *Body Counts*, 2.

23. Stoler, quoted in Sakai, "On Romantic Love and Military Violence," 212.

24. For an articulation of this position, see Martha Nussbaum, *Cultivating Humanity: A Classical Defense of Reform in Liberal Education* (Cambridge: Cambridge University Press, 1997); Nussbaum, *Not for Profit: Why Democracy Needs the Humanities* (Princeton, NJ: Princeton University Press, 2010).

25. David Palumbo-Liu, *The Deliverance of Others: Reading Literature in a Global Age* (Durham, NC: Duke University Press, 2012), 2.

26. He sees this most clearly in the case of the military sex camps for American soldiers as extensions of World War II–era Japanese Imperial "comfort women" or sex slave stations; Sakai, "On Romantic Love and Military Violence," 206.

27. Any kind of relief from American unhappiness that a single act of colonial domination can offer is at best a temporary one. As Sara Ahmed argues in the British imperial context, "To see happily is not to see violence, asymmetry, or force"; Ahmed, *The Promise of Happiness* (Durham, NC: Duke University Press, 2010), 132.

28. Luce, "American Century," 65.

29. Luce, "American Century," 65.

30. See Nikolas Rose, *The Politics of Life Itself: Biomedicine, Power, and Subjectivity in the Twenty-First Century* (Princeton, NJ: Princeton University Press, 2006).

31. As a time period, 1970–2000 is more popularly understood through neoliberal political, economic, and cultural frameworks, not militarism. Generally, the forces of neoliberalism between the 1970s and 1990s are understood as including post-Fordist economic structures, the intensification of communication and travel, the opening of national borders to capital, the closing of national inclusion to immigrants, and a challenge to the idea of a single language to define the nation. They create what Arjun Appadurai has called a "world of scapes" rather than a bounded nation-state; Appadurai, "Disjuncture and Difference in the Global Cultural Economy," *Theory, Culture and Society* 7, no. 2 (1990): 295–310. It has also become clear that in the twenty-first century we should add to Appadurai's fivescapes a religious scape and a military scape.

32. Reginald Horsman, *Race and Manifest Destiny: The Origins of American Racial Anglo-Saxonism* (Cambridge, MA: Harvard University Press, 1981).

33. Oscar V. Campomanes makes this argument in "1898 and the Nature of the New Empire," *Radical History Review*, no. 73 (1999): 130–46.

34. See Dylan Rodríguez, *Suspended Apocalypse: White Supremacy, Genocide, and the Filipino Condition* (Minneapolis: University of Minnesota Press, 2010).

35. Tammy Clewell, "Mourning beyond Melancholia: Freud's Psychoanalysis of Loss," *Journal of the American Psychoanalytic Association* 52, no. 1 (2004): 44.

36. Saidya Hartman discusses the fugitive status of slave women as she tries to retrace the route her ancestor took as she became a part of the Atlantic slave trade in *Lose Your Mother: A Journey Along the Atlantic Slave Route* (New York: Farrar, Straus and Giroux, 2007).

37. By invoking the palimpsestic as a coexisting of colonial and neoliberal states I am drawing from M. Jacqui Alexander's *Pedagogies of Crossing: Meditations on Feminism, Sexual Politics, Memory, and the Sacred* (Durham, NC: Duke University Press, 2005).

38. For discussions of how racial capitalism and neoliberal governance seek to turn all individuals into *homo oeconomicus*, see *Sylvia Wynter: On Being Human as Praxis*, ed. Katherine McKittrick (Durham, NC: Duke University Press, 2015); Wendy Brown, *Undoing the Demos: Neoliberalism's Stealth Revolution* (Cambridge, MA: MIT Press, 2015).

39. For Butler, the temporality of loss is connected to a fundamental loss that is connected to the unknown in the other, and thus death brings the threat of never knowing this loss in the other: "Freud says that we do not always know what it is in that person that has been lost"; Butler, *Precarious Life*, 21. This leads her to conclude that "mourning has involved knowing what was lost and melancholia to a certain extent not knowing" (22). Thus, "we are undone by each other; my narrative falters, as it must" (23). See also Diana Taylor, *Disappearing Acts: Spectacles of Gender and Nationalism in Argentina's "Dirty War"* (Durham, NC: Duke University Press, 2001); Chungmoo Choi, "The Politics of War Memories toward Healing," in *Perilous Memories: The Asia-Pacific War(s)*, ed. T. Fujitani, Geoffrey White, and Lisa Yoneyama (Durham, NC: Duke University Press, 2001), 395–410.

40. Grace M. Cho, *Haunting the Korean Diaspora: Shame, Secrecy, and the Forgotten War* (Minneapolis: University of Minnesota Press, 2008), 20. She borrows the term from literary scholar Lyndsey Stonebridge's work in "Bombs and Roses: The Writing of Anxiety in Henry Caught," *Diacritics* 28, no. 4: 25–43.

41. Lisa Yoneyama argues that they are imagined to be settled "by the San Francisco Peace Treaty and other state-to-state normalization treaties"; Yoneyama, *Cold War Ruins*, 154.

42. David L. Eng and David Kazanjian, eds., *Loss: The Politics of Mourning* (Berkeley: University of California Press, 2003).

43. Making value out of trauma has roots in the actuarial and insurance sciences that arise with industrialization and the rise in accidents and trauma in the factory and the city. For more on this, see Athena Athanasiou, "Technologies of Humanness,

Aporias of Biopolitics, and the Cut Body of Humanity," *differences: A Journal of Feminist Cultural Studies* 14, no. 1 (2003): 125–62; Gert Buelens, Sam Durrant, and Robert Eaglestone, eds., *The Future of Trauma Theory: Contemporary Literary and Cultural Criticism* (New York: Routledge, 2014).

44. Eng and Kazanjian, *Loss*, 3.

45. Their work is also in conversation with Anne Anlin Cheng's *The Melancholy of Race: Assimilation, Psychoanalysis, and Hidden Grief* (Oxford: Oxford University Press, 2000).

46. Wendy Brown, "Resisting Left Melancholia," in *Loss: The Politics of Mourning*, ed. Eng and Kazanjian, 459.

47. Brown, "Resisting Left Melancholia," 459.

48. Walden Bello, "Conclusion: From an American Lake to a People's Pacific in the Twenty-First Century," in *Militarized Currents*, 309–21. For example, the state's investment in controlling how its population mourns is clear in the post-9/11 "War on Terror" begun by George W. Bush. The decision of some newspapers to print photographs of flag-draped coffins — thus connecting the dead bodies beneath to the metonym for the U.S. nation — caused an uproar and was condemned by the Bush White House. Defense Department redactions to obscure the faces and insignia of honor guard members in many of the war casualty images since 9/11 similarly disinvite the gaze. This demonstrates how the state seeks to surround death, and thus its recognition of mourning, with silence and shadows; see Dian Million, *Therapeutic Nations: Healing in an Age of Indigenous Human Rights* (Tucson: University of Arizona Press, 2013).

49. See for example Nitasha Sharma's "Pacific Revisions of Blackness: Blacks Address Race and Belonging in Hawai'i," where she considers how the U.S. military mediates the relationship of Blackness in the Hawaiian islands: *Amerasia Journal* 37, no. 3 (2011): 43–60.

50. Jodi A. Byrd and Michael Rothberg, "Between Subaltern and Indigeneity: Critical Categories for Postcolonial Studies," *Interventions: International Journal of Postcolonial Studies* 31, no. 1 (2011): 5.

51. See Anne McClintock, "The Angel of Progress: The Pitfalls of the Term 'Postcolonialism,'" *Social Text* 31/32 (1992): 84–98; Ella Shohat, "Notes on the 'Post-Colonial,'" *Social Text* 31/32 (1992): 99–113. We can see the influence of Third World feminist scholarship in Ethnic Studies with the significance of *This Bridge Called My Back: Writings by Radical Women of Color*, ed. Cherríe Moraga and Gloria E. Anzaldúa, 2nd ed. (New York: Kitchen Table Press, 1983), to the critical ethnic studies canon. Their scholarship and activism also bridge anti-apartheid movements of the 1980s and the anti-Zionist movement in the 1990s, symbolized by Edward Said accused of stoning in South Lebanon, after he threw a rock over the Lebanon–Israeli wire fence border toward an Israeli watchtower while he was visiting the Lebanese border. See also Chandra Talpade Mohanty, "Under Western Eyes: Feminist Scholarship and Colonial Discourses," *Boundary 2* 12, no. 3/13, no. 1 (spring/fall 1984): 338–58.

52. Achille Mbembe, *On the Postcolony* (Berkeley: University of California Press, 2001). Collectively, this Third World postcolonialism shifted the postcolo-

nial modality from a static study of the Other to understanding how colonialism also changed the metropole through hybridity, subalterns, syncretism, and creolization — terms that came to influence the humanities and social sciences. See Néstor García Canclini, *Hybrid Cultures: Strategies for Entering and Leaving Modernity*, trans. Christopher Chiappari and Silvia López (Minneapolis: University of Minnesota Press, [1995] 2005); Homi K. Bhabha, "Of Mimicry and Man: The Ambivalence of Colonial Discourse," in *The Location of Culture* (New York: Routledge, 1994), 121–31. Also see Kobena Mercer, "Cosmopolitan Contact Zones," in *Afro Modern: Journeys through the Black Atlantic*, ed. Tanya Barson and Peter Gorschluter (London: Tate, 2010), 40–48.

53. They have instead rerooted the field in decolonization movements of the late nineteenth and early twentieth centuries, including the end of the African slave trade and decline of European colonies across the Americas and the Caribbean; Gayatri Chakravorty Spivak, "Can the Subaltern Speak?," from *Marxism and the Interpretation of Culture*, ed. C. Nelson and Lawrence Grossberg (Urbana: University of Illinois Press, 1988), 271–313; García Canclini, *Hybrid Cultures*; Katherine McKittrick, ed., *Sylvia Wynter: On Being Human as Praxis* (Durham, NC: Duke University Press, 2015). This is exemplified by the Negritude movement (led by Aimé Césaire and Leopold Senghor) against French colonialism, as well as Alejo Carpentier and José Marti against Spanish colonialism.

54. McClintock, "Angel of Progress." We can see the influence of Third World feminist scholarship in Moraga and Anzaldúa's *This Bridge Called My Back* and its significance to the critical ethnic studies canon.

55. Ann Laura Stoler, *Imperial Debris: On Ruins and Ruination* (Durham, NC: Duke University Press, 2013). See also Soyang Park, "Silence Subaltern Speech and the Intellectual in South Korea: The Politics of Emergent Speech in the Case of Former Sexual Slaves," *Journal for Cultural Research* 9, no. 2 (2005): 169–206.

56. An illustrative example is how in the United States and South Korea the end of World War II is remembered as the "U.S. rescue of South Korea from Japan and communism." The history of American direct occupation when the U.S. military ruled South Korea between September 8, 1945, and August 15, 1948, coupled with direct American military intervention into the 1980s, when military dictator Park Chung Hee ruled with U.S. support, is denied and is dangerous knowledge to this day. The military dictatorship was not to be spoken of well into the 1980s; see Mark Caprio and Yoneyiku Sugita, *Democracy in Occupied Japan: The U.S. Occupation and Japanese Politics and Society* (New York: Routledge, 2007).

57. Chungmoo Choi, "The Discourse of Decolonization and Popular Memory: South Korea," in *The Politics of Culture in the Shadow of Capital*, ed. Lisa Lowe and David Lloyd (Durham, NC: Duke University Press, 1997), 461.

58. As opposed to simply territorial expansion, the goal of hegemony is to enable the United States to dominate East Asian markets and get cheap labor for First World consumers. But even this can have disastrous results, as we saw in the Asian economic crisis in 1997, and can create completely new social and economic systems; see Jinah Kim and Neda Atanasoski, "Unhappy Desires and Queer Postsocialist

Futures: Hong Kong and Buenos Aires in Wong Kar-Wai's *Happy Together*," *American Quarterly* 69, no. 3 (2017): 697–718; Pheng Cheah, "The Crisis of Money," *positions: east asia cultures critique* 16, no. 1 (2008): 189–219.

59. See Byrd and Rothberg, "Between Subaltern and Indigeneity; Audra Simpson, *Mohawk Interruptus: Political Life across the Borders of Settler States* (Durham, NC: Duke University Press, 2014); Candace Fujikane and Jonathan Y. Okamura, eds., *Asian Settler Colonialism: From Local Governance to the Habits of Everyday Life in Hawai'i* (Honolulu: University of Hawai'i Press, 2008); Aloysha Goldstein, ed., *Formations of United States Colonialism* (Durham, NC: Duke University Press, 2014).

60. Fujikane, "Introduction: Asian Settler Colonialism in the U.S. Colony of Hawai'i," in *Asian Settler Colonialism*, 20.

61. While some places were more subject to displacement and resettlement—such as in Okinawa and Guam, where bases were made with bulldozers with the local population bullied off at gunpoint—other places, such as the Commonwealth of the Mariana Islands, Marshall Islands, Micronesia, and Palau, the goal is not settler colonialism, but to establish sites for launching and testing missiles.

62. Noenoe K. Silva in *Aloha Betrayed: Native Hawaiian Resistance to American Colonialism* (Durham, NC: Duke University Press, 2004) shows how this colonialism depended fundamentally on the degradation and erasure of native culture and language.

63. Patrick Wolfe, "Settler Colonialism and the Elimination of the Native," *Journal of Genocide Research* 8, no. 4 (2008): 387–409.

64. See Thomas Borstelmann, *The Cold War and the Color Line: American Race Relations in the Global Arena* (Cambridge, MA: Harvard University Press, 2001); George Lipsitz, "'Frantic to Join . . . the Japanese Army': Black Soldiers and Civilians Confront the Asia-Pacific War," in *Perilous Memories*, ed. Fujitani, White, and Yoneyama, 347–77; T. Fujitani, "*Go for Broke*, the Movie: Japanese American Soldiers in U.S. National, Military, and Racial Discourses," in *Perilous Memories*, ed. Fujitani, White, and Yoneyama, 239–66; Penny M. Von Eschen, *Race against Empire: Black Americans and Anticolonialism, 1937–1957* (Ithaca, NY: Cornell University Press, 1997); Yukiko Koshhiro, *Trans-Pacific Racisms and the U.S. Occupation of Japan* (New York: Columbia University Press, 1999); Nils Gilman, *Mandarins of the Future: Modernization Theory in Cold War America* (Baltimore: Johns Hopkins University Press, 2003).

65. Craig Santos Perez, *From Unincorporated Territory [Guma']* (Richmond, CA: Omnidawn, 2014), 5.

66. Michael Bevacqua sees the Guam–U.S. relationship as structured by "banal imperialism," which is an imperialist fantasy that the colonialized desire to be colonized. Michael Bevacqua. "The Exceptional Life and Death of a Chamorro Soldier: Tracing the Militarization of Desire in Guam, USA." In Shigematsu and Camacho, *Militarized Currents*, 33–62.

67. Elaine H. Kim and Chungmoo Choi, eds., "Introduction," in *Dangerous Women: Gender and Korean Nationalism* (New York: Routledge, 1998), 3.

68. See Leo T. S. Ching, *Becoming "Japanese": Colonial Taiwan and the Politics of*

Identity Formation (Berkeley: University of California Press, 2001); Gerald Horne, *Race War! White Supremacy and the Japanese Attack on the British Empire* (New York: New York University Press, 2004).

69. In 1898, Puerto Rico becomes a U.S. commonwealth at the same time as Guam, and in 1900, American Samoa is made into an unincorporated territory. For more on the Puerto Rican condition, see Christina Duffy Burnett, *Foreign in a Domestic Sense: Puerto Rico, American Expansion, and the Constitution* (Durham, NC: Duke University Press, 2001). See also Amy Kaplan, "'Left Alone with America': The Absence of Empire in the Study of American Culture," in *Cultures of United States Imperialism*, ed. Amy Kaplan and Donald Pease (Durham, NC: Duke University Press, 1993), 3–21.

70. Shigematsu and Camacho, "Introduction," in *Militarized Currents*, xviii.

71. Takashi Fujitani, *Race for Empire: Koreans as Japanese and Japanese as Americans in World War II* (Berkeley: University of California Press, 2011).

72. For the specific term, see Chalmers Johnson, *The Sorrows of Empire: Militarism, Secrecy, and the End of the Republic* (New York: Henry Holt, 2004). For a description of America's Pacific as a garrison state, see Bello, "Conclusion," in *Militarized Currents*, 309–21. For more global perspective on the rise in the number of U.S. military bases, see David Vine, *Base Nation: How U.S. Military Bases Abroad Harm America and the World* (New York: Metropolitan, 2015).

73. Byrd and Rothberg, "Between Subaltern and Indigeneity," 5.

74. Byrd and Rothberg, "Between Subaltern and Indigeneity," 4.

75. Peter J. Taylor, *Modernities: A Geohistorical Interpretation* (Minneapolis: University of Minnesota Press, 1999); Lisa Lowe, *The Intimacies of Four Continents* (Durham, NC: Duke University Press, 2015); Grace Kyungwon Hong, "Consumerism without Means," in *The Ruptures of American Capital: Women of Color Feminism and The Culture of Immigrant Labor* (Minneapolis: University of Minnesota Press, 2006), 107–42; Kumkum Sangari, "The Politics of the Possible," in *Theory of the Novel: A Historical Approach*, ed. Michael McKeon (Baltimore: Johns Hopkins University Press, 1993), 900–922.

76. Shigematsu and Camacho, "Introduction," in *Militarized Currents*, xxiii, emphasis in the original.

77. See Nan Kim, "Ruins of Global Militarism, Embodiment of Dissent: Gangjeong Village's Culture of Peace and Life Movement" (presentation, LandBody: Indigeneity's Radical Commitments Conference, University of Wisconsin, Milwaukee, May 7, 2016).

78. Simon Romero, "Slow-Burning Challenge to Chile on Easter Island," *New York Times*, October 6, 2012. Accessed October 7, 2012, http://www.nytimes.com/2012/10/07/world/americas/slow-burning-rebellion-against chile-on-easter-island.html?pagewanted=all. Also known as the Easter Islands, Rapa Nui in the South East Pacific held an important place within Polynesian cultural and economic circuits. In the 1800s as European trade across the Pacific increased, the island was an unwilling outpost for European navies and pirates with tragic consequences for the Rapa Nui people and land. Rapa Nui formally became a part of Latin America in 1888 when

Chile, after winning the War of the Pacific with Peru and Bolivia, annexed the island and abolished its monarchy. Also see Bruce W. Farcau, *The Ten Cents War: Peru, Chile, and Bolivia in the War of the Pacific, 1879–1884* (Westport, CT: Praeger, 2000).

79. Stoler, *Haunted by Empire: Geographies of Intimacy in North American History* (Durham, NC: Duke University Press, 2006); see also Stoler, *Along the Archival Grain: Epistemic Anxieties and Colonial Common Sense* (Princeton, NJ: Princeton University Press, 2010); Lowe, *Intimacies of Four Continents*.

80. Espiritu, *Body Counts*, 21, emphasis in the original.

81. See Fujitani, *Race for Empire*; Katharine H. S. Moon, *Sex among Allies: Military Prostitution in U.S.–Korea Relations* (New York: Columbia University Press, 1997).

82. See Bonnie Honig, *Antigone, Interrupted* (Cambridge: Cambridge University Press, 2013); Judith Butler, *Antigone's Claim: Kinship between Life and Death* (New York: Columbia University Press, 2000).

83. See Rachel Lee, "Asian American Cultural Production in Asia-Pacific Perspective," *boundary 2* 26, no. 2 (1999): 231–54.

84. Lee, "Asian American Cultural Production in Asian-Pacific Perspective," 253. The encounters among Euro-Americans, Asians, and Latinos are circumscribed by neoliberalism's demand for the opening of borders and reorganization of national economies that, in the U.S. context, have depended on the United States' particular post–World War II relationship to Asia and Latin America. As I detail in chapter 2, the dependence on Asian and Latino labor, market, and production capacity imagines essential differences among Euro-Americans, Asians, and Latinos. Euro-American/Asian/Latin American subjects are expected to inhabit exclusive states such as: free/indentured/slave; interiority/exteriority/primal; creative/hardworking/criminal; native born/immigrant/undocumented; and owner/manager/worker.

85. See Connery, "Pacific Rim Discourse"; Arif Dirlik, "Asia Pacific Studies in an Age of Global Modernity," *Inter-Asia Cultural Studies* 6, no. 2 (2005): 158–70. For an archive of print images that creates a sense of the space that is shared between these two "cultures of the periphery," see Erika Esau, *Images of the Pacific Rim: Australia and California, 1850–1935* (Sydney, Australia: Powerhouse, 2010).

86. Connery, "Pacific Rim Discourse."

87. See, for example, the *Oxford Online Dictionary*.

88. Shigematsu and Camacho, *Militarized Currents*, xxxiii.

89. Raúl Homero Villa and George J. Sánchez, "Introduction: Los Angeles Studies and the Future of Urban Cultures," *American Quarterly* special issue: Los Angeles and the Future of Urban Cultures, guest editors Raúl Homero Villa and George J. Sánchez, no. 3 (2004): 498–505. See also Paul Ong, Edna Bonacich, and Lucie Cheng, eds., *The New Asian Immigration in Los Angeles and Global Restructuring* (Philadelphia: Temple University Press, 1994), particularly the introduction, in which they argue that military connections first and foremost drive migration between East Asia and the United States.

90. Stoler, *Haunted by Empire*, 18.

91. The 1898 Spanish-American War and 1848 U.S.-Mexico War are two important

precursors to American attempts at battling Japanese colonialism in the Pacific and maintaining the lands grabbed from the Japanese since. See Rob Wilson, *Reimagining the American Pacific: From "South Pacific" to Bamboo Ridge and Beyond* (Durham, NC: Duke University Press, 2000); Keith L. Camacho, *Cultures of Commemoration: The Politics of War, Memory, and History in the Mariana Islands* (Honolulu: University of Hawai'i Press, 2011); Teresia K. Teaiwa, "Bikinis and Other S/Pacific N/Oceanism," in *Militarized Currents*, ed. Shigematsu and Camacho.

92. Stoler, *Along the Archival Grain*.

93. Rosanne Kennedy, "Indigenous Australian Arts of Return: Mediating Perverse Archives," in *Rites of Return: Diaspora Poetics and the Politics of Memory*, ed. Marianne Hirsh and Nancy Miller (Durham, NC: Duke University Press, 2011), 88–104.

94. According to Wikipedia, *dossier* comes from the French word for "back" (*dos*). As Fanon is describing, dossiers are central for profiling the colonial and racial subject. For example, the dossier has played a key role as a representation of espionage and is vital to the operations of the FBI's COINTELPRO.

95. Frantz Fanon, *Toward the African Revolution: Political Essays*, trans. Haakon Chevalier (New York: Grove, [1967] 1994), 49.

96. U.S. dossiers—for example, on COINTELPRO operations against the Black Panthers—are still difficult to access fully.

97. See David L. Eng and Shinhee Han, "A Dialogue on Racial Melancholia," *Psychoanalytic Dialogues* 10, no. 4 (2000): 667–700. See also the articles and artwork in the special issue on Asian American mental health edited by Mimi Khuc: "Open in Emergency: A Special Issue on Asian American Mental Health," *Asian American Literary Review* (2016); Min Hyoung Song, "Communities of Remembrance: Reflections on the Virginia Tech Shootings and Race," *Journal of Asian American Studies* 11, no. 1 (2008): 1–26, and Song, *The Children of 1965: On Writing, and Not Writing, as an Asian American* (Durham, NC: Duke University Press, 2013). The 1940s–60s U.S. Cold War rhetorical battle against Soviet Union racial liberalism represented the United States as liberators of all people. The institutionalization of antiracism in that period becomes a general national policy spanning "liberal multiculturalism" (1980–90) and neoliberal multiculturalism (2000s). It is this liberal humanism that has silenced the diaspora within U.S. national space. See Jodi Melamed, *Represent and Destroy: Rationalizing Violence in the New Racial Capitalism* (Minneapolis: University of Minnesota Press, 2011), 13–14; Marianne Hirsch and Nancy K. Miller, eds., *Rites of Return: Diaspora Poetics and the Politics of Memory* (New York: Columbia University Press, 2011); Viet Thanh Nguyen, *Nothing Ever Dies: Vietnam and the Memory of War* (Cambridge, MA: Harvard University Press, 2016).

98. See Eng and Han, "Dialogue on Racial Melancholia." This essay is a result of the dialogue between the two authors, who were also impacted by the deaths of the students at Columbia. They write, "In the final analysis, this essay has been an exercise for us to mourn the various passings of Asian American students who no longer felt tied to our present world, such as it is" (698).

99. Jay Caspian Kang is doing interesting work on Asian American necropolitics. See Kang, *The Dead Do Not Improve: A Novel* (New York: Hogarth, 2013); Kang,

"That Other School Shooting," *New York Times Magazine*, March 28, 2013, http://www.nytimes.com/2013/03/31/magazine/should-it-matter-that-the-shooter-at-oikos-university-was-korean.html?mcubz=3; Kang, "What a Fraternity Hazing Death Revealed About the Painful Search for an Asian-American Identity," *New York Times Magazine*, August 9, 2017, https://www.nytimes.com/2017/08/09/magazine/what-a-fraternity-hazing-death-revealed-about-the-painful-search-for-an-asian-american-identity.html?mcubz=3.

ONE. Melancholy Violence

1. Yoneyama, *Cold War Ruins*, 15.

2. The short story was first published in the Christmas edition of the 1985 *Rafu Shimpo*, a English-language Japanese American newspaper in Los Angeles and also included in a reprint of *Seventeen Syllables and Other Stories*, ed. King-Kok Cheung (New Brunswick, NJ: Rutgers University Press, 1988, 2nd ed.).

3. King-Kok, *Seventeen Syllables*, 15.

4. Frantz Fanon, *The Wretched of the Earth*, trans. Constance Farrington (New York: Grove, 1963).

5. Fanon, *The Wretched of the Earth*, 249–310.

6. Japanese American internment is regularly revived by white supremacists as an idealized state response to managing racial others during times of war. In November 2016 Carl Higbie, the head of the Great America Political Action Committee, suggested that the Korematsu decision could serve as a precedent for a registry of Muslim immigrants. In Virginia, Roanoke mayor David Bowers suspended local assistance for Syrian refugees and invoked mass internment as a response to the perceived threat. "I'm reminded that President Franklin D. Roosevelt felt compelled to sequester Japanese foreign nationals after the bombing of Pearl Harbor, and it appears that the threat of harm to America from ISIS now is just as real and serious as that from our enemies then," he said in a statement in November 2015; Matt Ford, "The Return of *Korematsu*," *Atlantic Magazine*, November 19, 2015, https://www.theatlantic.com/politics/archive/2015/11/the-shadow-of-korematsu/416634/.

7. Williams, *Divided World*, 98.

8. Nigel Gibson, "Why Frantz Fanon Still Matters," October 8, 2016, http://readingfanon.blogspot.com/2016/08/why-frantz-fanon-still-matters.html.

9. For a discussion how psychiatry and politics intertwined in his thinking produces a "critical ethnopsychiatry based on a new concept of culture," see Nigel Gibson and Roberto Beneduce, *Frantz Fanon, Psychiatry and Politics* (London: Rowman and Littlefield, 2017).

10. Lewis Gordon also calls for the need for renewed study of Fanon's medical practice given how Blacks and other colonized people are pathologized within psychiatry and medicine overall. *What Fanon Said: A Philosophical Introduction to His Life and Thought* (New York: Fordham University Press, 2015).

11. In the World War I era the term *forward psychiatry* was coined by European psychologists, particularly in France and England, to explain the experiences by sol-

diers in the front or "forward" of the action. This is the precursor to contemporary diagnosis of Post-Traumatic Stress Disorder (PTSD). This was a new phenomenon; shell shock and other related traumas were unique to the rising mechanization of warfare. If untreated, this meant that the soldiers were unable to return to the front. It was able to be "seen" because the trauma manifested itself physically, with shaking hands, sweating, and other physical manifestations. Fanon saw during his analysis that many of his patients realized they were still holding onto trauma because, although they could not recall it in their minds, their bodies manifested their trauma. The only female patient he discusses in the chapter "Colonial Wars and Mental Disorders," a young Frenchwoman, was diagnosed with anxiety disorder caused by the fact that her father, a leader in the French military, tortured Algerians in their home. Their screams through the night had manifested later in her life as clammy hands, and, alarmingly, it seemed to her that water "dripped from her hands." Frantz Fanon, *Wretched of the Earth*, 204.

12. As his biographer Alice Cherki writes, he presented regularly and participated in professional conferences even when he was ambassador for Algeria. One of his goals as a psychiatrist was to change the nature of psychiatric practice and show how different treatment is needed for the French occupation forces and colonized Algerians. Alice Cherki, *Fanon: A Portrait*, trans. Nadia Benabid (Ithaca, NY: Cornell University Press, 2006).

13. Cherki, *Fanon*, 253.

14. Fanon, *Wretched of the Earth*, 249.

15. Fanon, *Wretched of the Earth*, 252.

16. Fanon, *Wretched of the Earth*, 298–99.

17. Nigel Gibson offers a history of how white supremacy and racism has shaped the practice of psychiatry in the U.S. against Black people, and has led to a mental health crisis for Black people in the United States. Nigel Gibson, "Why Frantz Fanon Still Matters."

18. Adriana Cavarero, *Horrorism: Naming Contemporary Violence* (New York: Columbia University Press, 2008). Fanon's diagnosis remains prescient and demonstrates the longer genealogy in which the current twenty-first-century Muslim suicide bomber is rendered unmournable. For Cavarerro it is significant to recognize the specific gendered nature of insurgency's unmournability. Cavarero describes the rising European support of U.S.-led War against Terror as rooted in histories of European anti-Semitism and Islamophobia (as was leveraged against the Algerians in the period that Fanon writes about). In France the deadly ten-year period during which France waged war against decolonizing Algeria is considered the "dirty war" and a painful memory. This is punctuated by the fact that there is no memorial or public acknowledgment of French use of terror.

19. The violence of France's suppression of the Algerian war is still not publicly acknowledged in France. Nicolas Bancel, Pascal Blanchard, and Sandrine Lemaire, "Torture in Algeria: Past Acts that Haunt France," *Le Monde diplomatique*, June 2001. http://mondediplo.com/2001/06/10torture.

20. Fanon, *Wretched of the Earth*, 300.

21. In addition to Williams, see Julietta Hua for the ways this legal framework racialized Third World women: *Trafficking Women's Human Rights* (Minneapolis: University of Minnesota Press, 2011). Catherine Cole offers an important analysis of how performance becomes central to redress and truth and reconciliation, which emerge out of this liberal human rights project: *Performing South Africa's Truth Commission: Stages of Transition* (Bloomington: Indiana University Press, 2009).

22. In 1945, there were 51 states in the United Nations, and in 1965, there were 117. Regardless of the lingering on of colonialism, this post–World War II period is defined by the nation-state solely as a body with any political power.

23. Williams, *Divided World*, 105.

24. For a critique of liberal humanism that rises during U.S. interventions in the Serbian crisis and how war becomes a pretext for humanitarian violence, see Neda Atanasoski, *Humanitarian Violence: The U.S. Deployment of Diversity* (Minneapolis: University of Minnesota Press, 2013).

25. Williams, *Divided World*, xx.

26. Cherríe Moraga and Gloria E. Anzaldúa, eds., *This Bridge Called My Back: Writings by Radical Women of Color*, 2nd ed. (New York: Kitchen Table, 1983).

27. For more on how "A Fire in Fontana" speaks to the neoconservative period of the 1980s, see James Lee, *Urban Triage: Race and the Fictions of Multiculturalism* (Minneapolis: University of Minnesota Press, 2004).

28. For this argument see Grace Kyungwon Hong, "'Something Forgotten Which Should Be Remembered': Private Property and Cross-Racial Solidarity in the Work of Hisaye Yamamoto," *American Literature* 71, no. 2 (1999): 291–310.

29. Hong, "'Something Forgotten Which Should Be Remembered.'"

30. Yamamoto, "A Fire in Fontana," 157.

31. For the ways that Blackness is produced as a priori criminal by the state see Lisa Marie Cacho, *Social Death: Racialized Rightlessness and the Criminalization of the Unprotected* (New York: New York University Press, 2012).

32. In "A Fire in Fontana," Yamamoto does not portray any of the progressive things she did in her own life. She never describes her antiracist work with the Congress of Racial Equality (CORE) or her activism during the civil rights era. As she mentioned during an interview, before internment her dream was to go to Stanford University. But when that opportunity was presented to her in the 1950s, she chose to work for the *Catholic Worker* seeking to participate in social change. See Crow and Yamamoto, "A *MELUS* Interview."

33. Yamamoto, "A Fire in Fontana," 150.

34. Yamamoto, "A Fire in Fontana," 150.

35. Yamamoto, "A Fire in Fontana," 150.

36. Yamamoto, "A Fire in Fontana," 150.

37. For more on this legacy of figurative consuming the body in mourning practices in Western culture, see Geoffrey Gorer, *Death, Grief, and Mourning* (Salem, NH: Ayer, 1977).

38. See George Lipsitz, *The Possessive Investment in Whiteness: How White People Profit from Identity Politics* (Philadelphia: Temple University Press, 1998); Helen

Heran Jun, *Race for Citizenship: Black Orientalism and Asian Uplift from Pre-Emancipation to Neoliberal America* (New York: New York University Press, 2011).

39. Ta-Nehisi Coates, in "The Case for Reparations," explains how bank mortgages were effectively unavailable for Black people, making it impossible to own homes. See also Martha Biondi, "The Rise of the Reparations Movement," *Radical History Review*, no. 87 (2003): 5–18; "The Case for Reparations," *The Atlantic*, June 2014. See also Eric Avila, *Popular Culture in the Age of White Flight: Fear and Fantasy in Suburban Los Angeles* (Berkeley: University of California Press, 2004).

40. The Kerner Commission's (National Advisory Commission on Civil Disorders) was set up to explain the "summer of riots" across Brown and Black communities in the U.S. in 1967. The report's well-known statement that "Our nation is moving toward two societies, one Black, one white—separate and unequal" described a segregated United States where Blacks were systematically denied access to education, housing, and jobs and subject to white supremacist violence without any recourse to state protection. The National Advisory Commission on Civil Disorders, *The Kerner Report* (Princeton, NJ: Princeton University Press, 2016).

41. Yamamoto's influence in turning to this metaphor is likely as connected to her engagement with decolonial philosophy as it is to her faith developed during her service with the Catholic Worker Movement, to which she devoted her time and career after her work with the newspaper.

42. Fanon, *Black Skin, White Masks*, 11. Here he is discussing the alienation of the Black self. In his later writings he turns to metaphors of fire to discuss how the vanguard needs to step back so that peasant and rural classes have enough time to become ready to fully participate in rebuilding the newly decolonized nation.

43. Fanon, *Black Skin, White Masks*, 11.

44. Yamamoto, "Fire in Fontana," 154.

45. See Kaja Silverman, *The Acoustic Mirror: The Female Voice in Psychoanalysis and Cinema* (Bloomington: Indiana State University Press, 1988). She argues that girls do not leave melancholia fully because they do not stop identifying with the mother.

46. Marianne Hirsch first develops her idea of "postmemory" in "Family Pictures: *Maus*, Mourning and Post-Memory," *Discourse: Journal for Theoretical Studies in Media and Culture* 15, no. 2 (winter 1992–93): 3–29. *No-No Boy*, by John Okada, is another example of an internment narrative that doesn't explicitly discuss internment (Seattle: University of Washington Press, [1976] 2014). See Caroline Chung Simpson's *An Absent Presence: Japanese Americans in Postwar American Culture, 1945–1960* for how Japanese American internment's visibility is heavily structured by the compulsion to forget internment in national history (Durham, NC: Duke University Press, 2002).

47. Yamamoto, "Fire in Fontana," 152.

48. bell hooks, "Oppositional Gaze: Black Female Spectators," in *Feminist Film Theory: A Reader*, ed. Sue Thornham (New York: New York University Press, 1999), 307–20.

49. Yamamoto, "Fire in Fontana," 157.

50. Yamamoto, "Fire in Fontana," 156.

51. By subveillance I am referring to scholars of the Arab Spring (2010) who look at how youth used digital technologies to tape and document police brutality. See Jessica Lake, "*Red Road* (2006) and Emerging Narratives of 'Sub-veillance,'" *Continuum: Journal of Media and Cultural Studies* 24, no. 2 (2010): 231–40.

52. Charles L. Crow and Hisaye Yamamoto, "A *MELUS* Interview: Hisaye Yamamoto," *MELUS* 14, no. 1 (1987): 75, emphasis in the original. In the interview this incites one of the few moments of animation. Descriptions of dispossession are a central part of this interview. In addition to Poston, she talks about how her family's farm is now a part of Camp Pendleton Marine Corp Base.

53. The Poston Memorial Monument was built in 1992, on tribal land with tribal support, and still stands today. See Thomas Y. Fujita-Rony, "Poston (Colorado River)," *Densho Encyclopedia*, accessed September 6, 2017, http://encyclopedia.densho.org/Poston_%28Colorado_River%29/.

54. The War Relocation League becomes the Indian Management Organization, strengthening these links further.

55. Citizens Committee for Resettlement, Thomas R. Bodine Papers, http://www.oac.cdlib.org/findaid/ark:/13030/tf6w100515/dsc/.

56. Iyko Day, *Alien Capital: Asian Racialization and the Logic of Settler Colonial Capitalism* (Durham, NC: Duke University Press, 2016), 18. See also J. Kēhaulani Kauanui, *Hawaiian Blood: Colonialism and the Politics of Sovereignty and Indigeneity* (Durham, NC: Duke University Press, 2008).

57. As Victor Bascara put it: "In the 1970s, only an overly optimistic lunatic fringe entertained the possibility of actually obtaining monetary redress from the government that had incarcerated them." Bascara, "Cultural Politics of Redress: Reassessing the Meaning of the Civil Liberties Act of 1988 after 9/11." *Asian American Law Journal*, 10, no. 2 (2003): 185–214, 191.

58. For an excellent discussion of the idea of reparations through Melanie Klein in the context of Japanese American reparations see Joshua Takano Chambers-Letson, *A Race So Different: Performance and Law in Asian America* (New York: New York University Press, 2013).

59. By 1944, more than 2,000 Latin Americans of Japanese descent, 80 percent from Peru, were placed in internment camps in the United States. Many have not received reparations or apology under the 1988 Civil Rights Act, despite having won a historic apology from the Inter-American Human Rights Commission in 2017. See Evelyn Iritani's "His Family's Internment Earned Apologies from a Human Rights Commission. Will the U.S. Government Respond?" *Los Angeles Times*, March 24, 2017, http://www.latimes.com/opinion/op-ed/la-oe-iritani-update-shibayama-internment-20170323-story.html.

60. Bascara, "Cultural Politics of Redress," 198.

61. Yoneyama, *Cold War Ruins*, 7.

62. https://www.tulelake.org/history.

63. https://www.tulelake.org/history.

64. "Tule Lake," *Densho Encyclopedia*, http://encyclopedia.densho.org/Tule_Lake/.

65. Ellen Clare Kennedy looks at testimony during a hearing to consider "Bills to Expatriate Certain Nationals of the United States; To Create a Japanese Deportation Commission, and to Deport Disloyal Japanese which were held in January, 1944," and argues that the bill is led by clear racism. She cites Mr. Norrell of Arkansas who testifies: *"From the discussion here this morning I take it that there is no argument but what we will deport the noncitizen Japs. There has been no discussion as to that. There has been quite a discussion about the citizen Jap, the men and women who were born here. I do not believe it is so complicated. An American citizen loses his right to citizenship when he is convicted of a felony. A felony is what the statute says it is. I would give them a trial by this deportation commission and provide no bail. I think American citizens should run this country. They ought to take charge and run it."* From Ellen Clare Kennedy, "The Japanese-American Renunciants: Due Process and the Danger of Making Laws During Times of Fear," Japan-Pacific Research Institute Working Paper 110 (October 2006), http://www.jpri.org/publications/workingpapers/wp110.html.

66. Kennedy, "Japanese American Renunciants."

67. See Yuji Ichioka, ed., *Views from Within: The Japanese American Evacuation and Resettlement Study* (Los Angeles: Asian American Studies Center, University of California at Los Angeles, 1989). On the topic of the Immigration and Nationality Act of 1952 (McCarran-Walter Act) and how this impacted those previously considered "aliens ineligible for citizenship" see Mai Ngai's *Impossible Subjects: Illegal Aliens and the Making of Modern America* (Princeton, NJ: Princeton University Press, 2004).

68. Ellen Clare Kennedy, "The Japanese-American Renunciants."

69. This belated recognition is notable when compared to the Manzanar War Relocation Center, which received recognition in 1992. The designation of Tule Lake as part of the World War II Valor in the Pacific National War Monument does not occur until 2008, created by President George W. Bush. This designation was made possible by the advocacy of the Tule Lake Committee and JACL. This memorialization was preceded by H.R. 1492, which designated close to $38,000,000 in federal grant money to preserve the entirety of the sites that interned and imprisoned Japanese Americans.

70. Chris Iijima, quoted in Eric K. Yamamoto et al., *Race, Rights, and Reparation: Law and the Japanese-American Internment* (New York: Wolters Kluwer Law and Business, 2013).

71. For a study of Japanese Americans organizing in the 1970s to help members of their community suffering from drug addiction, see May Fu, "'Serve the People and You Help Yourself': Japanese-American Anti-Drug Organizing in Los Angeles, 1969 to 1972," *Social Justice* 35, no. 2 (2008): 80–99. Fu connects the demand for silence to an unhealthy relationship to internment, which is a foundational event for every Japanese American. See also Caroline Chung Simpson, *An Absent Presence*.

72. Matthew M. Briones, "Hardly 'Small Talk': Discussing Race in the Writing of Hisaye Yamamoto," *Prospects* 29 (2005): 435–72.

73. Sara Clarke Kaplan, "Souls at the Crossroads, Africans on the Water: The

Politics of Diasporic Melancholia," *Callaloo* 30, no. 2 (2007): 514, emphasis in the original.

74. For more on this, see Atanasoski, *Humanitarian Violence*; Julietta Hua, *Trafficking Women's Human Rights*; Michael Rogin, *Ronald Reagan, the Movie: And Other Episodes in Political Demonology* (Berkeley: University of California Press, 1988). As Melanie McAlister argues, in the 1980s, "Muslims as agents of terror" are seen in the development of a genre of anti-terrorist action films created to culturally conflate Islam, terrorism, and the Middle East after 1979; see McAlister, *Epic Encounters: Culture, Media, and U.S. Interests in the Middle East since 1945*, updated ed. (Berkeley: University of California Press, 2005), especially chap. 5.

75. For more on how transpacific redress culture in the case of Korean comfort women depend on strategies which bring arts, performance, and politics together see Elizabeth W. Son's *Embodied Reckoning: "Comfort Women," Performance, and Transpacific Redress* (Ann Arbor: University of Michigan Press, 2018), and Cathy Schlund-Vials, *War, Genocide, and Justice: Cambodian American Memory Work* (Minnesota: University of Minneapolis Press, 2012).

76. Mike Davis describes how 1980s neoconservative policies sought to decimate the city to reorganize it along the logic of economic integration; *City of Quartz: Excavating the Future in Los Angeles* (New York: Verso, 1990).

TWO. Racial Cognitive Mapping, Interregnum, and the LA Riots

1. For more on this, see Mike Davis, *City of Quartz: Excavating the Future in Los Angeles* (New York: Verso, 1990); Nancy Abelman and John Lie, *Blue Dreams: Korean Americans and the Los Angeles Riots* (Cambridge, MA: Harvard University Press, 1995); Lynn Mie Itagaki, *Racial Burnout: The Spatialization of Civility in the 1992 Los Angeles Crisis* (Minneapolis: University of Minnesota Press, 2015).

2. "California Counts," Public Policy Institute of California, 1995.

3. Dai Sil Kim-Gibson, *Sa-I-Gu*, documentary (San Francisco: Cross Current Media, National Asian American Telecommunications Association, 1993), DVD; Héctor Tobar, *The Tattooed Soldier* (New York: Penguin, 2000).

4. Min Hyoung Song, *Strange Futures: Pessimism and the 1992 Los Angeles Riots* (Durham, NC: Duke University Press, 2005), especially chap. 4.

5. Like the scene of burning imagined by Hisaye Yamamoto at the end of "A Fire in Fontana," *Gook* is framed by a burning store, in front of which a ghostly young Black girl, killed during the LA Riots, dances.

6. Antonio Gramsci, *Selections from the Prison Notebooks*, ed. Quintin Hoare, trans. Geoffrey Nowell Smith (New York: International Publishers, 1992), 276.

7. Philippe Theophanidis, "Interregnum as a Legal and Political Concept: A Brief Contextual Survey," *Synthesis*, no. 9 (fall 2016): 109–24.

8. For how both the prosecution and defense relied in the videos to make their case see Judith Butler, "Endangered/Endangering: Schematic Racism and White Paranoia," in *Reading Rodney King/Reading Urban Uprising*, ed. Robert Gooding

Williams, 15–22 (New York: Routledge, 1993). Elizabeth Alexander calls the lack of guilty verdict despite the clear evidence of Black pain the "ritualistic production of black bodies in pain" for white visual pleasure connected to the history of lynching as a public spectacle: "Can You Be BLACK and Look at This: Reading the Rodney King Video." In *Black Male: Representations of Masculinity in Contemporary American Art*, edited by Thelma Golden, 91–110 (New York: Whitney Museum of Art, 1994).

9. Fredric Jameson, "Cognitive Mapping," in *Marxism and the Interpretation of Culture*, ed. Cary Nelson and Lawrence Grossberg (Urbana: University of Illinois Press, 1988), 353.

10. Dai Sil Kim-Gibson, born in North Korea while it was under Japanese rule, creates films widely known for championing the compelling but neglected issues of human rights. They are marked by inventive formats and her particular style of humanizing the storytellers. Her critically acclaimed works include *Wet Sand: Voices from L.A.* (2004); *Silence Broken: Korean Comfort Women* (2000); *America Becoming* (1991); *A Forgotten People: The Sakhalin Koreans* (2000); *Olivia's Story* (2000); and *Motherland: Cuba, Korea, U.S.A.* (2006).

11. After the cease-fire was declared in 1996, neither side was brought to trial. Efrain Rios Montt, an army general who seized power in 1982 and under whose military leadership the brutality of the attacks against the Maya Ixtil occurred, did not face trial until 2013.

12. Itagaki, *Civil Racism: The 1992 Los Angeles Rebellion and the Crisis of Racial Burnout* (Minneapolis: University of Minnesota Press, 2016).

13. David L. Eng and David Kazanjian, eds., *Loss: The Politics of Mourning* (Berkeley: University of California Press, 2003); Song, *Strange Futures*, chap. 3.

14. Ji-Yeon Yuh, "Moved by War: Migration, Diaspora, and the Korean War," *Journal of Asian American Studies* 8, no. 3 (2005): 278.

15. For more on this history see Bruce Cumings, *Korea's Place in the Sun: A Modern History*, updated ed. (New York: W. W. Norton, 2005); and Akira Iriye, *After Imperialism: The Search for a New Order in the Far East, 1921–1931* (Chicago: Imprint, 1990).

16. The San Francisco Peace Treaty was criticized from the beginning by China and India because they felt it violated the Potsdam Agreement (1945), and that it was a bilateral treaty between the United States and Japan as opposed to Japan with the countries it had violated. India, for example, refused to attend because it was appalled by Okinawa being denied sovereignty and being turned over to U.S. military dominion. See John Price, "A Just Peace? The 1951 San Francisco Peace Treaty in Historical Perspective," *Japan Policy Research Institute*, Working Paper 78 (June 2001).

17. Price, "Just Peace?"

18. Price, "Just Peace?"

19. Price, "Just Peace?"

20. Yukiko Koshiro, *Trans-Pacific Racisms and the U.S. Occupation of Japan* (New York: Columbia University Press, 1999), 121.

21. Jodi Kim, "'I'm Not Here, If This Doesn't Happen': The Korean War and Cold War Epistemologies in Susan Choi's *The Foreign Student*, and Heinz Insu Fenkl's *Memories of My Ghost Brother*," *Journal of Asian American Studies* 11, no. 3 (2008): 281.

22. Bruce Cumings, *Parallax Vision: Making Sense of American–East Asian Relations at the End of the Century* (Durham, NC: Duke University Press, 2002); Mimi Thi Nguyen, *The Gift of Freedom: War, Debt, and Other Refugee Passages* (Durham, NC: Duke University Press, 2012).

23. See Kate Doyle and Peter Kornbluh, eds., "CIA and Assassinations: The Guatemala 1954 Documents," *The National Security Archive Electronic Briefing Book No. 4* (Washington, DC: National Security Archive, n.d.), http://nsarchive.gwu.edu/NSAEBB/NSAEBB4/index.html.

24. For more on this, see Greg Grandin, *The Blood of Guatemala: A History of Race and Nation* (Durham, NC: Duke University Press, 2000).

25. Commission for Historical Clarification, *Guatemala: Memory of Silence* (Guatemala City: Historical Clarification Commission, 1999), 9–13.

26. For more on this, see Nora Hamilton and Norma Stoltz Chinchilla, *Seeking Community in a Global City: Guatemalans and Salvadorans in Los Angeles* (Philadelphia, PA: Temple University Press, 2001). Studies conclude that 21 percent of the total Salvadoran population and 16 percent of the total Guatemalan population in the United States in 1990 came between 1981 and 1982, fleeing military violence in their respective countries. See David E. Lopez, Eric Popkin, and Edward Telles, "Central Americans: At the Bottom, Struggling to Get Out," in *Ethnic Los Angeles*, ed. Roger Waldinger and Mehdi Bozorgmehr (New York: Russell Sage Foundation, 1996), 279–304.

27. Christopher L. Connery, "Pacific Rim Discourse: The U.S. Global Imaginary in the Late Cold War Years," *boundary 2* 21, no. 1 (1994): 48.

28. For more on this critique, with a particular focus on China, the United States, and Argentina, see Jinah Kim and Neda Atanasoski, "Unhappy Desires and Queer Postsocialist Futures: Hong Kong and Buenos Aires in Wong Kar-Wai's *Happy Together*," *American Quarterly* 69, no. 3 (2017): 697–718.

29. Walter D. Mignolo offers a powerful critique of the ways that Third World others are hierarchized in "The Geopolitics of Knowledge and the Colonial Difference," *SAQ* 101, no. 1 (2003): 57–96.

30. Manthia Diawara, "Toward a Regional Imaginary in Africa," in *The Cultures of Globalization*, ed. Fredric Jameson and Masao Miyoshi (Durham, NC: Duke University Press, 1998), 103.

31. Diawara, "Toward a Regional Imaginary in Africa," 104.

32. Diawara, "Toward a Regional Imaginary in Africa," 107.

33. Diawara, "Toward a Regional Imaginary in Africa," 104.

34. For more on the differential racialization of Blacks and Koreans in neoliberal Los Angeles, see Helen Heran Jun, *Race for Citizenship: Black Orientalism and Asian Uplift from Pre-Emancipation to Neoliberal America* (New York: New York University Press, 2011).

35. For how Koreans become caught in the middle of a Black/White fight see Min Pyong, *Caught in the Middle: Korean Communities in New York and Los Angeles* (Berkeley: University of California Press, 1996). For a thorough structural analysis of the riots see Melvin L. Oliver, James H. Johnson Jr., and Walter C. Farrell Jr., "Anatomy of a Rebellion: A Political-Economic Analysis," in *Reading Rodney King/ Reading Urban Uprising*.

36. Comparisons have been made to the cordoning and isolating of survivors during Hurricane Katrina in 2005.

37. See particularly p. 43 of Lisa Lowe's "On Contemporary Asian American Projects," *Amerasia Journal* 21, nos. 1–2 (1995): 41–52.

38. Jodi Melamed, "Racial Capitalism," *Journal of Critical Ethnic Studies* 1, no. 1 (2015): 76–85; Denise Ferreira da Silva, "Globality," *Journal of Critical Ethnic Studies* 1, no. 1 (2015): 33–38.

39. The twenty-first-century interest in the extended interregnum created by the failure of capitalism is linked to 1990s concerns over the loss of utopic thinking. See the conceptual links and concerns in Zygmut Bauman's discussion on interregnum and the extended discussion by urban geographers (e.g., David Harvey, Edward Soja and Allen J. Scott, Doreen Massey) and postmodernists (e.g., Fredric Jameson and Francis Fukuyama) on the pessimism and lack of utopic thinking as a result of neoliberalism and the state's claim that capitalism has "won." See Zygmut Bauman, "Times of Interregnum," *Ethics and Global Politics* 5, no. 1 (2012): 49–56; David Harvey, *A Brief History of Neoliberalism* (Oxford: Oxford University Press, 2007); Edward Soja and Allen J. Scott, eds., *The City: Los Angeles and Urban Theory at the End of the Twentieth Century* (Berkeley: University of California Press, 1996); Fredric Jameson, *Postmodernism, or, the Cultural Logic of Late Capitalism* (Durham, NC: Duke University Press, 1991); Francis Fukuyama, *The End of History and the Last Man* (New York: Avon 1992).

40. See Raúl Villa and George J. Sánchez, guest eds., "Los Angeles and the Future of Urban Cultures," special issue, *America Quarterly* 56, no. 3 (2004).

41. See Amy Kaplan and Donald Pease, *Cultures of United States Imperialism* (Durham, NC: Duke University Press, 1993); Shelley Streeby, *American Sensations: Class, Empire, and the Production of Popular Culture* (Berkeley: University of California Press, 2002); Christian G. Appy, ed., *Cold War Constructions: The Political Culture of United States Imperialism, 1945–1966* (Amherst: University of Massachusetts Press, 2000); Karen Kuo, *East Is West and West Is East: Gender, Culture, and Interwar Encounters between Asia and America* (Philadelphia: Temple University Press, 2013).

42. For more on this racialization, see Melanie McAlister, *Epic Encounters: Culture, Media, and U.S. Interests in the Middle East Since 1945*, updated ed. (Berkeley: University of California Press, 2005); Herman Gray, *Cultural Moves: African Americans and the Politics of Representation* (Berkeley: University of California Press, 2005).

43. Chungmoo Choi, "The Discourse of Decolonization and Popular Memory: South Korea," *positions* 1, no. 1 (1993): 83.

44. Jodi Kim, "'I'm Not Here, If This Doesn't Happen'"; Kim, *Ends of Empire: Asian American Critique and the Cold War* (Minneapolis: University of Minnesota Press, 2010).

45. For more on this, see Edward J. W. Park, "Friends or Enemies? Generational Politics in the Korean American community in Los Angeles," *Qualitative Sociology* 22, no. 2 (1999): 161–75; Nancy Abelman and John Lie, *Blue Dreams: Korean Americans and the Los Angeles Riots* (Cambridge, MA: Harvard University Press, 1995).

46. See George Lipsitz, *The Possessive Investment in Whiteness: How White People Profit from Identity Politics* (Philadelphia: Temple University Press, 1998); T. Fujitani, *Race for Empire: Koreans as Japanese and Japanese as Americans during World War II* (Oakland: University of California Press, 2011).

47. See Jun, *Race for Citizenship*.

48. In *Further Selections from the Prison Notebooks*, Gramsci describes how "the old world is dying, the new world tardy (slow) to appear and in this chiaroscuro (light-dark) surge (emerge) monsters" (275–76). See also Choi, "Discourse of Decolonization and Popular Memory."

49. See Itagaki, *Racial Burnout*.

50. Jodi Kim, "'I'm Not Here, If This Doesn't Happen,'" 281.

51. In protest to martial law, a citizens' army pushed the martial law forces out of town by taking up arms. In response, the Korean army created a cordon around Kwangju; in the interregnum the Kwanju Commune came into being, and the city ran their own affairs.

52. There is growing scholarship on the contradictory conservative and progressive elements to diasporic scholarship across the Pacific. For example, see Helen Heran Jun, "Contingent Nationalisms: Renegotiating Borders in Korean and Korean American Women's Oppositional Struggles," *positions: asia critique* 5, no. 2 (1997): 325–55, and Min Jung Kim, "Moments of Danger in the (Dis)continuous Relation of Korean Nationalism and Korean American Nationalism," *positions* 5, no. 2 (1997): 361.

53. See Elaine H. Kim, "Myth, Memory, and Desire: Homeland and History in Contemporary Korea American Writing and Visual Art," in *Holding Their Own: Perspectives on the Multi-Ethnic Literatures of the United States*, ed. Dorothea Fischer-Hornung and Heike Raphael-Hernandez (Stauffenburg, Germany: Verlag, 2000).

54. Achille Mbembe, "Provisional Notes on the Postcolony," *Africa* 62, no. 1 (1992): 26.

55. Tobar, *Tattooed Soldier*, 241.

56. Tobar, *Tattooed Soldier*, 3.

57. Frantz Fanon, *Black Skin, White Masks*, trans. Charles Lam Markmann (New York: Grove Press, 1967), 21.

58. Tobar, *Tattooed Soldier*, 42.

59. Tobar, *Tattooed Soldier*, 41, original emphasis. For more on "tent city" and the growth of homeless communities in downtown Los Angeles, see Davis, *City of Quartz*.

60. Tobar, *Tattooed Soldier*, 185–89.

61. Tobar, *Tattooed Soldier*, 126.

62. Tobar, *Tattooed Soldier*, 233.

63. Tobar, *Tattooed Soldier*, 308.

64. Tobar, *Tattooed Soldier*, 13.

65. Kevin Lynch, *The Image of the City* (Cambridge, MA: MIT Press, 1960).

66. Jameson, *Postmodernism*, 51–52. For Jameson, cognitive mapping is a utopic project in postmodernism.

67. Tobar, *Tattooed Soldier*, 71.

68. Tobar, *Tattooed Soldier*, 288.

69. Tobar, *Tattooed Soldier*, 289.

70. Tobar, *Tattooed Soldier*, 273.

71. Tobar, *Tattooed Soldier*, 168.

72. Tobar, *Tattooed Soldier*, 66.

73. The movie ET was released in the United States in June 1982 and had reached most of Guatemala's movie theaters by December 1982. For an analysis of ET as representing the failures of masculinity in the Reagan post–Vietnam War era, see Michael Rogin, *Independence Day* (London: British Film Institute, 1998); Rogin, *Ronald Reagan, the Movie: And Other Episodes in Political Demonology* (Berkeley: University of California Press, 1988).

74. Tobar, *Tattooed Soldier*, 174.

75. Park, "Friends or Enemies?"

THREE. Transpacific Noir, Dying Colonialism

1. John Dower, in *War without Mercy: Race and Power in the Pacific War* (New York Pantheon, 1987), describes the brutality in U.S. military action against Japan driven by the desire to annihilate and decimate the Japanese empire.

2. Scholarship on the impact of the atomic bomb on knowledge production and cultural politics is rich. See Rey Chow, "The Age of the World Target," in *America's Wars in Asia: A Cultural Approach to History and Memory*, ed. Phillip West, Steven I. Levine, and Jackie Hilz (New York: M. E. Sharpe, 1998), 205–20; Michael Sherry, *The Rise of American Air Power: The Creation of Armageddon* (New Haven, CT: Yale University Press, 1987); Paul Virilio, *The Information Bomb*, trans. Chris Turner (New York: Verso, 2005); Lisa Yoneyama, *Hiroshima Traces: Time, Space, and the Dialectics of Memory* (Berkeley: University of California Press, 1999).

3. Omer Bartov, *Murder in Our Midst: The Holocaust, Industrial Killing, and Representation* (Oxford: Oxford University Press, 1996).

4. The history of the atomic bomb is about the assault on the Pacific Arena as a whole, conceived of as both bodies of land and bodies of water, unoccupied islands as well as industrial cities, all connected along the sharp edge of a killing machine. The Bikini Islands and the people who are a part of the atomic diaspora were displaced, like many other native peoples, in order to test the atomic bombs. This is completely invisible to most Americans. See Teresia K. Teaiwa, "Bikinis and Other S/Pacific N/Oceans," in *Militarized Currents: Toward a Decolonized Future in Asia*

and the Pacific, ed. Setsu Shigematsu and Keith L. Camacho (Minneapolis: University of Minnesota Press, 2010), 15–31.

5. Mikhail Bakhtin, *Speech Genres and Other Late Essays*, ed. Caryl Emerson and Michael Holquist, trans. Vern W. McGee (Austin: University of Texas Press, 1986), 170. For his discussion of the dialogic, heteroglossia, and refractive nature of discourses, see Bakhtin, "Discourse in the Novel," in *The Dialogic Imagination: Four Essays*, ed. Michael Holquist, trans. Caryl Emerson and Michael Holquist (Austin: University of Texas Press, 1992), 259–422.

6. Avery F. Gordon, *Ghostly Matters: Haunting and the Sociological Imagination*, 2nd ed. (Minneapolis: University of Minnesota, 2008), 8.

7. For the periodization of noir to the World War II era, see Raymond Borde and Étienne Chaumeton, *A Panorama of American Film Noir (1941–1953)*, trans. Paul Hammond (San Francisco: City Lights, 2002); Alain Silver and James Ursini, eds., *Film Noir Reader* (Pompton Plains, NJ: Limelight, 1996).

8. Bartov, *Murder in Our Midst*, 50.

9. Giorgio Agamben, *Homo Sacer: Sovereign Power and Bare Life*, trans. Daniel Heller-Roazen (Stanford, CA: Stanford University Press, 1998).

10. Cho, *Haunting the Korean Diaspora*, 26–27.

11. See Lisa Yoneyama, "Memory Matters: Hiroshima's Korean Atom Bomb Memorial and the Politics of Ethnicity," *Public Culture* 7, no. 3 (1995): 499–527. In this exploration of the highly charged 1999 political battle to move the Korean Atomic Bomb memorial into the official peace park in Hiroshima, Yoneyama analyzes the memorial as regressive nationalism.

12. For most of Korea's history its kingdoms have had to pay tribute to China and Japan. However, the modern Japanese rule of Korea begins with the Japan–Korea Treaty of 1876 and is consolidated by the Japan–Korea Treaty of 1905, in which the then-Korean Empire was declared a protectorate of Japan. See Bruce Cumings, *Korea's Place in the Sun: A Modern History*, updated ed. (New York: W. W. Norton, 2005).

13. A notable exception is Okinawa, to which India objected and gave as one of the reasons that the country refused to attend the San Francisco Peace Treaty.

14. For more on this, see Michael Bazyler, "Japan Should Follow the International Trend and Face Its History of World War II Forced Labor," *Asia-Pacific Journal: Japan Focus* 7, no. 5.3 (2009). http://apjjf.org/-Michael-Bazyler/3030/article.html.

15. For more on the San Francisco Peace Treaty and its impact on furthering Korea's colonial status, see Johnson, *Blowback*; John Price, "A Just Peace? The 1951 San Francisco Peace Treaty in Historical Perspective," *Japan Policy Research Institute*, Working Paper No. 78 (June 2001).

16. This includes settling pre-war Japanese imperial crimes against Koreans and making Korea's economy and military security dependent on Japan. For a historical account, see J. Mark Mobius, "The Japan–Korea Normalization Process and Korean Anti-Americanism," Asian Survey 6, no. 4 (1966): 241–48.

17. See Wendy Brown, *States of Injury: Power and Freedom in Late Modernity* (Princeton, NJ: Princeton University Press, 1995). Brown calls for ways to con-

ceive of forgiveness as beyond the "private" or "gift" exchange toward an individual that then ends the grievance toward a forgiveness that is opened to further critique in the future. This is the only model that does not seek merely to reconstitute the nation-state with forgiveness signaling the end of the formal inquiry itself, since the formal end of the inquiry does not mark the actual end of pain. This is a temporality that is in line with Hannah Arendt's description of a seeking of apology that solicits the kind of forgiveness "which does not merely re-act but acts anew and unexpectedly, unconditioned by the act which provoked it and therefore freeing from its consequences both the one who forgives and the one who is forgiven"; Arendt, *The Human Condition*, 2nd ed. (Chicago: University of Chicago Press, 1998), 241. For Arendt, forgiveness is possible only when punishable deeds are punished. Thus, for both Brown and Arendt, forgiveness as it exists within the liberal structure can only be a hopeful (im)possibility and instrumentalized political tool. Nation-states can force forgiveness from injured parties that serve the purpose of constructing a shared progressive history and linear narrative, making the "beneficiary" of the apology the nation.

18. For a discussion on the centrality of Los Angeles to the noir imaginary, see Kelly Olive and Benigno Trigo, *Noir Anxiety* (Minneapolis: University of Minnesota Press, 2002).

19. Sam Fuller, dir., *The Crimson Kimono* (Los Angeles: Columbia Pictures, 1959), DVD; Naomi Hirahara, *Summer of the Big Bachi* (New York: Bantam Dell, 2004).

20. Chi-Yun Shin and Mark Gallagher, eds., *East Asian Film Noir: Transnational Encounters and Intercultural Dialogue* (New York: I. B. Tauris, 2015), offer an important corrective to this tendency. People in the United States tend to be familiar with Japanese noir as a genre separate from American and European noir. Akira Kurosawa's *Stray Dog* (1949) is probably the first example of the genre in Japan; the *yakuza* (gangster) subgenre took off in the 1950s. Some of the notable films of that earlier period are Seijun Suzuki's *Underworld Beauty* (1958), *Tokyo Drifter* (1966), and *Branded to Kill* (1967).

21. Charlie Chan exemplifies this as literally a white man in yellowface speaking stolen lines. For fascinating studies of the character of Charlie Chan, see Yunte Huang, *Charlie Chan: The Untold Story of an Honorable Detective and His Rendezvous with American History* (New York: W. W. Norton, 2010); Robert G. Lee, *Orientals: Asian Americans in Popular Culture* (Philadelphia: Temple University Press, 1999). Another example is the racialization of the Japanese gardener and the stereotyping of his pronunciation of glass/grass in *Chinatown* (1974).

22. Lee Horsley, *The Noir Thriller* (New York: Palgrave Macmillan, 2001), 17.

23. Horsley, *Noir Thriller*, 17.

24. The noir protagonist is a twentieth-century adaptation of the nineteenth-century lone frontiersman, like James Fenimore Cooper's Natty Bumppo; their violence represents the work it takes to "tame" the frontier so that civilization can follow. This means that they can never fully live with civilized others.

25. Borde and Chaumeton, "Towards a Definition of Film Noir," 17–25.

26. This was partially established by using only two lights rather than the tradi-

tional three when setting up a scene. A sidelight was often missing, and only a front light and sometimes a backfill was used.

27. Paul Schrader, "Notes on Film Noir," *Film Comment* 8, no. 1 (1972): 11.

28. Manthia Diawara, ed., *Black American Cinema* (New York: Routledge, 1993).

29. Richard Dyer, "The Colour of Virtue: Lillian Gish, Whiteness, and Femininity," in *Women and Film: A Sight and Sound Reader*, ed. Pam Cook and Phillip Dodd (Philadelphia: Temple University Press, 1993), 1–9; Dyer, "Resistance through Charisma: Rita Hayworth and Gilda," in *Women in Film Noir*, ed. E. Ann Kaplan, rev. and expanded ed. (London: British Film Institute, 2008), 91–99.

30. Eric Lott, "The Whiteness of Film Noir," *American Literary History* 9, no. 3 (1997): 548.

31. Lott, "Whiteness of Film Noir," 551.

32. See Jennifer Fay and Justus Nieland, *Film Noir: Hard-Boiled Modernity and the Cultures of Globalization* (New York: Routledge, 2009), 26.

33. For more cultural history on the global dimensions of noir, see David Desser, "Global Noir: Genre Film in the Age of Transnationalism," in *Film Genre Reader IV*, ed. Barry Keith Grant (Austin: University of Texas Press, 2012), 628–48; James Naremore, "The Other Side of the Street," in *More Than Night: Film Noir in Its Contexts* (Berkeley: University of California Press, 1998), 220–53.

34. Marc Vernet, "Film Noir on the Edge of Doom," in *Shades of Noir: A Reader*, ed. Joan Copjec (New York: Verso, 1993), 24.

35. Vernet, "Film Noir on the Edge of Doom," 1. Studying noir has been central to groundbreaking theories in film as well as to the postcolonial theories of seminal figures such as Homi K. Bhabha, whose close reading of Orson Welles's *Touch of Evil* (1958) lays out the arguments that will become his formulation of mimicry. See Bhabha, "The Other Question: Stereotype, Discrimination, and the Discourse of Colonialism," *Screen* 24, no. 6 (1983): 18–36; Bhabha, *The Location of Culture* (New York: Routledge, 1994); Donald E. Pease, "Borderline Justice/States of Emergency: Orson Welles's *Touch of Evil*," *CR: The New Centennial Review* 1, no. 1 (2001): 75–105.

36. It is also clear that the wars in the Pacific influenced European noir films, most notably Josef von Sternberg's *Shanghai Express* (1933) and *The Shanghai Gesture* (1941), as well as Jean-Pierre Melville's *Le Samourai* (1967).

37. See Robert Serber, with Robert P. Crease, *Peace and War: Reminiscences of a Life on the Frontiers of Science* (New York: Columbia University Press, 1998), 104; Dashiell Hammett, *The Thin Man* (New York: Vintage, [1936] 1962). The fictional film *Fat Man and Little Boy* (1989) credits the names to Serber and Hammett. Other popular proposed originators for the names are Winston Churchill and Franklin Delano Roosevelt.

38. Chow, "Age of the World Target," 210.

39. This is a long tradition in American culture: the young country saw simple and complex machines as the way the nation would progress and expand. See Leo Marx, *The Machine in the Garden: Technology and the Pastoral Ideal in America* (Oxford: Oxford University Press, 1964).

40. Chow, "Age of the World Target," 210.

41. E. Ann Kaplan, ed., "Introduction," in *Women in Film Noir*, rev. and expanded ed. (London: British Film Institute, 1998), 15–35. See also Diane Waldman, "Film Theory and the Gendered Spectator: The Female or the Feminist Reader?" *Camera Obscura* 6, no. 318 (1988): 80–94. For a critical perspective that includes race, see Yvonne Tasker, "Women in Film Noir," in *A Companion to Film Noir*, ed. Andrew Spicer and Helen Hanson (Malden, MA: Wiley-Blackwell, 2013), 353–68.

42. E. Ann Kaplan, ed., "The 'Dark Continent' of Film Noir: Race, Displacement, and Metaphor in Tourneur's *Cat People* (1942) and Welles's *The Lady from Shanghai* (1948)," in *Women in Film Noir*, 185; emphases added.

43. For her assessment of feminist film criticism, see bell hooks, "The Oppositional Gaze: Black Female Spectators," in *Black Looks: Race and Representation* (New York: Routledge, 2015), 115–32. This is also a problem for Western knowledge production overall; see Ann Laura Stoler, *Race and the Education of Desire: Foucault's "History of Sexuality" and the Colonial Order of Things* (Durham, NC: Duke University Press, 1995); Denise Ferreira Da Silva, *Toward a Global Idea of Race* (Minneapolis: University of Minnesota Press, 2007).

44. See Copjec, "Introduction," in *Shades of Noir*, 26–27.

45. Lott, "Whiteness of Film Noir"; Diawara, "Noir by Noirs: Towards a New Realism in Black Cinema," in *Shades of Noir*, 261–78.

46. Fay and Nieland, *Film Noir*, x.

47. Rachel Adams, *Continental Divides: Remapping the Cultures of North America* (Chicago: University of Chicago Press, 2010); Pease, "Borderline Justice/States of Emergency"; Lott, "Whiteness of Film Noir"; Diawara, "Noir by Noirs."

48. For more on the racist and nationalist contours of noir, see Lott, "Whiteness of Film Noir"; Pease, "Borderline Justice/States of Emergency"; Bhabha, "Other Question"; Robert Crooks, "From the Far Side of the Urban Frontier: The Detective Fictions of Chester Himes and Walter Mosley," *College Literature* 22, no. 3 (1995): 68–90; Adams, *Continental Divides*; Copjec, *Shades of Noir*. In literary noir the traditional symbols identified with the frontier narrative are made clear through the racialized spatiality of noir narratives and the antihero and isolated hardboiled protagonist. A significant source for the American imagination of itself as a nation of boot-strapping and intrepid individuals, the formal incorporation of the lands west of the Mississippi into the national body by the end of the 1800s was the continental end of the frontier out West and South, and symbols such as the frontiersman—the lone individual whose brutality we excuse because it is what keeps back the hordes of barbarians—become unmoored from the Jacksonian frontier of the American West and displaced onto the emerging racial divide in American cities such as Los Angeles.

49. Amy Kaplan, "'Left Alone with America': The Absence of Empire in the Study of American Culture," in *Cultures of United States Imperialism*, ed. Amy Kaplan and Donald E. Pease (Durham, NC: Duke University Press, 1993), 16–17. For more on the links between frontier and noir narratives, see Crooks, "From the Far Side of the Urban Frontier."

50. Kaplan, "'Left Alone with America,'" 16–17. See also Gloria E. Anzaldúa, *Borderlands/La Frontera: The New Mestiza* (San Francisco: Aunt Lute, 1987). See

Richard Drinnon, *Facing West: The Metaphysics of Indian-Hating and Empire-Building* (Norman: University of Oklahoma Press, 1997); Amy Kaplan and Pease, *Cultures of United States Imperialism*.

51. This is an important site for Japanese American World War II–era history, as there is a Japanese American War Memorial and dedication to the Japanese American World War II 442nd Regiment.

52. Within the racial economy of Jim Crow and post-internment U.S. landscape, this representation of interracial love between a Japanese man and a white woman is remarkable, especially since yellowface representations of Asian masculinity was the convention of the time. For more on the politics of the film's interracial love story, see Calvin McMillian, "The Hardboiled and the Haunted: Race, Masculinity, and the Asian American Detective" (PhD diss., University of California, Santa Cruz, 2012).

53. Shuto is played by a Japanese American actor and stuntman who went by the professional name *Fuji*.

54. McMillian, "Hardboiled and the Haunted."

55. This happens early in the film. The lamps over the pool tables cast unpredictable and sinister shadows. Things turn violent quickly, and Charlie and Joe act in concert to take down Shuto. This joint attack is one of the last cases they investigate together as their competition for the same woman's love grows. The violence here parallels a scene near the end of the film wherein Joe, seemingly in a blind rage, knocks out Charlie during a charity boxing match. Whereas the irrationality lies with Shuto in the first scene, in the latter it is with Joe.

56. Stoler, *Imperial Debris: On Ruins and Ruination* (Durham, NC: Duke University Press, 2013).

57. Bruce Cumings, *The Origins of the Korean War* (Princeton, NJ: Princeton University Press, 1990), cited from Cho, *Haunting the Korean Diaspora*, 71.

58. For more on this see Bruce Cumings, *Parallax Vision: Making Sense of American–East Asian Relations at the End of the Century* (Durham, NC: Duke University Press, 2002).

59. This is the result of the United States having no legitimate reason to be in Korea; this was mostly to further U.S. domination over East Asia in the battle against Communism. Fighting the proxy war would come to a head in U.S. involvement in Vietnam, but the Korean War, between World War II and Vietnam, remained relatively erased. Like Japanese American internment, the Korean War remained a point of silence in the United States in the 1950s and 1960s. See Bruce Cumings, "The American Century and the Third World," *Diplomatic History* 23, no. 2 (1999): 355–70; Ji-Yeon Yuh, *Beyond the Shadow of Camptown: Korean Military Brides in America* (New York: New York University Press, 2002); Chalmers Johnson, *Blowback: The Costs and Consequences of American Empire* (New York: Henry Holt, 2000).

60. Grace M. Cho, *Haunting the Korean Diaspora: Shame, Secrecy, and the Forgotten War* (Minneapolis: University of Minnesota Press, 2008).

61. Cho, *Haunting the Korean Diaspora*, 19–20. She gets this term from Lyndsey

Stonebridge, "Bombs and Roses: The Writing of Anxiety in Henry Green's *Caught*," *Diacritics* 28, no. 4 (1998): 25–43.

62. Neel Ahuja, *Bioinsecurities: Disease Interventions, Empire, and the Government of Species* (Durham, NC: Duke University Press, 2016), describes "dread life" in similar terms.

63. Cho, *Haunting the Korean Diaspora*, 58.

64. Cho, *Haunting the Korean Diaspora*, 58.

65. Quoted from Charles J. Hanley, Sang-Hun Choe, and Martha Mendoza's *The Bridge at No Gun Ri: A Hidden Nightmare from the Korean War* (New York: Henry Holt, 2001), 189, from Cho, *Haunting the Korean Diaspora*, 81.

66. Fredric Jameson, "Magical Narratives: On the Dialectical Use of Genre Criticism," in *The Political Unconscious: Narrative as a Socially Symbolic Act* (Ithaca, NY: Cornell University Press, 1981), 103–50.

67. Naomi Hirahara, "Interview in *Pacific Citizen* with Caroline Aoyagi," May 14, 2005, http://news.newamericamedia.org/news/view_article.html?article_id=10a413b89de62529a74ae951db03b9ee, and Caroline Aoyagi, "Mystery Author Naomi Hirahara Looks to Her Community for Inspiration," *Pacific Citizen*, May 14, 2005, accessed December 2, 2010, http://news.newamericamedia.org/news/view_article.html?article_id=10a413b89de62529a74ae951db03b9ee.

68. In addition to Raymond Chandler's *The Big Sleep* (New York: Vintage, [1939] 1988), there are constant references to the Filipino "houseboy," in James M. Cain's 1936 novel version (1944 film released) of *Double Indemnity* (New York: Vintage, [1936] 1992). We should perhaps not be surprised that Carlos Bulosan's "lost noir novel"—*All the Conspirators* (Seattle: University of Washington Press, 2005)—is set in the late 1940s and features a Filipino houseboy as the noir protagonist.

69. Before he starred in sixteen films as Charlie Chan, he played the evil Fu Manchu four times.

70. Chandler, *The Big Sleep*, 29. The novel is replete with Oriental objects and décor that stand in for the implied lewd acts of the decadent pornographer Geiger. He is found dead in his studio, which we know is a place where horribly profane things are done, because it is covered with Chinese and Japanese art and screens. He himself is found "wearing Chinese slippers [and] a Chinese embroidered coat" (35) when discovered dead. Earlier in the novel, when the hardboiled detective Philip Marlowe asks the clerk at the rival bookstore across the street to give him a description of Mr. Geiger, she compares him to Charlie Chan. The comparison between Charlie Chan and Geiger is an ominous one, given that Geiger meets a violent death for his nonnormative desires. In Hawke's film version of *The Big Sleep* (1946), the director changes the way the Oriental theme in the scene is represented—femme fatale Carmen Sternwood wears a Chinese dress and is too drugged to prevent Geiger from taking pornographic pictures of her.

71. Huang, *Charlie Chan*, xvi.

72. Jessica Hagedorn, ed., *Charlie Chan Is Dead: An Anthology of Contemporary Asian American Fiction* (New York: Penguin, 1993).

73. Hirahara, *Summer of the Big Bachi*, 1.

74. Hirahara, *Summer of the Big Bachi*, 49.

75. This willingness to talk about cancer stands in contrast to the silence around the atomic bomb. Haruo encourages Mas to participate in medical studies and get free medical care. Then he tells Mas about people asking about the obvious damage to his face: "'I used to say, 'bomb, World War Two.' Then the people got real quiet; didn't wanna talk no more. Then I start changin' my story. 'Car crash.' Wife got mad. Fire. People start noddin' their head, tellin' me about same kind of accident their brother, sister, in-law was in.' Mas didn't know how Haruo was going to help anybody by giving his body to science. But there was no use asking more questions"; Hirahara, *Summer of the Big Bachi*, 132. Thus the atomic bomb represents the silencing power of the will to know, the will Mas is able to evade through his steadfast refusal to speak.

76. Hirahara, *Summer of the Big Bachi*, 163.

77. Hirahara, *Summer of the Big Bachi*, 7, 12.

78. Hirahara, *Summer of the Big Bachi*, 57.

79. Hirahara, *Summer of the Big Bachi*, 21.

80. Cho, "Diaspora of Camptown: The Forgotten War's Monstrous Family," *Women's Studies Quarterly* 34, no. 1/2 (2006): 310.

81. Cho, *Haunting the Korean Diaspora*, 58.

82. Ann S. Anagnost, "Strange Circulations," in *Beyond Biopolitics: Essays on the Governance of Life and Death*, ed. Patricia Ticineto Clough and Craig Willse (Durham, NC: Duke University Press, 2011), 223. Mas practices a kind of eugenics and creation of machines, not on himself but on cars: "He had replaced the engine with a Honda—the best—and every valve and spark plug was new and in top conditions"; Hirahara, *Summer of the Big Bachi*, 22.

83. Cho, *Haunting the Korean Diaspora*, 88.

84. Cho, *Haunting the Korean Diaspora*, 88.

85. Cho, *Haunting the Korean Diaspora*, 88.

86. The novel is likely referring to the growing movement by Korean forced laborers for back pay that gained some traction in the 1990s.

87. Chungmoo Choi, "The Politics of War Memories toward Healing," in *Perilous Memories: The Asia-Pacific War(s)*, ed. T. Fujitani, Geoffrey M. White, and Lisa Yoneyama (Durham, NC: Duke University Press 2001), 404.

88. Cho, *Haunting the Korean Diaspora*, 82.

89. Among other specific provisions, the rules governing reparations for Korean comfort women and forced laborers have been guided by shifting definitions set by the United Nations General Assembly. See UN General Assembly, Resolution 60/147, "Basic Principles and Guidelines of the Right to a Remedy and Reparation for Victims of Gross Violations of International Human Rights Law and Serious Violation of International Humanitarian Law," December 16, 2005, http://www.ohchr.org/EN/ProfessionalInterest/Pages/RemedyAndReparation.aspx.

90. For a critique of the liberal humanist models for reconciliation, like Truth and

Reconciliation emerging out of South Africa see Catherine Cole, *Performing South Africa's Truth and Reconciliation Commission: Stages of Transition* (Bloomington: Indiana University Press, 2009).

91. Brown, *States of Injury*.

FOUR. Destined for Death

1. Teresa Ralli and José Watanabe, *Antígona*, Performance, 2000. This is one of numerous performances and renditions of Antigone across the transpacific. See also *Antígona Vélez* (1951), by Leopoldo Marechal (Argentina); *La pasión según Antígona Pérez* (1968), by Luis Rafael Sánchez (Puerto Rico); *Antígona furiosa* (1986), by Griselda Gambaro (Argentina); *Antígona González* (2012), by Sara Uribe (Mexico); and *Antígona* (2000), by José Watanabe and Yuyachkani (Peru). See also Han Kang, *Human Acts: A Novel* (New York: Hogarth, 2016).

2. In addition to my extensive discussion on the Pacific Rim in the introduction, for more on the production of the Pacific Rim imaginary, see Rob Wilson and Arif Dirlik, eds., *Asia/Pacific as Space of Cultural Production* (Durham, NC: Duke University Press, 1995).

3. Diana Taylor, *Disappearing Acts: Spectacles of Gender and Nationalism in Argentina's "Dirty War"* (Durham, NC: Duke University Press, 1997), 123.

4. When Michael Brown was killed by the police in Ferguson, MO, on August 9, 2014, his uncovered body, left in the middle of the street for everyone in his community to see, sent an explicit message: "This could happen to you, anytime." The Family of Michael Brown, HandsUpUnited, Organization for Black Struggle (OBS), and Missourians Organizing for Reform and Empowerment (MORE), "Written Statement on the Police Shooting of Michael Brown and Ensuing Police Violence against Protesters in Ferguson, Missouri" (53rd Session of the United Nations Committee Against Torture, Geneva, 2014).

5. She is citing Alberto Moreiras, from *The Exhaustion of Difference* (Durham, NC: Duke University Press, 2001), 33. This quote is taken from Junyoung Kim's article "Asia-Latin America as Method: The Global South Project and the Dislocation of the West," *Verge: Global Asias* issue "Between Asia and Latin America: New Transpacific Perspectives," 3, no. 2 (fall 2017): 100.

6. For a discussion of the growth of a transpacific culture since the 1990s, see Naoki Sakai and Hyon Joo Yoo, eds., *The Trans-Pacific Imagination: Rethinking Boundary, Culture, and Society* (Singapore: World Scientific, 2012).

7. Evelyn Hu DeHart, "A&Q: Why Asia and Latin America?," *Verge: Global Asias* issue "Between Asia and Latin America," 10.

8. Kim, "Asia-Latin America as Method," 99. She is drawing on Rey Chow's insights.

9. Chris Connery characterizes the Pacific Rim's particular symbolic relationship to the U.S. in these terms: "Cold War is a bad story that drags on, and Pacific Rim is a deliverance; 1980s under Reagan was a high-powered domestic military economy, late Cold War's anti-teleology required a new spatial mythology for U.S. interna-

tional capital.... Appeals to national concerns, as in the rhetoric of the New Deal or the Great Society, were replaced by an extra-national trust in the market.... The United States could signify itself as a nation only militarily, hence the 'evil empire' and adventurism in Grenada, Lebanon, Panama, et cetera. The lack of a comprehensible fit, however, between militarism and any articulable global politics or economics, rendered this signification system unworkable at the level of mythology. Hence the turn to the Pacific Rim, and the psychic significance of Japan and the idea of the Pacific as a site of rejuvenation for America." With the rising dominance of the Pacific Rim idea, California and Los Angeles in particular play central roles in narratives about the rejuvenation and degeneration of the United States at the end of the century. Christopher L. Connery, "Pacific Rim Discourse: The U.S. Global Imaginary in the Late Cold War Years," *boundary 2* 21, no. 1 (1994): 32.

10. In addition to the 2017 *Verge: Global Asias* special issue *Between Asia and Latin America: New Transpacific Perspectives*, this broader scholarship in the 1990s and 2000s is indicative of the growing interest and a coherency in the growing study comparing these areas. See Lane Ryo Hirabayashi and Evelyn Hu-DeHart, guest eds. special issue, *Amerasia Journal* special issue: *Asians in the Americas: Transculturations and Power*, 28, no. 2 (2002); Hu-DeHart, "Huagong and Huashang: The Chinese as Laborers and Merchants in Latin America and the Caribbean," *Amerasia Journal* 28, no. 2 (2002): 63–91; Zelideth María Rivas and Debbie Lee-DiStefano, eds., *Imagining Asia in the Americas* (New Brunswick, NJ: Rutgers University Press, 2016); Lok C. D. Siu, *Memories of a Future Home: Diasporic Citizenship of Chinese in Panama* (Stanford, CA: Stanford University Press, 2005); Ignacio López-Calvo, *The Affinity of the Eye: Writing Nikkei in Peru* (Tucson: University of Arizona Press, 2013); and López-Calvo, *Dragons in the Land of the Condor: Writing Tusán in Peru* (Tucson: University of Arizona Press, 2014).

11. This is an account confirmed by unnamed government sources and from the hostages themselves, found in interviews and other accounts, who state that some captors were killed after they had surrendered.

12. Jennifer Egan, "The Liberation of Lori Berenson," *New York Times*, March 2, 2011, accessed March 2, 2011, http://www.nytimes.com/2011/03/06/magazine/06berenson-t.html?_r=1; Ann Patchett, *Bel Canto* (New York: Harper Collins, 2001).

13. David Palumbo-Liu, *The Deliverance of Others: Reading Literature in a Global Age* (Durham, NC: Duke University Press, 2012), 2.

14. See Martha Nussbaum, *Cultivating Humanity: A Classical Defense of Reform in Liberal Education* (Cambridge: Cambridge University Press, 1997); Nussbaum, *Not for Profit: Why Democracy Needs the Humanities* (Princeton NJ: Princeton University Press, 2010).

15. Palumbo-Liu, *Deliverance of Others*. For their theorization of the time-space continuum and its cultural dominant pastiche, see Pierre Bourdieu, *Acts of Resistance: Against the New Myths of Our Time*, trans. Richard Nice (Cambridge: Polity, 1998); David Harvey, *A Brief History of Neoliberalism* (Oxford: Oxford University Press, 2007); Fredric Jameson, *The Political Unconscious: Narrative as a Socially Symbolic Act* (Ithaca, NY: Cornell University Press, 1981).

16. This imperial common sense comes into meaning within a U.S. cultural, political, and economic context defined by what some scholars see as First World professional women's emergence as key players in neoliberal cultural politics and leads attempts to create structures that manage a global "sisterhood." For example, see Lauren Berlant, *The Female Complaint: The Unfinished Business of Sentimentality in American Culture* (Durham, NC: Duke University Press, 2008); Lisa Duggan, *The Twilight of Equality? Neoliberalism, Cultural Politics, and the Attack on Democracy* (Boston: Beacon Press, 2004); Julietta Hua, *Trafficking Women's Human Rights* (Minneapolis: University of Minnesota Press, 2011).

17. See Michael Taussig, "Culture of Terror, Space of Death: Roger Casement's Putumayo Report and the Explanation of Torture," *Comparative Studies in Society and History* 26, no. 3 (1984): 467–97; and Avery F. Gordon, *Ghostly Matters: Haunting and the Sociological Imagination*, 2nd ed. (Minneapolis: University of Minnesota Press, 2008).

18. Gordon, *Ghostly Matters*, 78.

19. Lieutenant General Jorge Rafael Videla, quoted in M. Florencia Nelli, "Identity, Dignity and Memory: Performing/Re-Writing *Antigone* in Post-1976 Argentina," *New Voices in Classical Reception Studies* 4 (2009): 70.

20. For more on reconciliation, see Kimberly Theidon, "Justice in Transition: The Micropolitics of Reconciliation in Postwar Peru," *Journal of Conflict Resolution* 50, no. 3, *Transitional Justice* (2006): 433–57. People I spoke with in Lima remember the 1980s and 1990s mainly in terms of how the war disrupted their lives. One young man recounts how his birthday stood out because it was a day when they had electricity in their house and they had to turn it off so he could blow out his candle. Electrical outages were common as insurgents targeted local power stations and other utilities to disrupt everyday life and the operations of the state and capital, with the ultimate goal of capturing the state.

21. Orin Starn, Carlos Iván Degregori, and Robin Kirk, eds., *The Peru Reader: History, Culture, Politics*, 2nd ed. (Durham, NC: Duke University Press, 2005), 319.

22. Mayer, "Peru in Deep Trouble."

23. Mayer, "Peru in Deep Trouble." See also Orin Starn, "Maoism in the Andes: The Communist Party of Peru—Shining Path and the Refusal of History," *Journal of Latin American Studies* 27, no. 2 (1995): 399–421.

24. Sendero Luminoso is described as being driven by a fierce sense of destiny, the belief that "laws of historical materialism" meant history was on their side and that a bloody insurgency was necessary in order to cleanse society of capitalism and its agents. MRTA was smaller and less militant, with a different understanding of Marxist-Maoist ideology than Maoist Sendero Luminoso. For most Limeños, however, the difference was unimportant, and they saw Sendero Luminoso and MRTA as a part of the same menace.

25. Duggan, *Twilight of Equality?*, ix.

26. C. Harvey Gardiner, *Pawns in a Triangle of Hate: The Peruvian Japanese and the United States* (Seattle: University of Washington Press, 1981).

27. For more on the racialization of Fujimori, see Nobuko Adachi, "Racial Jour-

neys: Justice, Internment and Japanese-Peruvians in Peru, the United States, and Japan," *Asia-Pacific Journal: Japan Focus* 5, no. 9 (2007); Eduardo González-Cueva, "Race and Political Representation in the Peruvian Public Sphere," presentation, Latin American Studies Association Conference, Chicago, September 1998, accessed March 19, 2008, http://lasa.international.pitt.edu/LASA98/Gonzalez-Cueva.pdf.

28. See Mayer, *Ugly Stories of the Peruvian Agrarian Reform* (Durham, NC: Duke University Press, 2009).

29. He had fled under cover of night amid growing demands that he resign and be charged with human rights violations, including murder and torture.

30. For more on Fujimori's controversial reign as president, see Moises Arce and Julio Carrion, "Presidential Support in a Context of Crisis and Recovery in Peru, 1985–2008," *Journal of Politics in Latin America* 2, no. 1 (2010): 31–51; Starn, Degregori, and Kirk, *Peru Reader*; Ellen Perry, dir., *The Fall of Fujimori* (Burbank, CA: Cinema Libre, 2004), DVD.

31. Despite Fujimori being found guilty of most of the charges of human rights abuses against him, his daughter Keiko Fujimori, who served as his first lady and whose politics is in line with his, is an immensely popular politician, almost winning the 2016 presidential elections. For more on his psychology and his relationship with his daughter, see Ellen Perry, dir. *The Fall of Fujimori* (PBS Films, 2005).

32. Robert J. Art and Louise Richardson, *Democracy and Counterterrorism Lessons from the Past* (Washington, DC: United States Institute of Peace Press, 2007), 208.

33. Jo-Marie Burt, "Guilty as Charged: The Trial of Former Peruvian President Alberto Fujimori for Human Rights Violations," *International Journal of Transitional Justice* 3, no. 3 (2009): 384–405.

34. Carlos Iván Degregori, "Peru: Challenges for the 21st Century, Summary and Synthesis," in *Peru: Challenges for the 21st Century*, ed. Inter-American Dialogue (Washington, DC: Inter-American Dialogue, 1997), 3, accessed November 2, 2016, http://archive.thedialogue.org/PublicationFiles/Peru%20Challenges%20for%20the%2021st%20Century.pdf.

35. For more on how Fujimori played up his Japanese ancestry even as he proclaimed himself to be the native son of Peru, see Eduardo González-Cueva, "Race and Political Representation in the Peruvian Public Sphere," Presentation for the *Latin American Studies Association Conference*, Chicago, September 1998; accessed March 19, 2008, http://lasa.international.pitt.edu/LASA98/Gonzalez-Cueva.pdf.

36. He made this case successfully against his main presidential opponent Mario Vargas Llosa, the Nobel Prize–winning novelist, who Fujimori represented as a European-identified elite out of touch with new economic realities across the transpacific.

37. Degregori, "Peru," 6, emphasis added. Fujimori is not a first-generation migrant, since he was born in Peru. But this kind of racial slipperiness frequently framed Fujimori and was seen as an advantage (and if Fujimori was actually born in Japan but wanted to become president, this was another instance of Fujimori defining his own rules). Known as "el chino" despite widespread knowledge of his

Japanese ancestry, he ran a campaign under the slogan "A President Like You"—a seemingly audacious claim in a country where Japanese Peruvians had limited visibility and political voice—and captured a majority of the popular vote; his presidency would rock the establishment and the old guard. The demands by MRTA that targeted Japan's relationship to Peru raised the specters of racism against Japanese Peruvians and highlighted the precarious nature of Japanese Peruvians' claims to essential Peruvian identity. As with the United States, Brazil, and Argentina, Peru has a twentieth-century history of Japanese immigration. Much like in other countries in the Americas, they were seen as inassimilable to the national whole, even when the nation was imagined as a *mestizo* and Creole body, as in Peru and Brazil. Thus, while MRTA made many demands, the targeting of the Japanese ambassador's home and the association of neoliberal economic reform to Japanese intervention in Peru caused concern for Japanese Peruvians. They feared the rise of anti-Japanese sentiment and the revitalization of racialization of Japanese Peruvians as forever foreigners and a mouthpiece for First and Second World interests.

38. Truth and Reconciliation Commission, Communications and Public Impact Office, "Press Release 226: TRC Final Report Was Made Public on August 28th, 2003 at Noon," August 28, 2003, accessed June 3, 2009, http://www.cverdad.org.pe/.

39. Enrique Mayer, "Peru in Deep Trouble: Mario Vargas Llosa's 'Inquest in the Andes' Reexamined," *Cultural Anthropology* 6, no. 4 (1991): 475.

40. This last number is particularly shocking, given that the same group counted for only 16 percent of Peru's total population. The TRC made five recommendations: (1) reconciliation and justice (which includes putting the perpetrators on trial); (2) national plan for Forensic Anthropological Interventions to find the bodies of more than 7,000 who "disappeared"; (3) reparations, which include symbolic, health, education, restoration of citizen status, and financial reparations; (4) Institutional reform; and (5) follow-up on the work of the committee. Amnesty International, "Peru: The Truth and Reconciliation Commission—A First Step towards a Country without Injustice," accessed August 10, 2011, http://www.amnesty.org/en/library/asset/AMR46/003/2004/en/4d8e52b4-d5e6-11ddbb24-1fb85fe8fa05/amr460032004en.html.

41. Jodi A. Byrd, *The Transit of Empire: Indigenous Critiques of Colonialism* (Minneapolis: University of Minnesota Press, 2012), xviii.

42. Egan, "Liberation of Lori Berenson."

43. Egan, "Liberation of Lori Berenson."

44. Egan, "Liberation of Lori Berenson."

45. Egan, "Liberation of Lori Berenson."

46. Egan, "Liberation of Lori Berenson."

47. Mary Louise Pratt, *Imperial Eyes: Travel Writing and Transculturation*, 2nd ed. (New York: Routledge, 2007), 7.

48. Through these public protests, the women "transformed themselves from 'traditional' women defined by their relationships with men (mothers, wives, daughters) into public protesters working on behalf of the whole society." Rita Arditti, *Search-*

ing for Life: The Grandmothers of the Plaza de Mayo and the Disappeared Children of Argentina (Berkeley: University of California Press, 1999), 97.

49. See Taussig, "Culture of Terror," 467–97.

50. Gordon, *Ghostly Matters*, 113; original emphasis.

51. In this way, "*Aparicion con vida*" mirrors Frantz Fanon's emphasis on the "rottenness of man, of his dreadful failure" against which even the dead are exhorted to speak; Fanon, *Toward the African Revolution: Political Essays*, trans. Haakon Chevalier (New York: Grove Press, [1964] 1994), 49.

52. Gordon, *Ghostly Matters*, 63.

53. Gordon, *Ghostly Matters*, 113.

54. Egan, "Liberation of Lori Berenson."

55. "An Interview with Ann Patchett," *bookbrowse.com*, accessed March 15, 2012, https://www.bookbrowse.com/author_interviews/full/index.cfm/author_number/645/ann-patchett.

56. "Interview with Ann Patchett."

57. As with Pratt's formulation of "anti-conquest narratives," Caren Kaplan argues that travel narratives, a genre to which *Bel Canto* is clearly drawing from, is a fecund site of imperialist desires and longing. *Questions of Travel: Postmodern Discourses of Displacement* (Durham, NC: Duke University Press, 2000).

58. Patchett, *Bel Canto*, jacket copy.

59. Patchett, *Bel Canto*, 13.

60. "Interview with Ann Patchett."

61. Doris Sommer, *Foundational Fictions: The National Romances of Latin America* (Berkeley: University of California Press, 1993).

62. The book won the PEN/Faulkner Award (2002), the Orange Prize for Fiction (2002), and the Book Sense Book of the Year (2003). It was a finalist for the National Book Critics Circle Award (2001) and was adapted by the Chicago Lyric Opera (2015).

63. Dylan Rodríguez, *Suspended Apocalypse: White Supremacy, Genocide, and the Filipino Condition* (Minneapolis: University of Minnesota Press, 2010), 36.

64. See Walter D. Mignolo, "Globalization, Civilization Processes, and the Relocation of Languages and Cultures," in *The Cultures of Globalization*, ed. Fredric Jameson and Masao Miyoshi (Durham, NC: Duke University Press, 1998), 32–53; David Harvey, *The Urbanization of Capital: Studies in the History and Theory of Capitalist Urbanization* (Baltimore: John Hopkins University Press, 1985).

65. Walter D. Mignolo further historicizes the Western production of any country in Latin America as a nameless "third world" in *The Idea of Latin America* (London: Blackwell, 2005).

66. Rodríguez, *Suspended Apocalypse*, 31.

67. Rodríguez, *Suspended Apocalypse*, 31.

68. Rodríguez, *Suspended Apocalypse*, 31.

69. Duggan, *Twilight of Equality?*, xii.

70. Ernesto Laclau, "Politics and the Limits of Modernity," in *Universal Abandon?*

The Politics of Postmodernism, ed. Andrew Ross (Minneapolis: University of Minnesota, 1988), 80.

71. Rachel Lee, "Notes from the (non)Field: Teaching and Theorizing Women of Color," *Meridians* 91, no. 1 (2000): 91.

72. This exemplifies how the event was seen globally and by many publics. Teresa Ralli, "Fragments of Memory," in *Holy Terrors: Latin American Women Perform*, trans. Margaret Carson, ed. Diana Taylor and Roselyn Costantino (Durham, NC: Duke University Press, 2003), 353.

73. Ralli, "Fragments of Memory," 360.

74. Ralli, "Fragments of Memory," 361.

75. Ralli, "Fragments of Memory," 360.

76. For more on the reconciliation aspect of the play, see Jill Lane, "*Antígona* and the Modernity of the Dead," *Modern Drama* 50, no. 4 (2007): 517–31; Nelli, "Identity, Dignity and Memory"; Francine M. A'ness, "Resisting Amnesia: Yuyachkani, Performance, and the Postwar Reconstruction of Peru," *Theatre Journal* 56, no. 3 (2004): 395–414; Taylor, *Disappearing Acts*.

77. See Michelle Har Kim, "José Watanabe—Part 1," *Asian American Literary Review*, March 6, 2011, accessed January 10, 2105, http://www.discovernikkei.org/en/journal/2011/3/6/jose-watanabe/.

78. Even Ralli's description of having seen the girl at the window disappeared by Fujimori inspiring her to look for Antígonas also participates in the act of testifying and not being a bystander.

79. A'ness, "Resisting Amnesia," 405.

80. Teresa Ralli, "Excerpts from *Antígona*," in *Holy Terrors: Latin American Women Perform*, trans. Margaret Carson, ed. Diana Taylor and Roselyn Costantino (Durham, NC: Duke University Press, 2003), 368.

81. Ralli, "Excerpts from *Antígona*," 369.

82. Ralli, "Excerpts from *Antígona*," 369–70.

83. Ralli, "Excerpts from *Antígona*," 367.

84. Judith Butler, *Antigone's Claim: Kinship between Life and Death* (New York: Columbia University Press, 2000), 24.

85. Butler, *Antigone's Claim*, 23.

86. A'ness, "Resisting Amnesia," 405.

87. Setsu Shigematsu and Keith L. Camacho, eds., *Militarized Currents: Towards a Decolonized Future in Asia and the Pacific* (Minneapolis: University of Minnesota Press, 2010), xxxiii.

88. Kyoung H. Park, *Mina*, in *Seven Contemporary Plays from the Korean Diaspora in the Americas*, ed. Esther Kim Lee (Durham, NC: Duke University Press, 2012), 321.

89. While Fujimori was often fondly called "el chino," Koreans were often misidentified as Japanese in Peru and as ethnic latecomers. The fact that Koreans are mistaken for their former colonizers means this colonial history is important knowledge for immigrants forging new identities. While there is an established scholarship about Japanese Peruvians, *Mina* is the only fictional work in English I know of which

centers a Korean Peruvian perspective. The *Asian Journal of Latin American Studies* is promising for the multilingual interdisciplinary scholarship on the links between Asia and Latin America: http://www.ajlas.org/ee the Latin American Studies Association of Korea.

90. Vijay Prashad, *The Darker Nations: A People's History of the Third World* (New York: New Press, 2007). See particularly his discussion of the historic Bandung Third World Conference in Indonesia in 1955.

EPILOGUE. Watery Graves

1. The U.S.–Japan Security Treaty of 1961 (signed at the same time as the San Francisco Peace Treaty), for example, where Japan gives up the right to wage war, then requires the U.S. to militarily act to "secure" the region. This treaty allowed the U.S. military to claim Okinawa from Japan as a matter of military security. George R. Packard, "The United States–Japan Security Treaty at 50," *Foreign Affairs*, March/April 2010 Issue, https://www.foreignaffairs.com/articles/japan/2010-03-01/united-states-japan-security-treaty-50.

2. Shigematsu and Camacho, in their introduction, criticize how President Barack Obama in 2010 authorized the move of 8,000–55,000 American military personal and hardware from Okinawa to Guam; *Militarized Currents*, xxiii. Also on the transnational dimensions of Okinawan antimilitary base politics, see Annamaria Shimabuku, "Transpacific Colonialism: An Intimate View of Transnational Activism in Okinawa." *CR: New Centennial Review* 12, no 1 (2012): 131–58.

3. See, for example, the statement from the Korean hibakusha written in "South Korean Hibakusha Urge Obama to Apologize in Hiroshima," *JapanTimes*, https://www.japantimes.co.jp/news/2016/05/20/national/history/south-korean-hibakusha-urge-obama-apologize-hiroshima/#.WlkKZVQ-feQ.

4. Many of the Korean hibakusha had worked for Mitsubishi's munitions plant in Hiroshima. Mitsubishi did offer an apology to U.S. WWII vets for forced labor, but has not made any moves to apologize to Koreans who were forcibly conscripted, including hibakusha. Sam Sanders, "Mitsubishi Apologies to U.S. WWII Veterans for Forced Labor," NPR Morning Edition, July, 20, 2015. https://www.npr.org/2015/07/20/424571375/mitsubishi-apologizes-to-u-s-world-war-ii-veterans-for-forced-labor.

5. Grace M. Cho, *Haunting the Korean Diaspora*, 59, quoting David Eng, from *Racial Castration: Managing Masculinity in America* (Durham, NC: Duke University Press 2001), 37.

6. Cho, *Haunting the Korean Diaspora*, 53, quoting Jill Bennett, *Emphatic Vision: Affect, Trauma, and Contemporary Art* (Stanford, CA: Stanford University Press, 2005).

7. See Nan Kim, "Korea on the Brink: Reading the Yŏnp'yŏng Shelling and Its Aftermath," *Journal of Asian Studies* 70, no. 2 (2011): 337–56.

8. Originally published in Japan as Fukagawa Munetoshi, *Umi ni kieta ni hibaku Chyousenjin chouyoukou—Chinkon no kaikyou* (Tokyo: Akashi Shoten, 1974); trans-

lations of the title vary. See David Palmer, "The Straits of Dead Souls: One Man's Investigation into the Disappearance of Mitsubishi Hiroshima's Korean Forced Labourers," *Journal of Japanese Studies* 26, no. 3 (2006): 335–51; Toyonaga Keisaburo, "Colonial and Atomic Bombs: About Survivors of Hiroshima Living in Korea," in *Perilous Memories: The Asia-Pacific War(s)*, ed. T. Fujitani, Geoffrey M. White, and Lisa Yoneyama (Durham, NC: Duke University Press, 2001), 378–94. Fukagawa is a celebrated Japanese hibakusha artist who has written poetry and music that explore hibakusha subjectivity and experiences. His crusade is widely known, and his personal transformation and devotion to the Korean hibakushas have made him an important figure within anticolonial Korean groups as well as in the atomic redress and disarmament movements.

9. They also criticized how right-wing state colluded with neoliberal capitalism to allow the dangerously unfit boat to set sail, which helped lead to the resignation and arrest of President Park Geun Hye, the daughter of the assassinated right-wing military president Park Chung Hee. In 2016 she was impeached and arrested for corruption and in 2016 she was sentenced to 24 years in prison. See Choe Sang-Hui's April 6, 2018, *New York Times* article on what she is charged with, "Park Geun-hye, South Korea's Ousted President, Gets 24 Years in Prison," https://www.nytimes.com/2018/04/06/world/asia/park-geun-hye-south-korea.html.

10. For more on Korean hibakusha and their legal battles, see David Palmer, "Korean Hibakusha, Japan's Supreme Court and the International Community: Can the U.S. and Japan Confront Forced Labor and Atomic Bombing?" *Asia-Pacific Journal: Japan Focus* 6, no. 2 (2008), accessed April 21, 2010, http://www.japanfocus.org/-David-Palmer/2670#sthash.KBykZbtN.dpuf.

11. See Min Hyoung Song, "Communities of Remembrance: Reflections on the Virginia Tech Shootings and Race," *Journal of Asian American Studies* 11, no. 1 (2008): 1–26.

· BIBLIOGRAPHY ·

Abelman, Nancy, and John Lie. *Blue Dreams: Korean Americans and the Los Angeles Riots*. Cambridge, MA: Harvard University Press, 1995.

Adachi, Nobuko. "Racial Journeys: Justice, Internment and Japanese-Peruvians in Peru, the United States, and Japan." *Asia-Pacific Journal: Japan Focus* 5, no. 9 (2007).

Adams, Rachel. *Continental Divides: Remapping the Cultures of North America*. Chicago: University of Chicago Press, 2010.

Agamben, Giorgio. *The Coming Community*. Translated by Michael Hardt. Minneapolis: University of Minnesota Press, 1993.

Agamben, Giorgio. "For a Theory of Destituent Power: Public Lecture in Athens, 16.11.2013." *Chronos*. Accessed December 12, 2015. http://www.chronosmag.eu/index.php/english.html.

Agamben, Giorgio. *Homer Sacer: Sovereign Power and Bare Life*. Translated by Daniel Heller-Roazen. Stanford, CA: Stanford University Press, 1998.

Agence France Press. "South Korea Ferry Victim's Father Ends 45-Day Hunger Strike." *Indian Express*. August 10, 2014. Accessed August 28, 2017. http://indianexpress.com/article/world/world-others/s-korea-ferry-victims-father-ends-45-day-hunger-strike/.

Ahmed, Sara. *The Promise of Happiness*. Durham, NC: Duke University Press, 2010.

Ahuja, Neel. *Bioinsecurities: Disease Interventions, Empire, and the Government of Species*. Durham, NC: Duke University Press, 2016.

Alexander, Elizabeth. "Can You Be BLACK and Look at This: Reading the Rodney King Video." In *Black Male: Representations of Masculinity in Contemporary American Art*, edited by Thelma Golden, 91–110. New York: Whitney Museum of Art, 1994.

Alexander, M. Jacqui. *Pedagogies of Crossing: Meditations on Feminism, Sexual Politics, Memory, and the Sacred*. Durham, NC: Duke University Press, 2005.

Amnesty International. "Peru: The Truth and Reconciliation Commission — A First Step towards a Country without Injustice." Accessed August 10, 2011. http://www.amnesty.org/en/library/asset/AMR46/003/2004/en/4d8e52b4-d5e6–11dd-bb24–1fb85fe8fa05/amr460032004en.html.

Anagnost, Ann S. "Strange Circulations." In *Beyond Biopolitics: Essays on the Governance of Life and Death*, edited by Patricia Ticineto Clough and Craig Willse, 213–37. Durham, NC: Duke University Press, 2011.

A'ness, Francine M. "Resisting Amnesia: Yuyachkani, Performance, and the Postwar Reconstruction of Peru." *Theatre Journal* 56, no. 3 (2004): 395–414.

Anzaldúa, Gloria E. *Borderlands/La Frontera: The New Mestiza*. San Francisco: Aunt Lute, 1987.

Appadurai, Arjun. "Disjuncture and Difference in the Global Cultural Economy." *Theory, Culture and Society* 7, no. 2 (1990): 295–310.

Appy, Christian G., ed. *Cold War Constructions: The Political Culture of United States Imperialism, 1945–1966*. Amherst: University of Massachusetts Press, 2000.

Arce, Moises, and Julio Carrion. "Presidential Support in a Context of Crisis and Recovery in Peru, 1985–2008." *Journal of Politics in Latin America* 2, no. 1 (2010): 31–51.

Arditti, Rita. *Searching for Life: The Grandmothers of the Plaza de Mayo and the Disappeared Children of Argentina*. Berkeley: University of California Press, 1997.

Arendt, Hannah. *The Human Condition*. 2nd ed. Chicago: University of Chicago Press, 1998.

Art, Robert J., and Louise Richardson. *Democracy and Counterterrorism Lessons from the Past*. Washington, DC: United States Institute of Peace Press, 2007.

Atanasoski, Neda. *Humanitarian Violence: The U.S. Deployment of Diversity*. Minneapolis: University of Minnesota Press, 2013.

Athanasiou, Athena. "Technologies of Humanness, Aporias of Biopolitics, and the Cut Body of Humanity." *differences: A Journal of Feminist Cultural Studies* 14, no. 1 (2003): 125–62.

Avila, Eric. *Popular Culture in the Age of White Flight: Fear and Fantasy in Suburban Los Angeles*. Berkeley: University of California Press, 2004.

Ayaogi, Caroline. "Mystery Author Naomi Hirahara Looks to Her Community for Inspiration." *Pacific Citizen*, May 14, 2005. Accessed December 2, 2010. http://news.newamericamedia.org/news/view_article.html?article_id=10a413b89de62529a74ae951db03b9ee.

Bakhtin, Mikhail. "Discourse in the Novel." In *The Dialogic Imagination: Four Essays*, edited by Michael Holquist, translated by Caryl Emerson and Michael Holquist, 259–422. Austin: University of Texas Press, 1992.

Bakhtin, Mikhail. *Speech Genres and Other Late Essays*. Edited by Caryl Emerson and Michael Holquist. Translated by Vern W. McGee. Austin: University of Texas Press, 1986.

Bancel, Nicolas, Pascal Blanchard, and Sandrine Lemaire. "Torture in Algeria: Past Acts that Haunt France." *Le Monde diplomatique*, June 2001. http://mondediplo.com/2001/06/10torture.

Bartov, Omer. *Murder in Our Midst: The Holocaust, Industrial Killing, and Representation*. Oxford: Oxford University Press, 1996.

Bascara, Victor. "Cultural Politics of Redress: Reassessing the Meaning of the Civil

Liberties Act of 1988 after 9/11." *Asian American Law Journal* 10, no. 2 (2003): 185–214.
Bauman, Zygmut. "Times of Interregnum." *Ethics and Global Politics* 5, no. 1 (2012): 49–56.
Bazyler, Michael. "Japan Should Follow the International Trend and Face Its History of World War II Forced Labor." *Asia-Pacific Journal: Japan Focus* 7, no. 5.3 (2009). http://apjjf.org/-Michael-Bazyler/3030/article.html.
Bello, Walden. "Conclusion: From American Lake to A People's Pacific in the Twenty-First Century." In Shigematsu and Camacho, *Militarized Currents*, 309–21.
Bennett, Jill. *Emphatic Vision: Affect, Trauma, and Contemporary Art*. Stanford, CA: Stanford University Press, 2005.
Berlant, Lauren. *The Female Complaint: The Unfinished Business of Sentimentality in American Culture*. Durham, NC: Duke University Press, 2008.
Bevacqua, Michael. "The Exceptional Life and Death of a Chamorro Soldier: Tracing the Militarization of Desire in Guam, USA." In Shigematsu and Camacho, *Militarized Currents*, 33–62.
Beverley, John, Jose Oviedo, and Michael Aronna, eds. *The Postmodernism Debate in Latin America*. Durham, NC: Duke University Press, 1995.
Bhabha, Homi K. *The Location of Culture*. New York: Routledge, 1994.
Bhabha, Homi K. "Of Mimicry and Man: The Ambivalence of Colonial Discourse." In *The Location of Culture*, 121–31. New York: Routledge, 1994.
Bhabha, Homi K. "The Other Question: Stereotype, Discrimination, and the Discourse of Colonialism." *Screen* 24, no. 6 (1983): 18–36.
Biondi, Martha. "The Rise of the Reparations Movement." *Radical History Review* 2003, no. 87 (2003): 5–18.
Borde, Raymond, and Étienne Chaumeton. *A Panorama of American Film Noir (1941–1953)*. Translated by Paul Hammond. San Francisco: City Lights, 2002.
Borde, Raymond, and Étienne Chaumeton. "Towards a Definition of *Film Noir*." In *Film Noir Reader*, edited by Alain Silver and James Ursini, 17–25. Pompton Plains, NJ: Limelight, 1996.
Borstelmann, Thomas. *The Cold War and the Color Line: American Race Relations in the Global Arena*. Cambridge, MA: Harvard University Press, 2001.
Bourdieu, Pierre. *Acts of Resistance: Against the New Myths of Our Time*. Translated by Richard Nice. Cambridge: Polity, 1998.
Brinkley, Alan. *The Publisher: Henry Luce and His American Century*. New York: Knopf, 2010.
Briones, Matthew M. "Hardly 'Small Talk': Discussing Race in the Writing of Hisaye Yamamoto." *Prospects* 29 (2005): 435–72.
Brivot, Marion, and Yves Gendron. "Beyond Panopticism: On the Ramifications of Surveillance in a Contemporary Professional Setting." *Accounting, Organizations, and Society* 36, no. 3 (2011): 135–55.
Brown, Wendy. "Resisting Left Melancholia." In *Loss: The Politics of Mourning*,

edited by David Eng and David Kazanjian, 458–66. Berkeley: University of California Press, 2003.
Brown, Wendy. *States of Injury: Power and Freedom in Late Modernity*. Princeton, NJ: Princeton University Press, 1995.
Brown, Wendy. *Undoing the Demos: Neoliberalism's Stealth Revolution*. Cambridge, MA: MIT Press, 2015.
Buelens, Gert, Sam Durrant, and Robert Eaglestone, eds. *The Future of Trauma Theory: Contemporary Literary and Cultural Criticism*. New York: Routledge, 2014.
Bulosan, Carlos. *All the Conspirators*. Seattle: University of Washington Press, 2005.
Burnett, Christina Duffy. *Foreign in a Domestic Sense: Puerto Rico, American Expansion, and the Constitution*. Durham, NC: Duke University Press, 2001.
Burt, Jo-Marie. "Guilty as Charged: The Trial of Former Peruvian President Alberto Fujimori for Human Rights Violations." *International Journal of Transitional Justice* 3, no. 3 (2009): 384–405.
Butler, Judith. *Antigone's Claim: Kinship between Life and Death*. New York: Columbia University Press, 2000.
Butler, Judith. "Endangered/Endangering: Schematic Racism and White Paranoia." In *Reading Rodney King/Reading Urban Uprising*, edited by Robert Gooding-Williams, 15–22. New York: Routledge, 1993.
Butler, Judith. *Precarious Life: The Powers of Mourning and Violence*. New York: Verso, 2004.
Byrd, Jodi A. *The Transit of Empire: Indigenous Critiques of Colonialism*. Minneapolis: University of Minnesota Press, 2012.
Byrd, Jodi A., and Michael Rothberg. "Between Subaltern and Indigeneity: Critical Categories for Postcolonial Studies." *Interventions: International Journal of Postcolonial Studies* 31, no. 1 (2011): 1–12.
"California Counts." Public Policy Institute of California, 1995.
Cacho, Lisa Marie. *Social Death: Racialized Rightlessness and the Criminalization of the Unprotected*. New York: New York University Press, 2012.
Cain, James M. *Double Indemnity*. New York: Vintage, [1936] 1992.
Camacho, Keith L. *Cultures of Commemoration: The Politics of War, Memory, and History in the Mariana Islands*. Honolulu: University of Hawai'i Press, 2011.
Campomanes, Oscar V. "1898 and the Nature of the New Empire." *Radical History Review* 1999, no. 73 (1999): 130–46.
Canclini, Néstor García. *Hybrid Cultures: Strategies for Entering and Leaving Modernity*. Translated by Christopher Chiappari and Silvia López. Minneapolis: University of Minnesota Press, [1995] 2005.
"The Candidates Debate; Transcript of the Reagan–Mondale Debate on Foreign Policy." *nytimes.com*. October 22, 1984. Accessed September 4, 2017. http://www.nytimes.com/1984/10/22/us/the-candidates-debate-transcript-of-the-reagan-mondale-debate-on-foreign-policy.html?pagewanted=all.
Caprio, Mark, and Yoneyiku Sugita. *Democracy in Occupied Japan: The U.S. Occupation and Japanese Politics and Society*. New York: Routledge 2007.

Cavarero, Adriana. *Horrorism: Naming Contemporary Violence*. New York: Columbia University Press, 2008.
Chambers-Letson, Joshua Takano. *A Race So Different: Performance and Law in Asian America*. New York: New York University Press, 2013.
Chandler, Raymond. *The Big Sleep*. New York: Vintage, [1939] 1998.
Cheah, Pheng. "Crisis of Money." *positions: east asia cultures critique* 16, no. 1 (2008): 189–219.
Chen, Mel Y. *Animacies: Biopolitics, Racial Mattering, and Queer Affect*. Durham, NC: Duke University Press, 2012.
Cheng, Anne Anlin. *The Melancholy of Race: Assimilation, Psychoanalysis, and Hidden Grief*. Oxford: Oxford University Press, 2000.
Cherki, Alice. *Fanon: A Portrait*. Translated by Nadia Benabid. Ithaca, NY: Cornell University Press, 2006.
Ching, Leo T. S. *Becoming "Japanese": Colonial Taiwan and the Politics of Identity Formation*. Berkeley: University of California Press, 2001.
Cho, Grace M. "Diaspora of Camptown: The Forgotten War's Monstrous Family." *Women's Studies Quarterly* 34, no. 1/2 (2006): 310.
Cho, Grace M. *Haunting the Korean Diaspora: Shame, Secrecy, and the Forgotten War*. Minneapolis: University of Minnesota Press, 2008.
Choe Sang-Huh. "Park Geun-hye, South Korea's Ousted President, Gets 24 Years in Prison." *The New York Times*, April 4, 2018. Accessed May 17, 2018. https://www.nytimes.com/2018/04/06/world/asia/park-geun-hye-south korea.html.
Choi, Chungmoo. *Comfort Women: Colonialism, War, and Sex*. Durham, NC: Duke University Press, 1997.
Choi, Chungmoo. "The Discourse of Decolonization and Popular Memory: South Korea." *positions* 1, no. 1 (1993): 83.
Choi, Chungmoo. "The Politics of War: Memories toward Healing." In Fujitani, White, and Yoneyama, *Perilous Memories*, 395–410.
Chow, Rey. "The Age of the World Target." In *America's Wars in Asia: A Cultural Approach to History and Memory*, edited by Phillip West, Steven I. Levine, and Jackie Hilz, 205–20. New York: M. E. Sharpe, 1998.
Chuh, Kandice. *Imagine Otherwise: On Asian Americanist Critique*. Durham, NC: Duke University Press, 2003.
Citizens Committee for Resettlement. Thomas R. Bodine Papers. http://www.oac.cdlib.org/findaid/ark:/13030/tf6w100515/dsc/.
Clewell, Tammy. "Mourning Beyond Melancholia: Freud's Psychoanalysis of Loss." *Journal of the American Psychological Association* 52, no. 1 (2004): 43–67.
Clinton, Hillary. "America's Pacific Century." Op-Ed for *Foreign Policy*, October 11, 2011. Accessed January 28, 2012. http://www.foreignpolicy.com/articles/2011/10/11/americas_pacific_century.
Coates, Ta-Nehisi. "The Black Family in the Age of Mass Incarceration." *Atlantic* 316, no. 3 (2015): 60–84.
Coates, Ta-Nehisi. "The Case for Reparations." *Atlantic Magazine*, June 2014.

https://www.theatlantic.com/magazine/archive/2014/06/the-case-for-reparations/361631/.
Cole, Catherine. *Performing South Africa's Truth Commission: Stages of Transition.* Bloomington: Indiana University Press, 2009.
Commission for Historical Clarification. *Guatemala: Memory of Silence.* Guatemala City: Historical Clarification Commission, 1999.
Connery, Christopher L. "Pacific Rim Discourse: The U.S. Global Imaginary in the Late Cold War Years." *boundary 2* 21, no. 1 (1994): 30–56.
Copjec, Joan, ed. *Shades of Noir: A Reader.* New York: Verso, 1993.
Crooks, Robert. "From the Far Side of the Urban Frontier: The Detective Fictions of Chester Himes and Walter Mosley." *College Literature* 22, no. 3 (1995): 68–90.
Crow, Charles L., and Hisaye Yamamoto. "A *MELUS* Interview: Hisaye Yamamoto." *MELUS* 14, no. 1 (1987): 73–84.
Cumings, Bruce. "The American Century and the Third World." *Diplomatic History* 23, no. 2 (1999): 355–70.
Cumings, Bruce. *Korea's Place in the Sun: A Modern History.* Updated edition. New York: W. W. Norton, 2005.
Cumings, Bruce. *The Origins of the Korean War.* Princeton, NJ: Princeton University Press, 1990.
Cumings, Bruce. *Parallax Vision: Making Sense of American–East Asian Relations at the End of the Century.* Durham, NC: Duke University Press, 2002.
Da Silva, Denise Ferreira. "Globality." *Journal of Critical Ethnic Studies* 1, no. 1 (2015): 33–38.
Da Silva, Denise Ferreira. *Toward a Global Idea of Race.* Minneapolis: University of Minnesota Press, 2007.
Daniels, Roger. "Words Do Matter: A Note on Inappropriate Terminology and the Incarceration of the Japanese Americans." In *Nikkei in the Pacific Northwest: Japanese Americans and Japanese Canadians in the Twentieth Century*, edited by Louis Fiset and Gail Nomura, 183–207. Seattle: University of Washington Press, 2005.
Davis, Mike. *City of Quartz: Excavating the Future in Los Angeles.* New York: Verso, 1990.
Day, Iyko. *Alien Capital: Asian Racialization and the Logic of Settler Colonial Capitalism.* Durham, NC: Duke University Press, 2016.
Degregori, Carlos Iván. "Peru: Challenges for the 21st Century, Summary and Synthesis." In *Peru: Challenges for the 21st Century*, edited by Inter-American Dialogue (Washington, DC: Inter-American Dialogue, 1997), 3–8. Accessed November 2, 2016. http://archive.thedialogue.org/PublicationFiles/Peru%20Challenges%20for%20the%2021st%20Century.pdf.
Desser, David. "Global Noir: Genre Film in the Age of Transnationalism." In *Film Genre Reader IV*, edited by Barry Keith Grant, 628–48. Austin: University of Texas Press, 2012.
Diawara, Manthia, ed., *Black American Cinema.* New York: Routledge, 1993.
Diawara, Manthia. "Noir by Noirs: Towards a New Realism in Black Cinema." In *Shades of Noir*, edited by Joan Copjec, 261–78. New York: Verso, 1993.

Diawara, Manthia. "Toward a Regional Imaginary in Africa." In *The Cultures of Globalization*, edited by Fredric Jameson and Masao Miyoshi, 103–24. Durham, NC: Duke University Press, 1998.

Dirlik, Arif. "Asia Pacific Studies in an Age of Global Modernity." *Inter-Asia Cultural Studies* 6, no. 2 (2005): 158–70.

Dirlik, Arif. "The Postcolonial Aura: Third World Criticism in the Age of Global Capitalism." *Critical Inquiry* 20, no. 2 (1994): 328–35.

Dower, John. *War without Mercy: Race and Power in the Pacific War*. New York: Pantheon, 1987.

Doyle, Kate, and Peter Kornbluh, eds. "CIA and Assassinations: The Guatemala 1954 Documents." *The National Security Archive Electronic Briefing Book No. 4*. Washington, DC: National Security Archive, n.d. http://nsarchive.gwu.edu/NSAEBB/NSAEBB4/index.html.

Drinnon, Richard. *Facing West: The Metaphysics of Indian-Hating and Empire-Building*. Norman: University of Oklahoma Press, 1997.

Duggan, Lisa. *The Twilight of Equality? Neoliberalism, Cultural Politics, and the Attack on Democracy*. Boston: Beacon Press, 2004.

Dyer, Richard. "The Colour of Virtue: Lillian Gish, Whiteness, and Femininity." In *Women and Film: A Sight and Sound Reader*, edited by Pam Cook and Phillip Dodd, 1–9. Philadelphia: Temple University Press, 1993.

Dyer, Richard. "Resistance through Charisma: Rita Hayworth and Gilda." In *Women in Film Noir*, edited by E. Ann Kaplan, 91–99. Revised and expanded edition. London: British Film Institute, 2008.

Editorial Board. "Congress has itself to blame for the 9/11 Bill." *The New York Times*, September, 30, 2016. Accessed January 15, 2017. https://www.nytimes.com/2016/10/01/opinion/congress-has-itself-to-blame-for-9-11-bill.html.

Egan, Jennifer. "The Liberation of Lori Berenson." *New York Times*, March 2, 2011. Accessed on March 2, 2011. http://www.nytimes.com/2011/03/06/magazine/06berenson-t.html?_r=1.

Eng, David L. *The Feeling of Kinship: Queer Liberalism and the Racialization of Intimacy*. Durham, NC: Duke University Press, 2010.

Eng, David L. *Racial Castration: Managing Masculinity in Asian America*. Durham, NC: Duke University Press, 2001.

Eng, David L., and Alice Y. Hom, eds. *Q and A: Queer in Asian America*. Philadelphia: Temple University Press, 1998.

Eng, David L., and David Kazanjian, eds. *Loss: The Politics of Mourning*. Berkeley: University of California Press, 2003.

Eng, David, and Shinhee Han. "A Dialogue on Racial Melancholia." *Psychoanalytic Dialogues* 10, no. 4 (2000): 667–700.

Esau, Erika. *Images of the Pacific Rim, Australia and California 1850–1935*. Sydney, Australia: Power, 2010.

Espiritu, Yen Le. *Body Counts: Vietnamese War and Militarized Refugees*. Oakland: University of California Press, 2016.

The Family of Michael Brown, HandsUpUnited, Organization for Black Struggle

(OBS), and Missourians Organizing for Reform and Empowerment (MORE). "Written Statement on the Police Shooting of Michael Brown and Ensuing Police Violence Against Protesters in Ferguson, Missouri." 53rd Session of the United Nations Committee Against Torture, Geneva, 2014.

Fanon, Frantz. *Black Skin, White Masks*. Translated by Charles Lam Markmann. New York: Grove, 1967.

Fanon, Frantz. *A Dying Colonialism*. Translated by Haakon Chevalier. New York: Grove, 1965.

Fanon, Frantz. *Toward the African Revolution: Political Essays*. Translated by Haakon Chevalier. New York: Grove, [1964] 1994.

Fanon, Frantz. *The Wretched of the Earth*. Translated by Constance Farrington. New York: Grove, 1963.

Farcau, Bruce W. *The Ten Cents War: Peru, Chile, and Bolivia in the War of the Pacific, 1879–1884*. Westport, CT: Praeger, 2000.

Fay, Jennifer, and Justus Nieland. *Film Noir: Hard-Boiled Modernity and the Cultures of Globalization*. New York: Routledge, 2009.

Ford, Matt. "The Return of *Korematsu*." *Atlantic Magazine*, November 19, 2015. https://www.theatlantic.com/politics/archive/2015/11/the-shadow-of-korematsu/416634/.

Foucault, Michel. *"Society Must Be Defended": Lectures at the Collège de France 1975–1976*, edited by Mauro Bertani and Alessandro Fontana, translated by David Macey. New York: Picador, 2003.

Freud, Sigmund. *The Ego and the Id*. Translated by Joan Riviere. London: Hogarth, Institute of Psycho-Analysis, [1923] 1950.

Freud, Sigmund. "Further Recommendations in the Technique of Psycho-Analysis: Recollection, Repetition, and Working Through." In *Collected Papers*, 2:366–76. New York: Basic Books, [1914] 1959.

Freud, Sigmund. "Mourning and Melancholia." In *The Freud Reader*, edited by Peter Gay, 584–88. New York: W. W. Norton, [1917] 1989.

Freud, Sigmund. "On Narcissism: An Introduction." In *Freud's "On Narcissism: An Introduction,"* translated by James Strachey, edited by Joseph Sandler, Ethel Spector Person, and Peter Fonagy, 1–32. London: Karnac, 2012.

Fu, May. "'Serve the People and You Help Yourself': Japanese-American Anti-Drug Organizing in Los Angeles, 1969 to 1972." *Social Justice* 35, no. 2 (2008): 80–99.

Fujikane, Candace. "Introduction: Asian Settler Colonialism in the U.S. Colony of Hawai'i." In *Asian Settler Colonialism: From Local Governance to the Habits of Everyday Life in Hawai'i*, edited by Candace Fujikane and Jonathan Y. Okamura, 1–42. Honolulu: University of Hawai'i Press, 2008.

Fujikane, Candace, and Jonathan Y. Okamura, eds. *Asian Settler Colonialism: From Local Governance to the Habits of Everyday Life in Hawai'i*. Honolulu: University of Hawai'i Press, 2008.

Fujita-Rony, Thomas Y. "Poston (Colorado River)." *Densho Encyclopedia*. Accessed September 6, 2017. http://encyclopedia.densho.org/Poston_%28Colorado_River%29/.

Fujitani, T. "*Go for Broke*, the Movie: Japanese American Soldiers in U.S. National, Military, and Racial Discourse." In Fujitani, White, and Yoneyama, *Perilous Memories*, 239–66.

Fujitani, T. *Race for Empire: Koreans as Japanese and Japanese as Americans during World War II*. Berkeley: University of California Press, 2011.

Fujitani, T., Geoffrey M. White, and Lisa Yoneyama, eds. *Perilous Memories: The Asia-Pacific War(s)*. Durham, NC: Duke University Press, 2001.

Fukagawa Munetoshi. *Umi ni kieta ni hibaku Chyousenjin chouyoukou—Chinkon no kaikyou*. Tokyo: Akashi Shoten, 1974.

Fukuyama, Francis. *The End of History and the Last Man*. New York: Avon, 1992.

Fuller, Sam, dir. *The Crimson Kimono*. Los Angeles: Columbia Pictures, 1959. DVD.

Gardiner, C. Harvey. *Pawns in a Triangle of Hate: The Peruvian Japanese and the United States*. Seattle: University of Washington Press, 1981.

Gibson, Nigel Gibson, "Why Frantz Fanon Still Matters." http://readingfanon.blogspot.com/2016/08/why-frantz-fanon-still-matters.html.

Gibson, Nigel and Roberto Beneduce. *Frantz Fanon, Psychiatry and Politics*. London: Rowman and Littlefield, 2017.

Gilman, Nils. *Mandarins of the Future: Modernization Theory in Cold War America*. Baltimore: Johns Hopkins University Press, 2003.

Gilmore, Ruth. "Terror Austerity Race Gender Excess Theater." In *Reading Rodney King/Reading Urban Uprising*, edited by Robert Gooding-Williams, 23–37. New York: Routledge, 1993.

Goldstein, Aloysha, ed., *Formations of United States Colonialism*. Durham, NC: Duke University Press, 2014.

González-Cueva, Eduardo. "Race and Political Representation in the Peruvian Public Sphere." Presentation for the *Latin American Studies Association Conference*, Chicago, September 1998. Accessed March 19, 2008. http://lasa.international.pitt.edu/LASA98/Gonzalez-Cueva.pdf.

Gooding-Williams, Robert, ed. *Reading Rodney King/Reading Urban Uprising*. New York: Routledge, 1993.

Gordon, Avery F. *Ghostly Matters: Haunting and the Sociological Imagination*. 2nd ed. Minneapolis: University of Minnesota Press, 2008.

Gordon, Bernard K. "Pacific Futures for the USA." In *Moving into the Pacific Century: The Changing Regional Order*, edited by Tiek Soon Lau and Leo Suryadinata. Singapore: National University of Singapore, 1988.

Gordon, Lewis. *What Fanon Said: A Philosophical Introduction to His Life and Thought*. New York: Fordham University Press, 2015.

Gorer, Geoffrey. *Death, Grief, and Mourning*. Salem, NH: Ayer, 1977.

Gotanda, Neil. "Reproducing the Model Minority Stereotype: Judge Karlin's Sentencing Colloquy in 'People V Soon Ja Du.'" In *Re-visioning Asian America: Locating Diversity*, edited by Soo-Young Chin. Pullman: Washington University Press, 1995.

Gramsci, Antonio. *Further Selections from the Prison Notebooks*. Edited and translated by Derek Boothman. Minneapolis: University of Minnesota Press, 1995.

Grandin, Greg. *The Blood of Guatemala: A History of Race and Nation*. Durham, NC: Duke University Press, 2000.
Gray, Herman. *Cultural Moves: African Americans and the Politics of Representation*. Berkeley: University of California Press, 2005.
Hagedorn, Jessica, ed. *Charlie Chan Is Dead: An Anthology of Contemporary Asian American Fiction*. New York: Penguin, 1993.
Hamilton, Nora, and Norma Stoltz Chinchilla. *Seeking Community in a Global City: Guatemalans and Salvadorans in Los Angeles*. Philadelphia: Temple University Press, 2001.
Hammett, Dashiell. *The Thin Man*. New York: Vintage, [1936] 1962.
Hanley, Charles J., Sang-Hun Choe, and Martha Mendoza. *The Bridge at No Gun Ri: A Hidden Nightmare from the Korean War*. New York: Henry Holt, 2001.
Haraway, Donna. "The Bio-Politics of Postmodern Bodies: Determination of Self in Immune System Discourse." In *Feminist Theory and the Body*, edited by Janet Price and Margrit Shildrick. New York: Routledge, 1999.
Hartman, Saidya. *Lose Your Mother: A Journey Along the Atlantic Slave Route*. New York: Farrar, Straus, and Giroux, 2007.
Harvey, David. *A Brief History of Neoliberalism*. Oxford: Oxford University Press, 2007.
Harvey, David. *The Urbanization of Capital: Studies in the History and Theory of Capitalist Urbanization*. Baltimore: John Hopkins University Press, 1985.
Hereniko, Vilsoni, and Rob Wilson, eds. *Inside Out: Literature, Cultural Politics, and Identity in the New Pacific*. Lanham, MD: Rowman and Littlefield, 1999.
Herman, Arthur. *Douglas MacArthur: American Warrior*. New York: Random House, 2016.
Hirabayashi, James. "Segregation." *Densho Encyclopedia*. Accessed March 14, 2014.
Hirabayashi, Lane Ryo, and Evelyn Hu-DeHart, guest eds. "*Asians in the Americas: Transculturations and Power*." Special Issue. *Amerasia Journal* 28, no. 2 (2002).
Hirahara, Naomi. *Summer of the Big Bachi*. New York: Bantam Dell, 2004.
Hirsch, Marianne. *The Generation of Postmemory: Writing and Visual Culture after the Holocaust*. New York: Columbia University Press, 2012.
"Family Pictures: *Maus*, Mourning and Post-Memory." *Discourse: Journal for Theoretical Studies in Media and Culture*, vol. 15, no. 2 (winter 1992–93): 3–29.
Hirsch, Marianne, and Nancy K. Miller, eds. *Rites of Return: Diaspora Poetics and the Politics of Memory*. New York: Columbia University Press, 2011.
Hoare, Quintin, ed. *Antonio Gramsci: Selections from the Prison Notebooks*, trans. Geoffrey Nowell Smith. New York: International Publishers, 1992.
Hondagneu-Sotelo, Pierrette. *Gender and U.S. Immigration: Contemporary Trends*. Berkeley: University of California Press, 2003.
Hong, Grace Kyungwon. "Consumerism without Means." In *The Ruptures of American Capital: Women of Color Feminism and the Culture of Immigrant Labor*, 107–42. Minneapolis: University of Minnesota Press, 2006.
Hong, Grace Kyungwon. *The Ruptures of American Capital: Women of Color Femi-*

nism and the Culture of Immigrant Labor. Minneapolis: University of Minnesota Press, 2006.

Hong, Grace Kyungwon. "'Something Forgotten Which Should Have Been Remembered': Private Property and Cross-Racial Solidarity in the Work of Hisaye Yamamoto." *American Literature* 71, no. 2 (1999): 291–310.

Honig, Bonnie. *Antigone, Interrupted*. Cambridge: Cambridge University Press, 2013.

hooks, bell. *Black Looks: Race and Representation*. New York: Routledge, 2015.

Horne, Gerald. *Race War! White Supremacy and the Japanese Attack on the British Empire*. New York: New York University Press, 2004.

Horsley, Lee. *The Noir Thriller*. New York: Palgrave Macmillan, 2001.

Horsman, Reginald. *Race and Manifest Destiny: The Origins of American Racial Anglo-Saxonism*. Cambridge, MA: Harvard University Press, 1981.

Hua, Julietta. *Trafficking Women's Human Rights*. Minneapolis: University of Minnesota Press, 2011.

Huang, Yunte. *Charlie Chan: The Untold Story of the Honorable Detective and His Rendezvous with American History*. New York: W. W. Norton, 2010.

Hu-DeHart, Evelyn. "Huagong and Huashang: The Chinese as Laborers and Merchants in Latin America and the Caribbean." *Amerasia Journal* 28, no. 2 (2002): 63–91.

Ichioka, Yuji, ed. *Views from Within: The Japanese American Evacuation and Resettlement Study*. Los Angeles: Asian American Studies Center, University of California at Los Angeles, 1989.

International Center for Transitional Justice, translation. *Truth and Reconciliation Commission of Peru: Final Report—General Conclusions*. 2003.

"An Interview with Ann Patchett." *bookbrowse.com*. Accessed March 15, 2012. https://www.bookbrowse.com/author_interviews/full/index.cfm/author_number/645/ann-patchett.

Iritani, Evelyn. "His Family's Internment Earned Apologies from a Human Rights Commission. Will the U.S. Government Respond?" *Los Angeles Times*, March 24, 2017. http://www.latimes.com/opinion/op-ed/la-oe-iritani-update-shibayama-internment-20170323-story.html. By 1944, more than 2,000 Latin Americans, 80% from Peru, were interned in the U.S.

Iriye, Akira. *After Imperialism: The Search for a New Order in the Far East, 1921–1931*. Chicago: Imprint, 1990.

Iriye, Akira, and Yonosuke Nagai, eds. *The Origins of the Cold War in Asia*. New York: Columbia University Press, 1977.

Irons, Peter. *Justice at War: The Story of Japanese American Internment Cases*. Berkeley: University of California Press, 1983.

Itagaki, Lynn Mie. *Civil Racism: The 1992 Los Angeles Rebellion and the Crisis of Racial Burnout*. Minneapolis: University of Minnesota Press, 2016.

Jameson, Fredric. "Cognitive Mapping." In *Marxism and the Interpretation of Culture*, edited by Cary Nelson and Lawrence Grossberg, 347–60. Urbana: University of Illinois Press, 1988.

Jameson, Fredric. "Magical Narratives: On the Dialectical Use of Genre Criticism." In *The Political Unconscious: Narrative as a Socially Symbolic Act*, 103–50. Ithaca, NY: Cornell University Press, 1981.

Jameson, Fredric. *Postmodernism, or, the Cultural Logic of Late Capitalism*. Durham, NC: Duke University Press, 1991.

The Japan Times. "South Korean Hibakusha Urge Obama to Apologize in Hiroshima." *The Japan Times*, May 20, 2016. Accessed May 20, 2016. https://www.japantimes.co.jp/news/2016/05/20/national/history/south-korean-hibakusha-urge-obama-apologize-hiroshima/#.WlkKZVQ-feQ.

Johnson, Chalmers. *Blowback: The Costs and Consequences of American Empire*. New York: Henry Holt, 2000.

Johnson, Chalmers. *The Sorrows of Empire: Militarism, Secrecy, and the End of the Republic*. New York: Henry Holt, 2004.

Julien, Isaac. *Frantz Fanon: Black Skin, White Mask* (documentary film). San Francisco: California Newsreel, 1996. DVD.

Jun, Helen Heran. "Contingent Nationalisms: Renegotiating Borders in Korean and Korean American Women's Oppositional Struggles." *positions: asia critique* 5, no. 2 (1997): 325–55.

Jun, Helen Heran. *Race for Citizenship: Black Orientalism and Asian Uplift from Pre-Emancipation to Neoliberal America*. New York: New York University Press, 2011.

Kang, Han. *Human Acts: A Novel*. New York: Hogarth, 2016.

Kang, Jay Caspian. *The Dead Do Not Improve: A Novel*. New York: Hogarth, 2013.

Kang, Jay Caspian. "That Other School Shooting." *New York Times Magazine*, March 28, 2013. http://www.nytimes.com/2013/03/31/magazine/should-it-matter-that-the-shooter-at-oikos-university-was-korean.html?mcubz=3.

Kang, Jay Caspian "What a Fraternity Hazing Death Revealed About the Painful Search for an Asian-American Identity." *New York Times Magazine*, August 9, 2017. https://www.nytimes.com/2017/08/09/magazine/what-a-fraternity-hazing-death-revealed-about-the-painful-search-for-an-asian-american-identity.html?mcubz=3.

Kang, Laura Hyun Yi. *Compositional Subjects: Enfiguring Asian/American Women*. Durham, NC: Duke University Press, 2002.

Kaplan, Amy. "'Left Alone with America': The Absence of Empire in the Study of American Culture." In *Cultures of United States Imperialism*, edited by Amy Kaplan and Donald Pease, 3–21. Durham, NC: Duke University Press, 1993.

Kaplan, Amy, and Donald E. Pease, eds. *Cultures of United States Imperialism*. Durham, NC: Duke University Press, 1993.

Kaplan, Caren. *Questions of Travel: Postmodern Discourses of Displacement*. Durham, NC: Duke University Press, 2000.

Kaplan, E. Ann, ed. "The 'Dark Continent' of Film Noir: Race, Displacement, and Metaphor in Tourneur's *Cat People* (1942) and Welles's *The Lady from Shanghai* (1948)." In *Women in Film Noir*, revised and expanded edition, 183–201. London: British Film Institute, 2008.

Kaplan, E. Ann. "Introduction." In *Women in Film Noir*, edited by E. Ann Kaplan. Rev. and expanded ed. London: British Film Institute, 2008.

Kaplan, E. Ann. *Trauma Culture: The Politics of Terror and Loss in Media and Literature*. New Brunswick, NJ: Rutgers University Press, 2005.

Kaplan, Sara Clarke. "Souls at the Crossroads, Africans on the Water: The Politics of Diasporic Melancholia." *Callaloo* 30, no. 2 (2007): 511–26.

Kauanui, J. Kēhaulani. *Hawaiian Blood: Colonialism and the Politics of Sovereignty and Indigeneity*. Durham, NC: Duke University Press, 2008.

Kauanui, J. Kēhaulani, and Vicente M. Diaz. "Native Pacific Cultural Studies on the Edge." *Contemporary Pacific* 13, no. 1 (2001): 315–41.

Keisaburo, Toyonaga. "Colonial and Atomic Bombs: About Survivors of Hiroshima Living in Korea." In Fujitani, White, and Yoneyama, *Perilous Memories*, 378–94.

Kennedy, Ellen Clare. "The Japanese-American Renunciants: Due Process and the Danger of Making Laws during Times of Fear." *Japan Policy Research Institute*, Working Paper 110, October 2006. Accessed May 10, 2016. http://www.jpri.org/publications/workingpapers/wp110.html.

Kennedy, Rosanne. "Indigenous Australian Arts of Return: Mediating Perverse Archives." In *Rites of Return: Diaspora Poetics and the Politics of Memory*, edited by Marianne Hirsh and Nancy Miller, 88–104. Durham, NC: Duke University Press, 2011.

Khuc, Mimi, guest ed. "Open in Emergency: A Special Issue on Asian American Mental Health." *Asian American Literary Review* (2016).

Kim, Elaine H. "Home Is Where the 'Han' Is: A Korean American Perspective on the Los Angeles Upheavals." *Social Justice* 20, nos. 1/2 (1993): 1–21.

Kim, Elaine H. "Myth, Memory, and Desire: Homeland and History in Contemporary Korea American Writing and Visual Art." In *Holding Their Own: Perspectives on the Multi-Ethnic Literatures of the United States*, edited by Dorothea Fischer-Hornung and Heike Raphael-Hernandez. Stauffenburg, Germany: Verlag, 2000.

Kim, Elaine H., and Chungmoo Choi, eds. "Introduction." In *Dangerous Women: Gender and Korean Nationalism*, 1–8. New York: Routledge, 1998.

Kim, Jinah, and Neda Atanasoski. "Unhappy Desires and Queer Postsocialist Futures: Hong Kong and Buenos Aires in Wong Kar-Wai's *Happy Together*." *American Quarterly* 69, no. 3 (2017): 697–718.

Kim, Jodi. *Ends of Empire: Asian American Critique and the Cold War*. Minneapolis: University of Minnesota Press, 2010.

Kim, Jodi. "'I'm Not Here, If This Doesn't Happen': The Korean War and Cold War Epistemologies in Susan Choi's *The Foreign Student* and Heinz Insu Fenkl's *Memories of My Ghost Brother*." *Journal of Asian American Studies* 11, no. 3 (2008): 279–302.

Kim, Junyoung. "Asia-Latin America as Method: The Global South Project and the Dislocation of the West." *Verge: Global Asias* issue, *Between Asia and Latin America: New Transpacific Perspectives* 3, no. 2 (fall 2017): 97–117.

Kim, Michelle Har. "José Watanabe." *Asian American Literary Review*, March 6,

2011. Accessed January 10, 2015. http://www.discovernikkei.org/en/journal/2011/3/6/jose-watanabe/.

Kim, Min Jung. "Moments of Danger in the (Dis)continuous Relation of Korean Nationalism and Korean American Nationalism." *positions* 5, no. 2 (1997): 357–89.

Kim, Nan. "Korea on the Brink: Reading The Yŏnp'yŏng Shelling and Its Aftermath." *Journal of Asian Studies* 70, no. 2 (2011): 337–56.

Kim, Nan. "Ruins of Global Militarism, Embodiment of Dissent: Gangjeong Village's Culture of Peace and Life Movement." Presentation at LandBody: Indigeneity's Radical Commitments Conference. University of Wisconsin, Milwaukee, May 7, 2016.

Kim-Gibson, Dai Sil. *Sa-I-Gu*. Documentary. San Francisco: Cross Current Media, National Asian American Telecommunications Association, 1993. DVD.

Klein, Christina. *Cold War Orientalism: Asian in the Middlebrow Imagination, 1945–1961*. Berkeley: University of California Press, 2003.

Koshiro, Yukiko. *Trans-Pacific Racisms and the U.S. Occupation of Japan*. New York: Columbia University Press, 1999.

Kuo, Karen. *East Is West and West Is East: Gender, Culture, and Interwar Encounters Between Asia and America*. Philadelphia: Temple University Press, 2013.

Laclau, Ernesto. "Politics and the Limits of Modernity." In *Universal Abandon? The Politics of Postmodernism*, edited by Andrew Ross, 80. Minneapolis: University of Minnesota, 1988.

Lake, Jessica. "*Red Road* (2006) and Emerging Narratives of 'Sub-veillance.'" *Continuum: Journal of Media and Cultural Studies* 24, no. 2 (2010): 231–40.

Lane, Jill. "*Antígona* and the Modernity of the Dead." *Modern Drama* 50, no. 4 (2007): 517–31.

Lee, Don. *Country of Origin*. New York: W. W. Norton, 2004.

Lee, James. *Urban Triage: Race and the Fictions of Multiculturalism*. Minneapolis: University of Minnesota Press, 2004.

Lee, Rachel. "Asian American Cultural Production in Asia-Pacific Perspective." *boundary 2* 26, no. 2 (1999): 231–54.

Lee, Rachel. "Notes from the (Non)Field: Teaching and Theorizing Women of Color." *Meridians* 91, no. 1 (2000): 85–109.

Lee, Robert G. *Orientals: Asian Americans in Popular Culture*. Philadelphia: Temple University Press, 1999.

Lim, Deborah K. *Research Report Prepared for Presidential Select Committee on JACL Resolution #7 (aka "The Lim Report")*. 1990/2002. http://www.resisters.com/study/LimTOC.htm.

Lipsitz, George. "'Frantic to Join . . . the Japanese Army': Black Soldiers and Civilians Confront the Asia-Pacific War." In Fujitani, White, and Yoneama, *Perilous Memories: The Asia-Pacific War(s)*.

Lipsitz, George. *The Possessive Investment in Whiteness: How White People Profit from Identity Politics*. Philadelphia: Temple University Press, 1998.

Lopez, David E., Eric Popkin, and Edward Telles. "Central Americans: At the Bot-

tom, Struggling to Get Out." In *Ethnic Los Angeles*, edited by Roger Waldinger and Mehdi Bozorgmehr, 279–304. New York: Russell Sage Foundation, 1996.
López-Calvo, Ignacio. *The Affinity of the Eye: Writing Nikkei in Peru*. Tucson: University of Arizona Press, 2013.
López-Calvo, Ignacio. *Dragons in the Land of the Condor: Writing Tusán in Peru*. Tucson: University of Arizona Press, 2014.
Lott, Eric. "The Whiteness of Film Noir." American Literary History 9, no. 3 (1997): 542–66.
Lowe, Lisa. *Immigrant Acts: On Asian American Cultural Politics*. Durham, NC: Duke University Press, 1996.
Lowe, Lisa. "The Intimacies of Four Continents," In *Haunted by Empire*, edited by Ann Laura Stoler, 191–212. Durham, NC: Duke University Press, 2006.
Lowe, Lisa. *The Intimacies of Four Continents*. Durham, NC: Duke University Press, 2015.
Lowe, Lisa. "On Contemporary Asian American Projects." *Amerasia Journal* 21, nos. 1–2 (1995): 41–52.
Luce, Henry R. "The American Century." *Life*, February 17, 1941, 61–65.
Lum, H. Y., and Bill Teter, eds. *Growing up Local: An Anthology of Poetry and Prose from Hawai'i*. Honolulu: Bamboo Ridge, 1998.
Lynch, Kevin. *The Image of the City*. Cambridge, MA: MIT Press, 1960.
Lyons, Paul. *American Pacificism: Oceania in the U.S. Imagination*. New York: Routledge, 2005.
Macey, David. *Frantz Fanon: A Biography*. New York: Picador, 2000.
Marx, Leo. *Machine in the Garden: Technology and the Pastoral Ideal in America*. Oxford: Oxford University Press, 1964.
Mayer, Enrique. "Peru in Deep Trouble: Mario Vargas Llosa's 'Inquest in the Andes' Reexamined." *Cultural Anthropology* 6, no. 4 (1991): 466–504.
Mayer, Enrique. *Ugly Stories of the Peruvian Agrarian Reform*. Durham, NC: Duke University Press, 2009.
Mbembe, Achille. "Necropolitics." Translated by Libby Meintjes. *Public Culture* 15, no. 1 (2003): 11–40.
Mbembe, Achille. "Necropolitics." In *Foucault in an Age of Terror: Essays on Biopolitics and the Defence of Society*, edited by Stephen Morton and Stephen Bygrave, 152–82. New York: Palgrave Macmillan, 2008.
Mbembe, Achille. *On the Postcolony*. Berkeley: University of California Press, 2001.
McAlister, Melanie. *Epic Encounters: Culture, Media, and U.S. Interests in the Middle East since 1945*. Updated ed. Berkeley: University of California Press, 2005.
McClintock, Anne. "The Angel of Progress: Pitfalls of the Term 'Postcolonialism.'" *Social Text* 31/32 (1992): 84–98.
McKittrick, Katherine, ed. *Sylvia Wynter: On Being Human as Praxis*. Durham, NC: Duke University Press, 2014.
McMillian, Calvin. "The Hardboiled and the Haunted: Race, Masculinity, and the Asian American Detective." PhD diss., University of California Santa Cruz, 2012.

Melamed, Jodi. "Racial Capitalism." *Journal of Critical Ethnic Studies* 1, no. 1 (2015): 76–85.
Melamed, Jodi. *Represent and Destroy: Rationalizing Violence in the New Racial Capitalism*. Minneapolis: University of Minnesota Press, 2011.
Mercer, Kobena. "Cosmopolitan Contact Zones." In *Afro Modern: Journeys through the Black Atlantic*, edited by Tanya Barson and Peter Gorschluter, 40–48. London: Tate, 2010.
Mignolo, Walter D. "The Geopolitics of Knowledge and the Colonial Difference." *SAQ* 101, no. 1 (2003): 57–96.
Mignolo, Walter D. "Globalization, Civilization Processes, and the Relocation of Languages and Cultures." In *The Cultures of Globalization*, edited by Fredric Jameson and Masao Miyoshi, 32–53. Durham, NC: Duke University Press, 1998.
Mignolo, Walter D. *The Idea of Latin America*. London: Blackwell, 2005.
Million, Dian. *Therapeutic Nations: Healing in an Age of Indigenous Human Rights*. Tucson: University of Arizona Press, 2013.
Mobius, J. Mark. "The Japan-Korea Normalization Process and Korean Anti-Americanism." Asian Survey 6, no. 4 (1966): 241–48.
Mohanty, Chandra Talpade. "Under Western Eyes: Feminist Scholarship and Colonial Discourses." *Boundary 2* 12, no. 3/13, no. 1 (spring/fall 1984): 338–58.
Moon, Katharine H. S. *Sex among Allies: Military Prostitution in U.S.-Korea Relations*. New York: Columbia University Press, 1997.
Moraga, Cherríe, and Gloria Anzaldúa, eds. *This Bridge Called My Back: Writings by Radical Women of Color*. 2nd ed. New York: Kitchen Table, 1983.
Moreiras, Alberto. *The Exhaustion of Difference*. Durham, NC: Duke University Press, 2001.
Morrison, Toni. *Playing in the Dark: Whiteness and the Literary Imagination*. New York: Vintage, 1993.
Muñoz, José Esteban. "Ghosts of Public Sex: Utopian Longings, Queer Memories." In *Policing Public Sex: Queer Politics and the Future of AIDS Activism*, edited by Dangerous Bedfellows, 355–72. Boston: South End, 1996.
Naremore, James. "The Other Side of the Street." In *More than Night: Film Noir in Its Contexts*, 220–53. Berkeley: University of California Press, 1998.
The National Advisory Commission on Civil Disorders. *The Kerner Report*. Princeton, NJ: Princeton University Press, 2016.
Nelli, M. Florencia. "Identity, Dignity and Memory: Performing/Re-Writing *Antigone* in Post-1976 Argentina." *New Voices in Classical Reception Studies* 4 (2009): 70–82.
Ngai, Mai. *Impossible Subjects: Illegal Aliens and the Making of Modern America*. Princeton, NJ: Princeton University Press, 2004.
Nguyen, Mimi Thi. *The Gift of Freedom: War, Debt, and Other Refugee Passages*. Durham, NC: Duke University Press, 2012.
Nguyen, Viet Thanh. *Nothing Ever Dies: Vietnam and the Memory of War*. Cambridge, MA: Harvard University Press, 2016.

Nussbaum, Martha. *Cultivating Humanity: A Classical Defense of Reform in Liberal Education*. Cambridge: Cambridge University Press, 1997.
Nussbaum, Martha. *Not for Profit: Why Democracy Needs the Humanities*. Princeton, NJ: Princeton University Press, 2010.
Okada, John. *No-No Boy*. Seattle: University of Washington Press, [1976] 2014.
Okihiro, Gary Y. *Island World: A History of Hawai'i and the United States*. Berkeley: University of California Press, 2009.
Oliver, Kelly, and Benigno Trigo. *Noir Anxiety*. Minneapolis: University of Minnesota Press, 2002.
Oliver, Melvin L., James H. Johnson Jr., and Walter C. Farrell Jr. "Anatomy of a Rebellion: A Political-Economic Analysis." In *Reading Rodney King/Reading Urban Uprising*, edited by Robert Gooding-Williams, 117–41. New York: Routledge, 1993.
Ong, Paul, Edna Bonacich, and Lucie Cheng, eds. *The New Asian Immigration in Los Angeles and Global Restructuring*. Philadelphia: Temple University Press, 1994.
Palmer, David. "Korean Hibakusha, Japan's Supreme Court and the International Community: Can the U.S. and Japan Confront Forced Labor and Atomic Bombing?" *Asia-Pacific Journal: Japan Focus* 6, no. 2 (2008). Accessed April 21, 2010. http://www.japanfocus.org/-David-Palmer/2670#sthash.KBykZbtN.dpuf.
Palmer, David. "The Straits of Dead Souls: One Man's Investigation into the Disappearance of Mitsubihi Hiroshima's Korean Forced Labourers." *Journal of Japanese Studies* 26, no. 3 (2006): 335–51.
Palumbo-Liu, David. *The Deliverance of Others: Reading Literature in a Global Age*. Durham, NC: Duke University Press, 2012.
Park, Edward J. W. "Friends or Enemies? Generational Politics in the Korean American Community in Los Angeles." *Qualitative Sociology* 22, no. 2 (1999): 161–75.
Park, Kyoung H. "Mina." In *Seven Contemporary Plays from the Korean Diaspora in the Americas*, edited by Esther Kim Lee, 321. Durham, NC: Duke University Press, 2012.
Park, Soyang. "Silence Subaltern Speech and the Intellectual in South Korea: The Politics of Emergent Speech in the Case of Former Sexual Slaves." *Journal for Cultural Research* 9, no. 2 (2005): 169–206.
Parreñas, Rhacel Salazar. *The Force of Domesticity: Filipina Migrants and Globalization*. New York: New York University Press, 2008.
Patchett, Ann. *Bel Canto*. New York: HarperCollins, 2001.
Pease, Donald E. "Borderline Justice/States of Emergency: Orson Welles' *Touch of Evil*." *CR: The New Centennial Review* 1, no. 1 (2001): 75–105.
Perry, Ellen, dir. *The Fall of Fujimori*. Burbank, CA: Cinema Libre, 2005. DVD.
Pilzer, Joshua. *Hearts of Pine: Songs in the Lives of Three Korean Survivors of the Japanese "Comfort Women."* Oxford: Oxford University Press, 2012.
Polanyi, Karl. *The Great Transformation: The Political and Economic Origins of Our Time*. Boston: Beacon Press, [1944] 2001.

Prashad, Vijay. *The Darker Nations: A People's History of the Third World*. New York: New Press, 2007.
Pratt, Mary Louise. *Imperial Eyes: Travel Writing and Transculturation*. 2nd ed. New York: Routledge, 2007.
Price, John. "A Just Peace? The 1951 San Francisco Peace Treaty in Historical Perspective." *Japan Policy Research Institute*. Working Paper 78. June 2001.
Puar, Jasbir. *Terrorist Assemblages: Homonationalism in Queer Times*. Durham, NC: Duke University Press, 2007.
Pyong, Min. *Caught in the Middle: Korean Communities in New York and Los Angeles*. Berkeley: University of California Press, 1996.
Ralli, Teresa. "Excerpts from *Antígona*." In *Holy Terrors: Latin American Women Perform*, translated by Margaret Carson, edited by Diana Taylor and Roselyn Costantino, 365–70. Durham, NC: Duke University Press, 2003.
Ralli, Teresa. "Fragments of Memory." In *Holy Terrors: Latin American Women Perform*, translated by Margaret Carson, edited by Diana Taylor and Roselyn Costantino, 355–64. Durham, NC: Duke University Press, 2003.
Ralli, Teresa, and José Watanabe. *Antígona*. Performance. 2000.
Rana, Junaid. *Terrifying Muslims: Race and Labor in the South Asian Diaspora*. Durham, NC: Duke University Press, 2011.
Richard, Nelly. "The Cultural Periphery and Postmodern Decentering: Latin America's Reconversion of Borders." In *Rethinking Borders*, edited by John C. Welchman, 71–84. Minneapolis: University of Minnesota Press, 1996.
Rivas, Zelideth María, and Debbie Lee-DiStefano, eds. *Imagining Asia in the Americas*. New Brunswick, NJ: Rutgers University Press, 2016.
Rodríguez, Dylan. *Forced Passages: Imprisoned Radical Intellectuals and the U.S. Prison Regime*. Minneapolis: University of Minnesota Press, 2006.
Rodríguez, Dylan. *Suspended Apocalypse: White Supremacy, Genocide, and the Filipino Condition*. Minneapolis: University of Minnesota Press, 2010.
Rogin, Michael. *Independence Day*. London: British Film Institute, 1998.
Rogin, Michael. *Ronald Reagan, the Movie: And Other Episodes in Political Demonology*. Berkeley: University of California Press, 1988.
Romero, Simon. "Slow-Burning Challenge to Chile on Easter Island." *New York Times*, October 6, 2012. Accessed October 7, 2012. http://www.nytimes.com/2012/10/07/world/americas/slow-burning-rebellion-against-chile-on-easter-island.html?pagewanted=all.
Rose, Nikolas. *The Politics of Life Itself: Biomedicine, Power, and Subjectivity in the Twenty-First Century*. Princeton, NJ: Princeton University Press, 2006.
Said, Edward W. *Orientalism*. New York: Vintage, 1979.
Sakai, Naoki. "On Romantic Love and Military Violence: Transpacific Imperialism and U.S.–Japan Complicity." In Shigematsu and Camacho, *Militarized Currents*, 205–31.
Sakai, Naoki, and Hyon Joo Yoo, eds. *The Trans-Pacific Imagination: Rethinking Boundary, Culture, and Society*. Singapore: World Scientific, 2012.

Saldana, Maria Josefina. *Revolutionary Imaginations in the Age of Development*. Durham, NC: Duke University Press, 2003.
Sanders, Sam. "Mitsubishi Apologies to U.S. WWII Veterans for Forced Labor." NPR Morning Edition, July, 20, 2015. https://www.npr.org/2015/07/20/424571375/mitsubishi-apologizes-to-u-s-world-war-ii-veterans-for-forced-labor.
Sangari, Kumkum. "The Politics of the Possible." In *Theory of the Novel: A Historical Approach*, edited by Michael McKeon, 900–922. Baltimore: Johns Hopkins University Press, 1993.
Santos Perez, Craig. *From Unincorporated Territory [Guma']*. Richmond, CA: Omnidawn, 2014.
Sassen, Saskia. *Globalization and Its Discontents*. New York: New Press, 1998.
Sater, William F. *Andean Tragedy: Fighting the War of the Pacific, 1879–1884*. Lincoln: University of Nebraska Press, 2009.
Scarry, Elaine. *The Body in Pain: The Making and Unmaking of the World*. Oxford: Oxford University Press, 1985.
Schrader, Paul. "Notes on Film Noir." *Film Comment* 8, no. 1 (1972): 8–13.
Schlund-Vials, Cathy. *War, Genocide, and Justice: Cambodian American Memory Work*. Minnesota: University of Minneapolis Press, 2012.
Schueller, Malini Johar. "Techno-Dominance and Torturegate: The Making of U.S. Imperialism." In *Exceptional State: Contemporary U.S. Culture and the New Imperialism*, edited by Ashley Dawson and Malini Johar Schueller, 162–88. Durham, NC: Duke University Press, 2007.
Seltzer, Mark. "Wound Culture: Trauma in the Pathological Public Sphere." *October* 80 (1997): 3–26.
Serber, Robert, with Robert P. Crease. *Peace and War: Reminiscences of a Life on the Frontiers of Science*. New York: Columbia University Press, 1998.
Sharma, Nitasha. "Pacific Revisions of Blackness: Blacks Address Race and Belonging in Hawai'i." *Amerasia Journal* 37, no. 3 (2011): 43–60.
Shatz, Adam. "The Torture of Algiers." *New York Review of Books*, November 21, 2002. http://www.algeria-watch.org/farticle/analyse/shatz_torture.htm.
Sherry, Michael. *The Rise of American Air Power: The Creation of Armageddon*. New Haven, CT: Yale University Press, 1987.
Shigematsu, Setsu, and Keith L. Camacho, eds. *Militarized Currents: Towards a Decolonized Future in Asia and the Pacific*. Minneapolis: University of Minnesota Press, 2010.
Shimabuku, Annmaria. "Transpacific Colonialism: An Intimate View of Transnational Activism in Okinawa." *CR: New Centennial Review* 12, no 1 (2012): 131–58.
Shin, Chi-Yun, and Mark Gallagher, eds. *East Asian Film Noir: Transnational Encounters and Intercultural Dialogue*. New York: I. B. Tauris, 2015.
Shohat, Ella. "Notes on the 'Post-Colonial.'" *Social Text* 31/32 (1992): 99–113.
Silva, Noenoe K. *Aloha Betrayed: Native Hawaiian Resistance to American Colonialism*. Durham, NC: Duke University Press, 2004.

Silver, Alain, and James Ursini, eds. *Film Noir Reader*. Pompton Plains, NJ: Limelight, 1996.
Silverman, Kaja. *The Acoustic Mirror: The Female Voice in Psychoanalysis and Cinema*. Bloomington: Indiana University Press, 1988.
Simpson, Audra. *Mohawk Interruptus: Political Life across the Borders of Settler States*. Durham, NC: Duke University Press, 2014.
Simpson, Caroline Chung. *An Absent Presence: Japanese Americans in Postwar American Culture, 1945–1960*. Durham, NC: Duke University Press, 2002.
Siu, Lok C. D. *Memories of a Future Home: Diasporic Citizenship of Chinese in Panama*. Stanford, CA: Stanford University Press, 2005.
Soja, Edward, and Allen J. Scott, eds. *The City: Los Angeles and Urban Theory at the End of the Twentieth Century*. Berkeley: University of California Press, 1996.
Sommer, Doris. *Foundational Fictions: The National Romances of Latin America*. Berkeley: University of California Press, 1993.
Son, Elizabeth W. *Embodied Reckoning: "Comfort Women," Performance, and Transpacific Redress*. Ann Arbor: University of Michigan Press, 2018.
Song, Min Hyoung. *The Children of 1965: On Writing, and Not Writing, as an Asian American*. Durham, NC: Duke University Press, 2013.
Song, Min Hyoung. "Communities of Remembrance: Reflections on the Virginia Tech Shootings and Race." *Journal of Asian American Studies* 11, no. 1 (2008): 1–26.
Song, Min Hyoung. *Strange Futures: Pessimism and the 1992 Los Angeles Riots*. Durham, NC: Duke University Press, 2005.
Spivak, Gayatri Chakravorty. "Can the Subaltern Speak?" In *Marxism and the Interpretation of Culture*, edited by Carey Nelson and Lawrence Grossberg, 271–313. Urbana: University of Illinois Press, 1988.
Starn, Orin. "Maoism in the Andes: The Communist Party of Peru—Shining Path and the Refusal of History." *Journal of Latin American Studies* 27, no. 2 (1995): 399–421.
Starn, Orin, Carlos Iván Degregori, and Robin Kirk, eds. *The Peru Reader: History, Culture, Politics*. 2nd ed. Durham, NC: Duke University Press, 2005.
Stoler, Ann Laura. *Along the Archival Grain: Epistemic Anxieties and Colonial Common Sense*. Princeton, NJ: Princeton University Press, 2010.
Stoler, Ann Laura. *Carnal Knowledge and Imperial Power: Race and the Intimate in Colonial Rule*. Berkeley: University of California Press, 2002.
Stoler, Ann Laura, ed. *Haunted by Empire: Geographies of Intimacy in North American History*. Durham, NC: Duke University Press, 2006.
Stoler, Ann Laura. "Imperial Debris: On Ruins and Ruination." *Cultural Anthropology* 23, no. 2 (2008): 191–219.
Stoler, Ann Laura. *Race and the Education of Desire: Foucault's "History of Sexuality" and the Colonial Order of Things*. Durham, NC: Duke University Press, 1995.
Stonebridge, Lyndsey. "Bombs and Roses: The Writing of Anxiety in Henry Green's *Caught*." *Diacritics* 28, no. 4 (1998): 25–43.

Streeby, Shelley. *American Sensations: Class, Empire, and the Production of Popular Culture*. Berkeley: University of California Press, 2002.

Sturken, Marita. *Tangled Memories: The Vietnam War, the AIDS Epidemic, and the Politics of Remembering*. Berkeley: University of California Press, 1997.

Suh, Jae Jung. "The Failure of the South Korean National Security State: The Sewol Tragedy in the Age of Neoliberalism." *Asia-Pacific Journal: Japan Focus* 12, no. 40 (2014): http://apjjf.org/2014/12/40/Jae-Jung-Suh/4195.html.

Tasker, Yvonne. "Women in Film Noir." In *A Companion to Film Noir*, edited by Andrew Spicer and Helen Hanson, 353–68. Malden, MA: Wiley-Blackwell, 2013.

Taussig, Michael. "Culture of Terror, Space of Death: Roger Casement's Putumayo Report and the Explanation of Torture." *Comparative Studies in Society and History* 26, no. 3 (1984): 467–97.

Taylor, Diana. *Disappearing Acts: Spectacles of Gender and Nationalism in Argentina's "Dirty War."* Durham, NC: Duke University Press, 2001.

Taylor, Diana, and Roselyn Costantino, eds. *Holy Terrors: Latin American Women Perform*. Durham, NC: Duke University Press, 2003.

Taylor, Peter J. *Modernities: A Geohistorical Interpretation*. Minneapolis: University of Minnesota Press, 1999.

Teaiwa, Teresia K. "Bikinis and Other S/Pacific N/Oceans." In Shigematsu and Camacho, *Militarized Currents*, 15–31.

Theidon, Kimberly. "Justice in Transition: The Micropolitics of Reconciliation in Postwar Peru." *Journal of Conflict Resolution* 50, no. 3, *Transitional Justice* (2006): 433–57.

Theophanidis, Philippe. "Interregnum as a Legal and Political Concept: A Brief Contextual Survey." *Synthesis*, no. 9 (fall 2016): 109–24.

Tobar, Héctor. *The Tattooed Soldier*. New York: Penguin, 2000.

Trask, Haunani-Kay. *A Native Daughter: Colonialism and Sovereignty in Hawai'i*. Honolulu: University of Hawai'i Press, 1999.

Truth and Reconciliation Commission, Communications and Public Impact Office. "Press Release 226: TRC Final Report Was Made Public on August 28th, 2003 at Noon," August 28, 2003. Accessed June 3, 2009. http://www.cverdad.org.pe/.

UN General Assembly. Resolution 60/147, "Basic Principles and Guidelines of the Right to a Remedy and Reparation for Victims of Gross Violations of International Human Rights Law and Serious Violation of International Humanitarian Law," December 16, 2005. http://www.ohchr.org/EN/ProfessionalInterest/Pages/RemedyAndReparation.aspx.

Vermeulen, Pieter. "The Biopolitics of Trauma." In *The Future of Trauma Theory: Contemporary Literary and Cultural Criticism*, edited by Gert Buelens, Samuel Durrant, and Robert Eaglestone, 141–56. New York: Routledge, 2014.

Vernet, Marc. "Film Noir on the Edge of Doom." In *Shades of Noir: A Reader*, edited by Joan Copjec, 1–32. New York: Verso, 1993.

Villa, Raúl Homero, and George J. Sánchez. "Introduction: Los Angeles Studies and the Future of Urban Cultures." *American Quarterly* special issue, guest editors Raúl Homero Villa and George J. Sánchez, vol. 56, no. 3 (2004): 498–505.

Vine, David. *Base Nation: How U.S. Military Bases Abroad Harm America and the World*. New York: Metropolitan, 2015.
Virilio, Paul. *The Information Bomb*. Translated by Chris Turner. New York: Verso, 2005.
Von Eschen, Penny M. *Race Against Empire: Black Americans and Anticolonialism, 1937–1957*. Ithaca, NY: Cornell University Press, 1997.
Waldman, Diane. "Film Theory and the Gendered Spectator: The Female or the Feminist Reader?" *Camera Obscura* 6, no. 318 (1988): 80–94.
Williams, Randall. *The Divided World: Human Rights and Its Violence*. Minneapolis: University of Minnesota Press, 2010.
Wilson, Rob. *Reimagining the American Pacific: From "South Pacific" to Bamboo Ridge and Beyond*. Durham, NC: Duke University Press, 2000.
Wilson, Rob, and Arif Dirlik, eds. *Asia/Pacific as Space of Cultural Production*. Durham, NC: Duke University Press, 1995.
Wolfe, Patrick. "Settler Colonialism and the Elimination of the Native." *Journal of Genocide Research* 8, no. 4 (2008): 387–409.
Yamamoto, Eric K., Margaret Chon, Carol L. Izumi, Jerry Kang, and Frank H. Wu. *Race, Rights, and Reparation: Law and the Japanese-American Internment*. New York: Wolters Kluwer Law and Business, 2013.
Yamamoto, Hisaye. "A Fire in Fontana." In *Seventeen Syllables and Other Stories*, edited by King-Kok Cheung. New Brunswick, NJ: Rutgers University Press, 1988.
Yoneyama, Lisa. *Cold War Ruins: Transpacific Critique of American Justice and Japanese War Crimes*. Durham, NC: Duke University Press, 2016.
Yoneyama, Lisa. *Hiroshima Traces: Time, Space, and the Dialectics of Memory*. Berkeley: University of California Press, 1999.
Yoneyama, Lisa. "Memory Matters: Hiroshima's Korean Atom Bomb Memorial and the Politics of Ethnicity." *Public Culture* 7, no. 3 (1995): 499–527.
Yúdice, George. *The Expediency of Culture: Uses of Culture in the Global Era*. Durham, NC: Duke University Press, 2004.
Yuh, Ji-Yeon. *Beyond the Shadow of Camptown: Korean Military Brides in America*. New York: New York University Press, 2002.
Yuh, Ji-Yeon. "Moved by War: Migration, Diaspora, and the Korean War." *Journal of Asian American Studies* 8, no. 3 (2005): 277–91.

· INDEX ·